NOLO *Products & Services*

"In Nolo you can trust." —THE NEW YORK TIMES

Books & Software

Nolo publishes hundreds of great books and software programs on the topics consumers and business owners want to know about. And every one of them is available in print or as a download at Nolo.com.

Plain-English Legal Dictionary

Free at Nolo.com. Stumped by jargon? Look it up in America's most up-to-date source for definitions of cutting edge legal terminology. Emphatically not your grandmother's law dictionary!

Legal Encyclopedia

Free at Nolo.com. Here are more than 1,200 free articles and answers to frequently asked questions about everyday consumer legal issues including wills, bankruptcy, small business formation, divorce, patents, employment and much more. As *The Washington Post* says, "Nobody does a better job than Nolo."

Online Legal Forms

Make a will or living trust, form an LLC or corporation or obtain a trademark or provisional patent at Nolo.com, all for a remarkably affordable price. In addition, our site provides hundreds of high-quality, low-cost downloadable legal forms including bills of sale, promissory notes, nondisclosure agreements and many more.

Lawyer Directory

Find an attorney at Nolo.com. Nolo's unique lawyer directory provides in-depth profiles of lawyers all over America. From fees and experience to legal philosophy, education and special expertise, you'll find all the information you need to pick a lawyer who's a good fit.

Nolo's Aim:

 **affordable**

 **hassle free**

Keep Up to Date!

*Old law is often bad law. That's why Nolo.com has free updates for this and every Nolo book. And if you want to be notified when a revised edition of any Nolo title comes out, sign up for this free service at **nolo.com/legalupdater**.*

"Nolo is always there in a jam."
—NEWSWEEK

Please note

We believe accurate, plain-English legal information should help you solve many of your own legal problems. But this text is not a substitute for personalized advice from a knowledgeable lawyer. If you want the help of a trained professional—and we'll always point out situations in which we think that's a good idea—consult an attorney licensed to practice in your state.

1st edition

Estate Planning for Blended Families

Providing for Your Spouse & Children in a Second Marriage

By Attorney Richard E. Barnes

NOLO

FIRST EDITION	MAY 2009
Editor	MARY RANDOLPH
Cover Design	SUSAN PUTNEY
Proofreading	ROBERT WELLS
Index	JULIE SHAWVAN
Printing	DELTA PRINTING SOLUTIONS, INC.

Barnes, Richard E.
  Estate planning for blended families : providing for your spouse and children in a second marriage / by Richard E. Barnes. -- 1st ed.
      p. cm.
  Includes bibliographical references and index.
  ISBN-13: 978-1-4133-1018-4 (pbk. : alk. paper)
  ISBN-10: 1-4133-1018-4 (pbk. : alk. paper)
  1. Estate planning--United States. 2. Trusts and trustees--Untied States. I. Title.
  KF750.Z9B36 2009
  346.7305'2--dc22

                        2009004829

Quantity sales: For information on bulk purchases or corporate premium sales, please contact the Special Sales Department. For academic sales or textbook adoptions, ask for Academic Sales. Call 800-955-4775 or write to Nolo, 950 Parker Street, Berkeley, California 94710.

To my wife, Bridgett, and our son, Tucker, who are wonderful.

Acknowledgments

I have the privilege of practicing in Georgia, which is the home of a very fine and collegial group of estate planning attorneys. I have benefited from my participation over the years in the Georgia State Bar's Fiduciary Law Section. Bob Edge, Bert Levy, Bill Linkous, Mil Hatcher, Professor Verner Chaffin, Professor Jeffrey Pennell, Albert Reichert, and John Wallace—these are giants who have paved the way for many others. I owe these lawyers and the Section a great deal.

I also am indebted to—

Alan Rothschild, of Columbus, Georgia, for his guidance and encouragement

Professor Mary Radford, Georgia State University School of Law, for her gracious and continuing support

Bob Grout, my mentor and friend

The "young guns"—Jim Spratt, Ed Manigault, Nick Djuric, Patricia Friedman, Mary Galardi, Ben Pruett, Adam Gaslowitz, Conrad Bates, Melissa Walker, Mark Williamson, and Lee Wiseley

My law partners, for their support while I was AWOL writing this book

Stacy Wagner, for encouraging me to write this book

My editor, Mary Randolph, for her patient blue pen

My in-laws, Autrey and Elizabeth Moore, who cared for our son, carried hay to our horses, and did about a million other things to help keep the house running while I was pondering matters great and small

My mother, for instilling in me a love of reading, and my father, whose love for bad puns and rhymes prompted the poetry in this book, and

My clients, who make my practice so rewarding. I am grateful to and blessed by them.

Table of Contents

Your Estate Planning Companion 1

1 The View From the Mountaintop...5

What Is Estate Planning?...6

Your Path to Successful Estate Planning.......................................7

Keeping It All Together..12

2 Identifying Your Goals and Concerns..13

What Are Your Goals?...17

What Do You Want to Avoid? 19

3 Balancing Your Planning for Spouses,
Children, and Stepchildren...25

Making Your Wishes Clear..28

How Big Is Your Pie?...29

Who Gets a Slice of the Pie?...37

How Big Are the Slices?...39

Getting Down to the Nitty-Gritty: Specific Assets.......................46

Building Relationships With Children and Stepchildren 52

4 You and Your Spouse: Talking It Through,
Working It Out...55

Talking About the Tough Stuff..58

Tips for Resolving Differences 63

Common Roadblocks—And How to Get Around Them....................65

5   Taxes 69

Federal Estate Tax 73

State Estate Taxes 87

The Federal Gift Tax 87

Gift Tax vs. Estate Tax: Why It's Better to Give Now Than Later 92

The Generation-Skipping Transfer Tax 95

6   Tools and Techniques for Blended Families 97

Understanding Probate and Nonprobate Assets 99

Will or Trust? Get This Right and Things Start to Fall Into Place 104

Providing for Your Spouse but Making Sure Your
    Children Ultimately Get Your Stuff 117

Providing Cash for Loved Ones With Life Insurance 136

Sharing the Wealth Now: Making Gifts During Your Life 139

Other Tax-Saving Tools 142

7   Spouses of Unequal Wealth 151

Talk, Talk, and Keep on Talking 154

Should You Help Out the Stepchildren? 156

Good Tools for Spouses of Unequal Means 157

8   The May-December Romance 165

Providing for the Younger Spouse 167

Providing for the Older Spouse's Children 171

Providing for Children From the Current Relationship 173

9   Family Property 175

Heirlooms 176

Real Estate 181

The Family Farm 185

A Family Business 188

Trust Assets 193

10 Choosing Executors and Trustees 197

What Do Executors and Trustees Do? 200

Potential Candidates for Executor or Trustee 203

Helping Your Executor and Trustee 215

11 Preparing for Disability and End-of-Life Decisions 219

Premature Disability: How Would You Pay the Bills? 222

Age-Related Disability 227

12 Working With Lawyers 243

How to Find the Right Lawyer for You 244

You Are the Client 248

How Lawyers Advise Couples 249

How Lawyers Bill 251

How Much Should It Cost? 253

The Estate Planning Process 253

Pulling Together the Information You Need 255

How to Help Your Lawyer (and Lower Your Bill) 260

Other Members of the Team: Accountants and Financial Advisers 262

13 Keeping Your Plan Current 265

Where to Keep Your Important Documents 266

When to Update Your Plan 268

G Selected Glossary...277

Appendixes

A Sample Estate Planning Questionnaire.................................281

B Sample Estate Plans...303

Pete and Cynthia: Young Couple of Modest Means 304

Randy and Andrea: Grandparents Whose House Is
  Their Primary Asset...308

Tom and Callie: Young Couple With Wealth..............................314

Jack and Lynn: Successful Couple With Age and Wealth Differences........319

Index

Your Estate Planning Companion

A new ring
A new house
A new life
A new spouse

He has kids
She does, too

Welcome to second marriage
With no clue what to do

Second marriages can be wonderful things. Seasoned by age and experience, your relationship can bring untold joy and fulfillment and the realization of something you could only have dreamt of before. Many people find greater comfort, connection, and intimacy in a blended family than in previous relationships.

And yet … and yet. And yet, for the second time, no one gave you the instruction manual when you walked down the aisle. Nothing prepared you for how to deal with the host of personalities (spouse, children, stepchildren, and in-laws), your relationship with them, and their relationships with each other.

That's why I sometimes say it's not just a second marriage—it's marriage squared. Somehow, it seems like there's a geometric progression of personalities and challenges from the first to the second marriage. Even in an ideal second marriage, there's just more stuff to deal with.

And now you have this nagging feeling that you need to do something about your estate planning—perhaps update an old will that predates your current relationship, buy some life insurance, something. But where to start? What should you do to make sure your wishes will be respected should something happen to you? The chorus of voices and issues can be daunting.

That's why I wrote this book. Its purpose is to guide you through the process of planning your estate. We'll start by looking at where you and your spouse want to go (your goals) and what you want to avoid (your concerns). We'll look at ways to discuss issues with your spouse and ways to resolve any competing desires. I'll talk about how to plan for children and stepchildren and how to discuss these issues with them if you so choose. When you've settled on your goals, you'll be ready to look at some techniques that often work well in second marriage estate planning, with an eye to special circumstances (a family business, disparities in age or wealth, and so on) that may affect your planning.

By reading this book, you're going to know a whole lot more about estate planning than when you started. Try to keep your spouse with you as you go, so you're not at the end of the book while your spouse is grappling with the table of contents.

Estate planning is fulfilling because it's something you do for the people you love. Having seen more ugly disputes than I'd care to remember, I cannot overemphasize the tremendous gift you are giving your family by getting your affairs in order.

Completing your estate plan can give you a great feeling of accomplishment. Many people, though, find themselves in a lawyer's office with only a vague feeling of what they want to accomplish. And what happens? Without preparation or a fine book such as the one you're holding, you may find the process takes a lot of time, is expensive, and can be emotionally jarring.

My goal is to make it as smooth as it can be by giving you a firm grasp of what you want to accomplish and knowledge of the various tools and techniques that may work best for you. The better prepared you are, the less expensive, less time consuming, and less draining your estate planning should be. Hey, you've come through a lot to get where you are. Let's not make it any harder than it needs to be.

At the end of the day, by following the process described in this book, you'll have a customized estate plan that balances your goals and concerns and provides for your loved ones, all in a design that represents the approach that's best for you.

Finally, remember that "the relentless pursuit of perfection" is... relentless. For many years, Lexus sold a lot of cars by promoting them as the product of "the relentless pursuit of perfection." While perfection may be an admirable goal when building automobiles and nuclear power plants, if you strive for perfection, and only perfection, in your estate planning, then you may be setting yourself up for trouble. Trying to take care of every possible contingency can keep you from ever completing your estate plan or can result in a plan that's so complicated its original purpose quickly becomes obscured.

The medical term for this is "making you and everyone around you crazy." A few deep breaths and a little discernment about what is and what is not a big deal can go a long way. Remember, it's *not* a nuclear power plant—if Aunt Olivia doesn't get Mama's teaspoon collection, Manhattan's not going to be reduced to a pile of rubble. Take your time, plan carefully, but know when to let go and finish up.

Some years ago, my wife heard a retired neighbor gravely proclaim, "I've just bought my last truck." Apparently, he thought there was no way he was going to live long enough to outlast the vehicle. Well, three trucks and an RV later, he's still going strong, he and his wife are traveling in the RV, and by all appearances they are having a ball. The point is, you never know. Most likely, you'll have plenty of time to fine-tune, change, or throw out some of the arrangements you make now. So don't worry that you're not getting everything exactly perfect.

> *Do the best you can,*
> *Then close the book.*
> *If something should change,*
> *Take another look.*

The View From the Mountaintop

What Is Estate Planning? 6

Your Path to Successful Estate Planning 7

    Step 1. Prepare 7

    Step 2. Discover the Tools and Techniques Available to You 9

    Step 3. Work with Your Lawyer and Other Advisers 9

    Step 4. Finalize Your Plan 10

Keeping It All Together 12

E ach summer my wife, our son, and I travel to Highlands, North Carolina, for a long weekend. While we're there, we stop by the little grocery store on the edge of town and stock up on sodas and homemade cookies. With our provisions in a backpack, we head to the trailhead and take the short, steep hike up Whiteside Mountain. On a clear day, the view to the valley below is incredible—lush trees, houses large and small, every year a little more development, but still unspoiled.

As part of our ritual, we take lots of pictures and then I hoist our son on my shoulders (not quite as easy now as it used to be!) and we hike back down into town for ice cream and pizza.

Whenever I think of Whiteside Mountain, I think of the view from the top, looking down, serene, at peace.

When beginning your estate planning, you're standing on a mountaintop of life experiences, looking down at the valley below, which represents your goals and dreams about what you'd like to have happen when you're gone. So here you are, with a vision of what you'd like to accomplish, some of it a little murky. But how do you get there from here?

Whether you've been through the estate planning process before or this is your first time, whether you're neat as a pin or searching beneath the cushions for a pen, the estate planning process is pretty much the same—an orderly path you take to achieve what you want.

But before I describe the path you'll take, let's look at what estate planning is.

What Is Estate Planning?

Put simply, estate planning is the process of communicating your wishes about your care and property—real estate, cash, treasured possessions, the stuff in the bottom of your closet—in a manner in which they'll be respected should you be unable to speak for yourself. At the end of your planning (yes, there is an end in sight!), you'll have a folder stuffed full of signed documents—typically, a will or trust, powers of attorney, and a living will or advance directive—all designed to bring about what you want to accomplish. I'll talk in later chapters about what these documents are and the place they may have in your planning.

To be effective, your estate planning must be:

Informed. You need enough information to make intelligent decisions—to know why certain techniques are better for you than others, and the pros and cons of these techniques.

Coordinated. The documents you sign in your lawyer's office aren't the only ones that affect your estate planning. A host of other documents, such as beneficiary designations on life insurance and retirement plans, joint accounts, and real estate deeds are also very important. You'll need to be aware of how these other documents affect your planning and make sure they are consistent with your overall plan.

Concluded. Let's face it, most folks would rather do just about anything other than plan for their mortality. There's a real tendency to put off planning as long as possible—so congratulations on beginning the process. Try not to get bogged down somewhere along the way, because failing to complete your estate planning doesn't leave you a whole lot farther along than if you never took it up in the first place—you just have less money after paying for something you can't use.

Your Path to Successful Estate Planning

Let's look at the path you'll take to get to an effective estate plan as part of a blended family. There are four primary steps along the way: Prepare, Discover, Meet, and Finalize.

Step 1. Prepare

Preparing for the process includes identifying your goals and concerns, assembling the necessary information, and talking about the issues with your spouse.

Identify your goals and concerns. Identifying your goals and concerns will guide your estate planning choices. For example, your primary goal could be to provide for your children at your death, or it could be to provide for a surviving spouse. You might be concerned about giving your children too much too soon or about your assets winding up in the hands of a former spouse. Moving from the general to the specific—from the vague (provide for loved ones) to the concrete (provide for Bob, Cindy, and Tonya, but not your ex)—lets you make choices that will ultimately achieve what you wish to accomplish. You'll also want to review your goals and concerns from time to time to remind yourselves why you are going through the process and encourage you to stay on track.

Assemble the necessary information. Beginning your estate planning is like tackling a home repair project or a recipe: you want to make sure you have all of the materials and ingredients at hand to ensure an orderly process. Preparation can help save you time and frustration spent looking for misplaced items, and can save you expensive attorney's time as well.

If you do a lot of cooking, you may have come across a wonderful French expression, *mise en place*, which is loosely translated as "everything in its place." When you're starting a recipe, it's helpful to get all of your ingredients, pans, and gadgets together up front so you're not hunting for the coriander just as the sauce is beginning to burn. Similarly, with your estate planning, it's a whole lot easier if you'll take the time to collect the information you'll need at the beginning, rather than arriving at the lawyer's office without a deed or an agreement or a retirement plan statement that you need. (Chapter 12 has a list of what to gather.)

Talk about the issues. After the both of you get a good handle on your goals and concerns and your financial picture, you and your spouse will want to sit down together and talk. You may find a lot of common ground; you may find some of your goals will differ. One spouse may wish to see family assets pass exclusively to that spouse's children; another spouse may say, "let's just throw everything all into one big pot and divide it among the kids." I'll give you suggestions on how to address and reconcile these issues.

Will Your Estate Planning Be the Eisenhower Tunnel or the Stumphouse Tunnel?

The Eisenhower Memorial Tunnel, about 60 miles west of Denver, is an engineering marvel. At over 11,000 feet elevation, it's the highest road tunnel in the world. It is approximately 1.7 miles long and crosses the Western Continental Divide. Almost 12 million vehicles passed through the tunnel in 2007.

The Stumphouse Tunnel, on the other hand, is located outside of Walhalla, South Carolina. Originally intended to be a railroad tunnel 5,863 feet in length, tunnel construction was abandoned in 1859 with 4,363 feet completed. Its intended use frustrated by lack of completion and periodic landslides, the tunnel found a brief renaissance as a place to store and age blue cheese by Clemson University. It's now a lovely place to visit and hike—but it's not a working tunnel.

The point? Just having the vision to get started on a grand project isn't enough.

Step 2. Discover the Tools and Techniques Available to You

Once you've discussed your goals and concerns, you'll want to think further about how you may wish to provide for the children in your blended family. Also, you'll want to learn more about taxes and the tools that you'll use in your planning. I'll describe basic estate planning devices such as wills and revocable living trusts and introduce you to more specialized techniques used in blended family estate planning. I'll also point out techniques that work well if you and your spouse have ever lived in a community property state.

Step 3. Work with Your Lawyer and Other Advisers

Once you and your spouse have decided on a general course of action, you'll want to select the lawyer who's right for you. You'll meet with the lawyer to go over your goals, concerns, and financial information. Your lawyer will have recommendations to help you achieve your goals. You also will want to make your accountant, if you have one, part of the team since he or she has an intimate knowledge of your finances, as well as any financial adviser you regularly consult. (Chapter 12 offers tips about how to select and work with attorneys and other experts, as well as what to look for when you review the documents produced by your attorney.)

Many of my married estate planning clients come to me as a couple. Some prefer to work on their own. Either way, one person generally takes the lead and is the contact person for questions, information, and scheduling meetings. If you are the leader, your responsibilities are to:

- work through the book
- keep your spouse informed throughout, and
- set aside time for you and spouse to work on exercises together.

Why Do You Need a Lawyer?

Nolo's philosophy is to help you do what you can for yourself and point you to a professional when necessary. In blended family estate planning, a lawyer is often necessary. Why? Because in blended families, each spouse might have different goals. Sorting through and reconciling these goals often warrants an impartial, experienced counselor to bring the parties together. Plus, although we hope and expect that everyone will get along, once one of the spouses has died, there is a potential for challenge by a disgruntled spouse, child, or stepchild. A lawyer's prior assistance in the process can increase the likelihood that the estate plan holds up.

Step 4. Finalize Your Plan

Once you've met with your lawyer, you will want to carefully review any documents your lawyer prepares, reading them closely to make sure your wishes are being respected. Don't be afraid to ask questions!

After you've given any changes to your lawyer and received answers to all of your questions, your lawyer will finalize the documents and invite you to the office to sign them. The signing ceremony will be very formal, with witnesses and a notary present to make sure all of the state law requirements are followed.

Once your estate planning documents have been signed, you should take time to rest and celebrate your accomplishment. Over time, you'll want to continue to make sure that your joint checking accounts, life insurance beneficiaries, retirement plan beneficiaries, and property titles are set up in ways that are consistent with the new plan and that you make any transfers (into a trust, for example) recommended by your attorney. Should you have a significant life event (birth or adoption of a child, change in marital or financial status), you'll want to look at your plan to make sure that it is still current and reflects your desires. Even if you don't think there have been any big changes to your life, you should review your plan about every three to five years.

Same-Sex Relationships

If you are in a same-sex relationship and you or your partner has adopted children or has children from a previous relationship, your issues are probably very similar to other couples in blended families. This book may be of help in sorting out what you'd like to accomplish. Issues of fairness to the children and fairness to your partner in the use and disposition of joint and separate assets will be important considerations in the preparation of your estate plan.

States differ in their recognition and treatment of same-sex relationships—some allow marriage, others civil unions or domestic partnership, and some do not recognize same-sex relationships at all. There are also varying rules as to the enforceability of agreements entered into by same-sex couples.

Federal law doesn't recognize any kind of same-sex relationship sanctioned by a state. That can affect your estate planning in many ways—for example, you can't leave property to your partner free of federal estate tax, as other married couples can. It's is important to consult an attorney experienced in such matters in your state of residence.

Keeping It All Together

This book contains some exercises and worksheets that you and your spouse will want to complete when designing your estate plan. You also will collect financial information that your lawyer will need. Without a system in place, it may be tough keeping everything together.

You may want to purchase a three-ring binder, some pockets that will fit into it, and a three-hole punch so you can corral the information in a central place. It's a good place for you to keep notes and a running list of questions to ask your lawyer, your accountant, and your financial adviser.

What Is a Blended Family?

Throughout this book, I use "blended families" to mean married couples and their children where one or both of the couple has children from a previous relationship. Individuals in second and third marriages can be in blended families, as can individuals in a first marriage if there are children from a prior relationship.

Identifying Your Goals and Concerns

What Are Your Goals? 17

What Do You Want to Avoid? 19

    Family Concerns 19

    Financial Concerns 19

    Looking at Concerns More Closely 20

Your estate planning will be much
More effective if you can get in touch
With and voice your choices, goals, and concerns
To make the most of lessons learned

I f you were planning a vacation, you'd start by thinking about where you wanted to go:

- The beach or the mountains?
- A remote cabin or Rio at Carnaval?
- Paragliding in Pamplona or pampering at a spa?

As you were putting together your dream trip, you might also consider what you'd like to avoid:

- "Oh, I don't want to go to the beach then, because that's spring break week and it'll be packed."
- "I want to make sure I avoid booking the last flight out that evening to avoid getting stranded if it gets canceled."
- "Can I really stand a summer of septuagenarians in Speedos?"

Once you have your goals in mind and you know what you'd like to avoid, planning the trip gets much easier. Estate planning is similar—you want to ensure that you end up where you want to be and that you and your loved ones don't get stuck somewhere along the way in a mess you could have avoided.

So before you start thinking about wills and trusts, or insurance and property arrangements, think about what it is, really, that you are trying to accomplish—and what you are really trying to avoid. Your feelings for your spouse, children, and stepchildren can pull you in different directions. By identifying the goals and concerns that are truly important to you, you can reconcile these competing feelings and dramatically increase the chances that your final estate plan will reflect your true desires.

Remember, this is YOUR plan. Within the limits of the law and your wallet, you have the freedom to do what you want to do.

By the end of this chapter you should know:

- your top five estate planning goals, and
- the top five things you want to avoid.

Is It a Goal or a Concern?

Goals are the positive things you're trying to accomplish with your planning: educating your children, maximizing inheritances, providing for spouses. *Concerns* are what you're trying to avoid: battles over your estate, having assets wind up in the hands of an ex-spouse, or having your estate ravaged by taxes like termites in a pile of wood shavings. Don't get too hung up on whether something is a goal or a concern. Many can be expressed both ways: maximize your children's inheritance (goal) vs. avoid unnecessary loss to your children's inheritance through estate taxes (concern).

Blended families present particular challenges, such as how each spouse will provide for the other, how each spouse will provide for children born into the relationship, and how each spouse will provide for children from previous relationships. You and your spouse will likely share common ground on many, if not most, points, but may have different opinions in certain areas. Despite the differences, you should be able to align each of your goals and concerns and come up with a coordinated plan.

For example, consider Nan and Roger. Both have children from a previous relationship. Roger's net worth is greater than Nan's. Nan's planning goals are to provide for her children at her death and leave little to Roger, because he has sufficient assets of his own. Roger's goals are to provide for Nan and his children equally at his death. Despite the differences in goals, there can still be a unified plan.

Knowing your goals and concerns helps your estate planning attorney prepare a customized, tailor-made plan. Obtaining an estate plan requires a significant investment of your time and money, so you want to make sure you get what's right for you and your family.

Consider the following two couples and how different their estate plans might need to be based on their goals and concerns.

Sally and John are in their mid-30s and are recently married. Sally has two children from a previous relationship; John has one. They plan on having more children. Sally's children are young, and she wants to make sure that they finish their education should she die prematurely. She is concerned that there wouldn't be enough money to fund her children's education, particularly if she stops working and takes time off to have children with John.

John's goals are to provide for Sally during her lifetime and to provide for his child and any later children to inherit his estate once she is gone. John doesn't want any of his assets to end up in the hands of his ex-wife should he die while his child is still a minor.

Sally and John don't feel the need to provide for one another's children because they've agreed they'll provide for their own children. Their goals and concerns might look like those outlined below.

Sally and John's Goals and Concerns		
	Goals	**Concerns**
Sally	Paying for college	Not having enough money to go around
	Providing for her children from her previous relationship	
	Providing for any children she and John might have	
John	Providing for Sally at his death or disability	Assets coming into hands of his ex-spouse
	Providing for his child from his previous relationship	
	Providing for any children from the current relationship	

Teresa and Randy married when Teresa was in her late 50s with two grown children. Randy is a sculptor in his mid-60s who also has adult children from his first marriage. Teresa inherited substantial property from her parents when they died; Randy has limited means. Teresa's goals are to provide for Randy's comfortable (not lavish) lifestyle should she die before he does, but ensure that any family property she inherited pass to her children and grandchildren. Teresa is concerned about Randy's money-managing abilities and worries that her assets may be depleted if she has to pay for Randy's health care, as he is a lifelong smoker with a family history of cardiac illness. Randy, knowing that Teresa is financially comfortable, wants his children to inherit what he has at his death. He remembers the fights over his father's estate when his father died and wants to avoid any disagreements between his children and Teresa at his death.

Randy and Teresa's Goals and Concerns		
	Goals	Concerns
Randy	Leaving assets to his children	Having disputes following death
Teresa	Providing for Randy Keeping family assets in the family	Randy's lacks of financial expertise and judgment Depleting her estate (and her children's inheritance) for Randy's health care

As you can imagine, the right estate plan for Sally and John will look very difference from the estate plan for Randy and Teresa. The difference lies in the couples' goals and concerns. Throughout this book, I'll show you sample plans and tools and techniques that will allow you to incorporate your goals and concerns into your plan.

What Are Your Goals?

You can probably find your big estate planning goals on the list below. So, as a starting point, select the five goals that most closely match yours. Try to avoid "shoulds" and "ought tos" and focus on your actual goals as of this moment. For example, if your children are most important to you, don't check "providing for charity" just because you think you "should" want to give to charity. You can rank your goals later.

The comprehensive estate planning questionnaire in Appendix A asks you to select from the following common goals:

- providing for your spouse at your death
- providing for your spouse if you become disabled
- providing for children from your current relationship
- providing for children from a previous relationship
- providing for stepchildren
- providing for grandchildren
- protecting children from losing their inheritance if the surviving spouse remarries
- ensuring a child won't lose their inheritance in divorce
- protecting assets from the claims of your creditors
- protecting children from losing their inheritance to their creditors
- providing a college education for your children
- being fair to your spouse, children, and stepchildren in the division of your estate
- keeping property, art, jewelry, or mementos you've inherited in the family
- keeping a business in the family
- minimizing estate tax
- providing for a child with special needs
- providing for children in a manner that avoids "too much/too soon" and gives each child the incentive to get an education and establish a career
- providing for charity, and
- avoiding probate.

Spaces are also provided for goals which are not already listed. This exercise will be most helpful if you and your spouse each work through it.

Now, again using the questionnaire in Appendix A, rank the ones you've chosen, listing from most important to least important.

Prioritizing your goals is important in case of conflicts, either in your goals or in helping to resolve any different choices you and your spouse may have made. You'll use this list of goals throughout the process, as you learn about the tools that will be best for you, in communicating your wishes with your attorney, and as your motivation to keep going and see the planning through.

What Do You Want to Avoid?

Concerns can be a powerful force; often, people's worries give them the needed push to tackle their estate planning. Sometimes, the drive to plan stems from a fear of what will happen under an existing, out-of-date plan. Other times, it may be a worry over what will happen if a person dies without a will or trust in place. To tap into this powerful motivator, you need to identify what you're trying to avoid.

For example, people in blended family relationships typically don't want to have their assets under the control of an ex-spouse, which can easily happen if assets are left outright to minor children and the ex-spouse is the children's guardian.

Most concerns arise in one of two areas: family or finances. Start by looking at these broad categories and writing down what comes to mind. The underlined items are common responses, but not exclusive.

Family Concerns

- I am concerned that if I were to die or become disabled today, my children might *not be adequately provided for; never receive their inheritance; or receive "too much/too soon."*
- I am concerned that if I were to die or become disabled today, my spouse might *not be adequately provided for; receive too much at the expense of my children; not be able to continue paying for our home.*
- I am concerned that if I were to die or become disabled today, my family might *quarrel with one another or fight over my estate.*

Financial Concerns

- I am concerned that if I were to die or become disabled today, my assets might *become subject to the control of my ex-spouse; or go entirely to my current spouse, with no guarantee that my children would be provided for or ultimately get the money.*

- I am concerned that if I were to die or become disabled today, my business might *suffer and have to be sold at a loss; be liquidated in a fire sale to pay estate tax; or pass to children who aren't prepared to run it properly.*

Looking at Concerns More Closely

Now that you've articulated your high-level concerns, let's take a closer look at the specific outcomes you want to avoid in your estate planning. These are the wake-you-up-in-the-middle-of-the-night, 3 a.m. kinds of concerns.

For starters, you need to assess how likely it is that any of these possible bad outcomes might actually happen. Sometimes people get so hung up on things that are unlikely to happen that they fail to address issues that may pose a more imminent threat. (See "Top Ten Nontax Mistakes People Make in Estate Planning for Blended Families," below.) One of the benefits of using an experienced estate planning attorney is that the attorney can help you decide whether to devote resources to resolving these concerns or to focus on matters that are more important to you.

For example, I sometimes see healthy couples with blended families who become almost paralyzed by what I call the "catastrophe scenario"— that is, "What happens to our stuff, if we (couple, children, stepchildren, couple's parents and siblings) all die?" Even as they acknowledge the remoteness of the possibility, they want to see it addressed in their estate planning documents. Because clients frequently find this issue so important, I encourage them to address it rather than dismissing it because of its low probability.

How seriously to take other concerns may depend on where you live. For example, if a couple coming to my office is already convinced about the horrors of probate, I generally try to dissuade them from focusing on it. That's because in my home state of Georgia, probate is not an ordeal, and the cost of the most widely offered alternative to probate (a revocable trust) outweighs the likely benefits. In states where probate is more expensive and time-consuming (California, for example), your adviser may well recommend a trust, even if it costs more up front.

Focusing on the Rewards of Completing Your Estate Planning

Sometimes, the only way to keep going through a difficult project—
whether it's seeing a dream home to completion, planning a wedding,
potty-training a child, or completing a spreadsheet at work—is to focus on
the rewards you'll get when you're done: cool drinks on the new deck; the
honeymoon; dry, happy children; or speeding through the next spreadsheet
with your hard-won efficiency.

Many people use the visualization, the process of imagining—
vividly—a desired outcome so that it becomes as real in their minds as
possible, down to sights, sounds, and tastes. Visualization can lend energy
and direction toward the goal you want. Sports psychologists use it with
top athletes to help them make the winning basket or sink the clutch putt.

As you work through your estate planning, picturing your family getting
along and appreciating the legacy you've left can be an important motivation. Many successful people are justifiably proud of the sacrifices they've
made so their families will live in the best neighborhoods, their children
attend the best schools, and so on. I tell my clients that their estate planning
and forethought—or the lack thereof—will probably be a lasting memory
for their spouses and children. What will your legacy be in this regard?

Take a moment to think about and write down how you expect to
feel when your estate planning is done. Will you feel relieved? Have peace
of mind? Be able to say "yes" if your children ask whether you've done any
estate planning?

From time to time, if the process begins to seem overwhelming,
review your goals and this list of feelings. It should remind you why you are
undertaking this process and encourage you to keep moving.

And if the good feelings aren't enough, don't underestimate the
motivating power of tangible rewards. Think about how you can reward
yourself and your spouse when you get this done: an exotic trip, new shoes,
exotic trip to buy new shoes, new golf club, new bike, new toy?

So, as you are sorting through your concerns, make sure you raise them with your attorney. Your attorney can't address them if your attorney doesn't know about them. If your attorney has convincing reasons to dissuade you from addressing a particular issue, then you can drop it. If it's still important to you, ask to have it addressed. Either way, you get peace of mind, which is what this process is all about.

You and your spouse should find your biggest concerns on the questionnaire in Appendix A. You can choose from the following common concerns or add your own:

- your assets going to someone other than your children
- assets coming under the control of an ex-spouse
- assets coming under the control of a stepchild instead of your children
- assets winding up in the hands of a new spouse should your spouse survive you and remarry
- not having enough money to meet everyone's needs
- estate taxes
- putting assets in the hands of someone who lacks the financial expertise or maturity to handle them properly
- losing control of your assets during your life
- children losing their inheritance through their own divorce or to creditors
- disputes among your loved ones, and
- depletion of your estate because of nursing home costs.

Once you have chosen your concerns, you should rank them, listing from most important to least important.

Top Ten Nontax Mistakes People Make in Estate Planning for Blended Families

1. Failing to have an up-to-date plan reflecting current goals and concerns.

2. Leaving everything outright to the surviving spouse with the expectation that the surviving spouse will take care of, and ultimately leave everything to, the first-to-die spouse's children. The funds that the first-to-die spouse thought were ultimately going to children may be consumed by the surviving spouse's lifestyle creditors, or left to a new spouse or to the spouse's children.

3. Failing to update beneficiary designations on nonprobate assets (life insurance, retirement plans, and payable on death accounts). I have seen situations where years after the divorce, the ex-spouse was still listed as the beneficiary—clearly not the intended result!

4. Leaving everything outright to one child with the expectation that the child will distribute it wisely among the surviving spouse and other children. That child is then hounded by siblings and the surviving spouse and subject to challenge in the way the child divides the property.

5. Leaving significant property outright to minor children. If the ex-spouse is the guardian of the children, the ex-spouse will likely have significant control over the assets.

6. Choosing an unqualified or biased executor or trustee or choosing cotrustees or coexecutors who cannot agree, leading to deadlock.

7. Making their children wait to inherit the bulk of their inheritance until the death of the surviving spouse. If the surviving spouse is their stepparent, children may grow to resent the stepparent and may receive their inheritance long after it could have been of most use to them and their families.

8. Leaving large amounts of money or property outright to a surviving spouse or child who is not prepared to handle it.

9. Not taking into account the surviving spouse's right to make a claim against the deceased spouse's estate for a statutory or elective share.

Top Ten Nontax Mistakes People Make in Estate Planning for Blended Families, cont'd.

Many states give a surviving spouse rights to a percentage of the estate or rights to use a house or other assets. This may limit one spouse's right to leave the bulk of his or her estate to children from a previous or the current relationship. If this right is not taken into account and planned for, the surviving spouse might make a successful claim against the estate, and the children could receive much less.

10. Failing to communicate their plans during life to their spouse and loved ones. At their death, some beneficiaries receive an unpleasant surprise. The executor becomes the bearer of bad news and target of the disappointed beneficiaries.

Don't Forget About Prenups, Postnups, or Divorce Settlements

In a second marriage, you're not starting with a blank slate. Divorce settlement agreements or pre- or postnuptial agreements frequently affect your estate planning—and just as frequently, people forget about them. If your divorce decree obligates you to maintain life insurance, for example, your estate planning attorney needs to know that. If there's a court order or court-approved settlement still in effect from your divorce, a judge could find you in contempt if you fail to follow it.

Similarly, if you and your spouse agreed in a prenup as to the division of your assets on death, your lawyer will want to incorporate (or amend, if that's your intention) those provisions in the estate plan to minimize conflict down the road. You don't want to create an estate plan that is inconsistent with an existing prenuptial agreement. If the estate plan is more generous to the surviving spouse than the prenuptial agreement is, the deceased spouse's children might challenge the estate plan. That would pit them squarely against the surviving spouse, who would be forced to defend the plan.

Balancing Your Planning for Spouses, Children, and Stepchildren

Making Your Wishes Clear 28

How Big Is Your Pie? 29

    Common Law States...30

    Community Property States..31

Who Gets a Slice of the Pie? 37

How Big Are the Slices?...39

    Your Spouse..41

    Your Children...42

    Your Stepchildren..44

    Charities or Other Beneficiaries...45

Getting Down to the Nitty-Gritty: Specific Assets 46

    Roughing Out a Plan...46

    Young Beneficiaries: When and How Should They Inherit?..........................49

Building Relationships With Children and Stepchildren..................................52

Living well,
Then leaving well
To the ones you love
Is the best reward.

One of the most rewarding parts of estate planning is making provisions for your loved ones that will last long after you're gone. It's really why people take up their estate planning—they want the peace of mind of knowing they've made the best choices for their loved ones. Helping blended families make those choices is what this book is all about.

In estate planning for blended families, there's often an unstated tension. Spouses, children, and stepchildren (and maybe grandchildren) are all candidates for your limited resources. You may feel torn as you try to decide how to divide your estate. Creating the right plan for your family will probably mean making some hard choices. It's what the economists call a zero-sum game: Every dollar you give to your spouse is a dollar that your child doesn't get, and vice versa. In many families, there just may not be enough to go around to satisfy everyone.

This risks disappointing family members. And unfortunately, lawsuits seem to be more common in blended families than in traditional nuclear ones. Once the biological parent is gone, disappointed children may be more likely to sue a stepparent than their own parent. These disputes are extremely personal and can destroy families.

The good news is that by working through the challenges today, you can spare your loved ones from needless strife once you are gone. This chapter will help you answer some key questions that parents in blended families often struggle with:

- How do I fairly divide my estate among my spouse and children?
- Should I include my stepchildren in my planning?
- When should I give property to my children and stepchildren—during my life, at my death, or when each reaches a certain age?
- Should I leave property with strings attached, or free and clear?

First, you need to think about who among your spouse, children, and stepchildren should inherit from your estate. It's not just a matter of money—you'll take into account not only financial need but also emotional maturity and your relationships with your children and stepchildren. Then, you get to put it all together in an exercise that lets you plan a rough division of your estate by taking specific assets and allocating them among your intended beneficiaries.

Dos and Don'ts When Planning for Your Spouse and Kids	
Do:	**Don't:**
Incorporate your wishes into your plan to make them legally binding.	Just tell your children and your surviving spouse what you want and leave it up to them.
Leave your children something immediately at your death.	Leave everything to your surviving spouse and make your children wait for the surviving spouse's death to receive an inheritance.
Assess your loved ones' needs and maturity before leaving them large sums of money.	Leave everything outright to your spouse or children if they're not ready to handle the wealth.
Leave something to your children that demonstrates your love for them, even if it's in the form of a letter.	Let your final communication be only your will, which can read as an impersonal, legalese-filled document.
Be open and honest about your plans, even if your spouse or children might not be entirely pleased. If they're adults, talk frankly with them about your intentions and how you've set things up. If they're too young for a heart-to-heart, begin to prepare them and set their expectations.	Let the person who sends out your will or trust after your death be the bearer of unpleasant surprises.
Make time for your children and stepchildren and let them know you love them.	Wait until it's too late.

Making Your Wishes Clear

No matter how you decide to leave your property, you need to make sure that your wishes are clear and binding. Children become angry or hurt when they don't receive something they expected to inherit from their parent. It may be as minor (in monetary terms) as a memento or as significant as the childhood home, but if their parent does not leave it to the child and the stepparent takes it, spends it, or leaves it to the stepparent's children, the disappointed child might sue the stepparent over the omission.

> **EXAMPLE:** Mary promises Todd she'll leave her mother's china to him. But in her will, Mary simply leaves everything to her second husband, George, who gives the china to his daughter. Todd is hurt and feels that George has violated his mother's wishes by not giving him the china. George says he never knew that Todd wanted the china or that Mary promised it to him.

A situation like this is probably the number-one cause of disputes between children and stepparents. The children are convinced that their parent wanted them to inherit something, but their parent dies and leaves it outright to the spouse. If the spouse sells it and keeps the money or gives the item or money to the spouse's children, the first spouse's children are cut out of the inheritance—and become angry and resentful.

So don't leave it to chance. Let your intentions be known, in as much detail as is necessary. If you want a particular asset to pass to your children, say so in your estate planning documents. Don't just leave it to your spouse with an unwritten understanding of what you wish to have happen.

Whenever you leave something to someone without any strings attached, it's an outright gift. The recipient is generally free to do with it what the recipient wants to do *even if you wanted the recipient to do something else.* So, if you want to make sure your daughter ultimately ends up with the family china, you can't just leave it to your second husband in your will and hope that he will give or leave it to her.

> **TIP**
>
> **Avoid surprises.** An important follow-up to making your wishes clear is communicating them to your family members. Children really don't like bringing this up with you, but they really do want to know. And by communicating now, you may be sparing your executor some grief down the road that would otherwise come from challenges to the plan. Surprises can breed lawsuits.

How Big Is Your Pie?

Dividing your estate can be like slicing a pie: you have to know how big the pie is, how many slices you want, and how big to make them. Completing the questionnaire in Exhibit A will help you determine how big your pie is—that is, what you own that you can leave freely. If you haven't yet worked through the questionnaire, take a few minutes to do so or make a rough "back of the envelope" estimate of your net worth by adding up all of your assets and subtracting your liabilities. What remains is your pie—what you have to leave. Don't forget to include in your calculation your share of any jointly owned assets, any joint liabilities, any retirement plan assets, any life insurance benefits payable as a result of your death, and any inheritances you expect to receive. To know what you can leave, you have to know what is yours to leave and what is your spouse's. This is especially important in blended families, where each spouse may want to leave property to different beneficiaries.

To determine what is yours to leave, you need to look at where you and your spouse have lived and where you live now.

Community Property States

The states listed below are community property states. All others are common law states.

Alaska*	Louisiana	Texas
Arizona	Nevada	Washington
California	New Mexico	Wisconsin
Idaho		

* In Alaska, couples can elect to treat their property as community property.

Common Law States

In common law states, when you want to know what you own (and so what you can convey), you look in whose name the assets are titled at the time of transfer. If the property's in your name—for example, your name is on the deed to your house or a bank account statement—it's yours to give away or leave. The rules are pretty simple:

- if the assets are solely in one spouse's name, that spouse can dispose of a 100% interest in the assets
- if the assets are held jointly by both spouses, each can dispose of a half interest.

> EXAMPLE: Bob and Alicia live in a common law state. For assets titled in Alicia's name alone at death, she can leave them to Bob, her children, or anyone else as she wishes.

The principal exception to this rule is for certain retirement plan benefits, where federal law mandates that you get your spouse's consent if you name someone else as the beneficiary. This applies to 401(k)s and other "qualified" plans and pensions.

This doesn't mean that your spouse has no rights when it comes to how you leave your property. It's very important to understand that despite these rules, your spouse will probably have the right to claim some of your property after your death. Depending on your state's laws, a surviving spouse might be able to claim a significant portion of your estate. (Few do, but it's an option.) These rights are guaranteed by laws called "elective share" or "forced share" statutes.

In many states, these laws entitle the surviving spouse to claim between a third and a half of the deceased spouse's estate. The spouse's share may be limited to a portion of what's in the probate estate or may include both probate and nonprobate assets, such as assets held in a trust. In some states, the share depends on how long you were married. Some state statutes give the surviving spouse certain lifetime rights with respect to real estate or the right to support for a certain time.

For blended families, these laws can be especially important, because you probably don't want to leave your spouse everything (as is common in first marriages). For example, say you have decided to leave your spouse 10% of your estate and no more because your spouse has independent resources. You're expecting the other 90% to go to your children from your previous marriage. If your spouse can instead make a claim at your death for a third to a half of your estate, your plan has suffered a major setback, and your children will get far less than you intended.

> CAUTION
>
> **Know what your spouse is entitled to claim.** The key is to talk with your lawyer and have your lawyer calculate each spouse's share in the other's estate under applicable law. If that's more than you intend to leave each other, all of you will need to work together to make a plan that will accomplish your goals. You and your spouse might need to sign a postnuptial agreement (discussed in Chapter 6).

Community Property States

In community property states, property owned by a married person is either separate property or community property. To determine which is which, you have to look beyond whose name the property is in.

You need to look at when and how the property was acquired. Even if the property is held in only one spouse's name, if you've lived in a community property state, it may belong jointly to the two of you.

Generally, you can dispose of your separate property as you wish, without getting the consent of the other spouse.

> **EXAMPLE:** Ben lives in Arizona and owns a valuable watercolor he inherited from his mother. He can give it or leave it in his will to his daughter without his wife's consent.

If an asset is community property, however, then each spouse owns a half interest in it, whether the asset is held in the name of the husband, the wife, or both. Community property states don't look at who the record owner is, but focus on when and how the asset was acquired. There's a presumption that most property acquired during the marriage is community property. (More on that below.)

In blended families, it is crucial for you to understand community property rules—otherwise, you might create unintended and undesired consequences. In a community property state, your ability to convey property outright to a child or anyone other than the other spouse can be limited in ways you might not expect. If you are thinking you are providing generously for your children by leaving them a significant asset, but in actuality are leaving them much less—possibly only a half interest—because the asset is community property, then your estate plan will not accomplish what you wish.

> **EXAMPLE:** Jeannie inherited a horse farm from her mother. The farm is Jeannie's separate property. As long as she keeps the farm her separate property, if Jeannie wants to leave it to her child, she can do so, and her husband will have no claim against it. However, if Jeannie and her second husband Ronnie use income from their jobs to improve the farm, then a portion of the farm is now community property, because salaries are community property. Now, Jeannie can't leave the farm to her child unless Ronnie agrees to give up his community property interest.

Same-Sex Couples

Just two community property states, California and Washington, currently let same-sex couples register with the state as domestic partners. In California, community property laws apply to registered domestic partners just as they do to married couples. In Washington, however, domestic partners cannot own community property.

Community Property Basics

Community property is generally property acquired by either spouse during the marriage while a resident of a community property state. Each spouse's salary and bonuses during the marriage are community property, as is any income generated by community property.

The big exception to this rule is that property one spouse receives as a gift or inherits is not community property; it's that spouse's separate property. Another exception is property that you and your spouse have agreed will be one spouse's separate property. State laws vary on what's required for an agreement, but it generally needs to be in writing.

Community property states *presume* that all property is community property unless you can prove that it should be treated as separate. So if your Aunt Betty gave you the property, you need to keep records to have proof.

Community property gives each spouse equal ownership regardless of how the asset is titled. Each spouse owns half of the couple's community property.

> EXAMPLE 1: Sinjin and Judy, a married couple, live in New Mexico, a community property state. Sinjin uses his bonus one year to buy a general store in downtown Las Cruces. The general store is community property, because Sinjin's bonus was community property. Even though the store may be titled only in Sinjin's name, Judy is an equal owner. Sinjin can't give the store away without Judy's consent, nor can he leave the children from his first

marriage a 100% interest in the store at his death if he dies before Judy, because Judy owns a half interest in the store.

EXAMPLE 2: Deborah and Allen, a married couple, live in California. If Deborah wishes to use her bonus one year to buy a car to give to her daughter, then she'll have to get Allen's consent, because her bonus is community property.

Some community property states allow each spouse to make reasonable gifts of community property to others without consent. If there's any doubt or if the gift is significant, make the gift from your separate property or get your spouse's consent.

EXAMPLE: Craig and his second wife Janet live in Washington state. Craig wants to give his son a car that he bought while married to Janet, but doesn't want Janet's children to make a fuss about it later. He asks Janet to sign a document agreeing that the gift is from both of them.

Classifying property as separate or community can be quite a challenge and can require the guidance of an experienced adviser. About half of the community property states (Idaho, Louisiana, Texas, and Wisconsin) treat income on separate assets as separate property; the others (Arizona, California, Nevada, New Mexico, and Washington) treat that income as community property.

EXAMPLE: Rose and Benny live in Texas. Benny has a working ranch he inherited from his family. Income from the ranch is Benny's separate property. If Rose and Benny lived in Arizona, income from the ranch would be their community property.

If you're not sure what's community property, ask your lawyer. These questions are easiest to answer while your records are still available. For example, say you have a business that you started before your marriage. If you use some income from the business to support your spouse and you during your marriage, but reinvest the rest in your business, under some states' rules your spouse would have an interest in the business. The extent of that interest would be hard to value. Presumably, your spouse's interest would relate to the amount of income you reinvested in the business during your marriage.

If it's important for you to leave the business to your children, then you don't want this uncertainty. You can override the community property rules if you and your spouse sign an agreement (called a community property agreement) stating what is separate and what is community property. Consult your attorney to make sure that you get the right result. Or, if you and your spouse signed a prenuptial agreement, it may have provisions in it as to what's separate and what's community property.

Keeping Assets Separate

If you and your spouse want to keep your assets separate, you can do it. You're free to make an agreement stating that some or all of your property, which state law would otherwise classify as community property, is separate property. This agreement needs to be in writing. And you need to follow up by scrupulously keeping your assets separate.

Good record keeping and being disciplined about keeping separate property separate are keys to avoiding disputes down the road. So don't mix community and separate property if you want to preserve the character of each. For example, if your state provides that income on separate assets during marriage is community property (and you wish to keep the separate assets separate), then deposit the income into a separate account to keep the whole account from becoming a joint asset.

> EXAMPLE 1: Bob and Samantha live in a community property state. Before their marriage, Samantha saved $200,000. Because it was hers before the marriage, it's her separate property. But if she puts it in the joint checking account she has with Bob, where they also deposit their salaries and out of which they pay all their bills, then it's going to be hard (impossible, really) to determine at Samantha's death whether the account contains $200,000 that

is still her separate property. There might be $300,000 in the account or there might be $10,000.

EXAMPLE 2: When Matt marries Elizabeth, he has $100,000 saved up. They live in a community property state. Matt keeps the money in a separate account and periodically puts the interest from the account into a joint account he opens with Elizabeth. The $100,000 will likely remain his separate property.

If you don't know whether a particular asset might be deemed community or separate property, check with your tax adviser. You and your spouse can resolve any ambiguity by entering into an agreement with one another now as to what is community property and what is separate property. Otherwise, keep in mind that you, your spouse, or your heirs may have to scour your records years from now to try to figure out whether your property was community or separate.

Commingling

Commingling is what happens when you combine separate and community property in one account or piece of property. Once you've commingled assets, the account or property is going to be presumed to be community property unless you can prove otherwise, which can be very difficult to do. If you want to keep your community property separate from your separate property, treat it like you would your laundry: Wash your whites and colors separately.

Tax Advantages of Community Property

It might make life simpler for you and your spouse to keep certain assets separate, and it might reassure your children to know that your second spouse isn't an equal owner of all your property. But consider the financial consequences before you decide. Owning community property can be advantageous for tax purposes. (I talk about taxes in Chapter 5.)

That's because if the asset has gone up in value since you acquired it, the tax basis for all of the community property—not just the half owned by the deceased spouse—steps up to fair market value at the first spouse's death. (Internal Revenue Code Section 1014.)

> **EXAMPLE:** Renee and Kel, a married couple, have a house worth $300,000 with a tax basis of $120,000. Under the community property laws of their state, Renee and Kel own the house equally. At Kel's death, the tax basis of the entire property steps up to $300,000.

Even though the value of the entire property is stepped up for capital gains tax purposes, only half of its value is included in the deceased spouse's gross estate for estate tax purposes.

> **EXAMPLE:** Kel's estate will include only his half interest in the property, or $150,000, so he's not taxed on the entire $300,000. If Kel leaves his one-half interest in the house to Renee, and she immediately sells the house for $300,000, then Renee will not have to pay any tax on the sale, even though she and Kel only had a basis of $120,000 in the property.

If the property's value has decreased since the date of purchase, you might not want it to be treated as community property because at the first spouse's death, the tax basis will go down to the lower fair market value.

Remember: Higher basis generally means less tax when the property is someday sold. Think of basis as riding an elevator in a high-rise: you'd generally rather ride the elevator up to your penthouse suite than down to the basement.

Who Gets a Slice of the Pie?

Once you know how big the pie is, the next step is to determine who gets a slice—that is, who are the people and charities you're going to benefit in your planning. These are the beneficiaries of your estate. After you determine who your beneficiaries are going to be, you need to determine the size of the slices, which we'll talk about in the next section.

Here, take a moment to list your potential beneficiaries. You and your spouse should each make a list. For this list, think just of the people you want to benefit, not the size of your pie. These are the people on your "must-inherit" list.

Must-Inherit List

The people whom I feel strongly must inherit from my estate are:

_____

_____

_____

_____

Next, list anyone whom you could have included, but didn't, on your must-inherit list, but would like to provide for if there's enough to go around. For example, if your spouse does not survive you, there may be other people or charities you would be able to provide for.

Maybe-Inherit List

If there's enough to go around, I would also like to leave something to:

_____

_____

_____

_____

If you're like most people, your must-inherit list consists of your spouse and your children. It may also include your grandchildren and one or more of your stepchildren. Your optional list likely includes grandchildren, stepchildren, other loved ones, and charities.

> **Enlarging and Protecting the Pie**
>
> If you're worried that the pie's not big enough to go around, see if you can make it bigger. If you can buy life insurance or set aside some savings for your children, you can boost your legacy. You may also want to look at tax-free retirement accounts and college savings plans to maximize the gift.
>
> Protect the pie with disability insurance and long-term care insurance. The costs of a premature disability or extended stay in a nursing home can be devastating. If you can tap into a group plan through work or an organization to which you belong, the rates may be significantly cheaper. (This is discussed more in Chapter 11.)

How Big Are the Slices?

Now that you know the size of your pie and whom you want to share it, you're ready to determine the size of everyone's slice. Start by looking at the beneficiaries on your must-inherit list. Put a star by the name of anyone on the list who has a particular need to inherit from you because of limited resources.

Focus first on these beneficiaries; they are the people among whom you will balance your resources. Think in rough percentages, such as "I'd like to leave my wife 50% of my estate, have my children split 40%, and give the rest to my stepchildren." You'll have an opportunity to go asset by asset in the next section.

Remember, this is YOUR unique plan. No one else can make the choices for you. But if you're casting about, wondering what other blended families are doing, here are some rules of thumb based on my experience:

It's okay to support a surviving spouse, even if the kids get less. Most of my clients want to support their spouses should they pass away first: they consider it part of the "love, honor, and cherish" of their marriage vows. This is particularly true when one spouse is financially dependent on the other: The financially stronger spouse wants to provide for the other throughout the remainder of the surviving spouse's life and still provide for children. As part of balancing the needs of the surviving spouse and the children, their priority is for the spouse to live comfortably, even if some of those dollars could have gone to the children.

If there's plenty to go around, it's good to divide the estate at the first spouse's death. You don't have to leave everything to your surviving spouse. With sufficient assets, you can provide for both your spouse and your children if you should pass away first. You'll have the chance in your planning to set some boundaries around what your spouse gets so that what's left ultimately ends up in the hands of your children, if that's your intention.

> **EXAMPLE:** Ricky leaves half of his substantial estate outright to his children. The other half he places in trust for his wife Lucy, who gets supported for the rest of her life, and then what's left goes to Ricky's children.

Once the couple's larger goals are met, each spouse should get to determine what to do with his or her assets. In other words, you should get to decide what to do with your stuff, and your spouse should get to do the same. If you want to leave your car to your child and not to your spouse, that's your decision. On the other hand, there are limits. If your spouse is reasonably relying on your plan for support, then you need to take that into account. (And, as discussed above, in most states a surviving spouse has the right to claim some share of the deceased spouse's estate anyway.) By and large, most spouses I've met recognize that subject to their responsibilities, they can leave their money as they wish.

Being fair to your children doesn't mean that you have to treat them all equally. Treat each child as an individual and think how best you can meet the needs of that child, while still taking care of your other beneficiaries. Your children have different needs and different resources. You may have put a star by the name of one or more children on your must-inherit list, but not others. Focus on those children you starred on the list: What is it that made you want to give them special treatment?

Is it a medical condition? A need based on occupation or lifestyle choice? Look at whether those children should get a bigger share. (For more on treating children according to need, see "Should You Treat Your Children Equally?" below.)

Make sure that personal items that mean a great deal to your children (but not necessarily to your spouse) go to your children at your death. Don't assume your spouse is going to appreciate the value to your children of all of your stuff or know which child is supposed to receive which item. Things have a way of getting lost, which can alienate your children from your spouse.

Don't forget any commitments you have made or are subject to. Some divorce decrees, settlement agreements, and child support agreements have specific requirements as to what may be required to be in the estate plan. If you are subject to one of these agreements, make sure you comply.

> EXAMPLE: Bennie is obligated by his divorce settlement to maintain a life insurance policy for his former wife Bonnie and to leave her an additional $10,000 in his will. As part of his estate planning, Bennie needs to keep the policy in place and make sure the $10,000 gets addressed in his will or trust.

In sum, think of each beneficiary's needs and resources, how much each is relying on you, how much you can expect to leave the beneficiary while meeting the other demands on your estate, and how much each may receive from another person (such as a parent or grandparent). Let's take a look at specific beneficiaries.

Your Spouse

Is your spouse relying on you for support? What other resources does your spouse have? If your spouse depends on you now and likely will continue to need support following your death, then you will want to make a significant provision for your spouse. If your spouse has independent wealth, you are probably less concerned, except that you might wish to leave your spouse certain rights to the house you share.

For example, if the house is in your name or both of your names, your estate plan may include leaving your spouse the right to use the house for life. (Chapter 6 discusses ways to do this.)

Your Children

Take a look at your situation. Do your children still rely on you for support? What other resources do they have? Are your children young, with their education well ahead of them? Are they in the midst of their education or already are out in the workforce? What legal obligations do you have to them in a divorce or settlement agreement or child support agreement?

Most people provide for their children as part of their estate planning, even if they're not legally required to do so. But if your children are adults and the divorce decree doesn't obligate you to provide for them, then you do not have to leave a portion of your estate to your children. Similarly, they won't be able to make a claim for any of your estate. If your children are minors and you don't provide for them in your estate plan, they may be able to make a claim against your estate even if your divorce decree doesn't specifically require you to provide for them. It depends on state law and your particular circumstances.

Parents generally like to make sure that their children have roughly equivalent opportunities given their interests, gifts, and needs. This doesn't necessarily mean that we treat our children identically when it comes to financial distributions. If Bobby needs braces, but Cindy doesn't, most parents don't write a check to Cindy to make sure they're spending the same amount of money on each child (a good thing, given the cost of orthodontists).

Yet when people begin their estate planning, a common tendency is to split up what's going to the children in identical shares. This kind of arrangement looks fair. But what if your children have vastly different needs? Would an even split be fair? Or should the less well-off child get a little more? These are questions you will have to answer for yourself and your children.

EXAMPLE 1: Jane has two children, Johnny and JoLyn. Johnny won the lottery some years back; JoLyn struggles to make ends meet and keep the heat on while juggling her work at the women's shelter and the food bank. Jane decides to leave 25% of her assets to Johnny and 75% to JoLyn. Jane sits down with each child explaining her reasoning and her love for both her children.

EXAMPLE 2: Jeremy has two children, Katie and Jake. Katie is a successful neurosurgeon; Jake is disabled as a result of a serious accident. Jeremy decides to split his assets in half and leave Jake's portion in a special needs trust and leave Katie her portion in a trust that pays out based on the trust's income earned, Katie's needs, and her age.

In each of these examples, despite the differing plans, the parent is comfortable that the result is fair, based on the needs of the children. Jane chose a split that was not 50/50, but let her children know why and reconfirmed her love for them. That gave her children insight into why she did what she did and lessened the likelihood of a rift based on hurt feelings. Jeremy chose a 50/50 split, but tailored the form of the inheritance to the needs of each child.

Children With Special Needs

If you have a child who will require support for his or her entire life, you should look into options that are especially designed to provide for the child while preserving his or her eligibility for important government benefits, particularly health insurance. For many families, a special needs trust is an effective method. For more information, see *Special Needs Trusts: Protect Your Child's Financial Future*, by Stephen Elias (Nolo).

Your Stepchildren

Start with the same basic questions: Do your stepchildren rely on you for support? What other resources do they have? If a stepchild has a realistic expectation of an inheritance from another parent or a grandparent, that can be incorporated in your planning.

Are your stepchildren in the midst of their education, or in the working world? Are you close to them? The closer the relationship and the greater the need, the more likely it is that you'll want to provide for your stepchildren.

> **EXAMPLE:** Bob, an architect, is married to Yvette, an anesthesiologist. Bob has two children from a previous relationship, Yvette has one. Bob's ex-wife, Marteel, works at a nonprofit organization and barely gets by. Yvette has shared custody of her child with her former husband, Todd, a successful phlebotomist. Bob and Yvette also have a child together. Bob's five potential beneficiaries are:
> - his wife, Yvette
> - his two children with Marteel
> - his child with Yvette, and
> - Yvette's child with Todd.
>
> Bob decides to divide his estate among Yvette, his children from his previous relationship, and his child with Yvette. Because Yvette's child with Todd will be adequately provided for, Bob makes a only small bequest to her under his will.

I've had a number of clients who provided for their stepchildren just as fully as if they were their natural children. For all intents and purposes, the stepchildren *are* their natural children, because when the clients entered into the relationship the stepchildren were young, and the stepparents were there all the way from skinned knees to puberty, from puberty to prom dresses, from prom dresses to wedding gowns. For these clients, it was a natural expression of their love for their stepchildren gained over many years to include them in their estate plan.

EXAMPLE: Don and Juanita marry when Juanita's daughter, Mary Claire, is four. Juanita has primary custody of Mary Claire, who lives with Don and Juanita until she leaves for college. Don wishes to provide in his will for Mary Claire equally with his children from his previous marriage.

Couples who meet and marry later in life typically have less desire and feel less familial pressure to provide for children who were adults at the time of the marriage. Of course, it depends on the circumstances. If your children are riding around in brand-new luxury cars while your spouse's children are collecting cans by the highway, then you're likely going to be under some not-so-subtle familial pressure to make some sort of provision for the can collectors. And that's okay—you're part of a blended family, there's a need, and you can help address that need. If there's a significant disparity and you can substantially improve the quality of life of your loved one's loved ones, then it makes sense to do so. (Chapter 7 talks more about what's fair when there's a substantial disparity in wealth between spouses.)

In the absence of such dire circumstances or a commitment you've made ("If anything ever happens to me, I want to pay for your child's education"), you should feel free to be honest about what you would like to leave to your stepchildren, just like you should with any other beneficiary.

If you don't have a commitment or legal obligation to support someone, then it is up to you to decide what you wish to do. It is your stuff and your plan.

Charities or Other Beneficiaries

Many people choose to leave something to a charity, a more distant relative, or a beloved friend. If that is your intention, make sure to include the charity or friend in your plan. If you want a friend or relation to inherit a certain item of sentimental value, be sure to leave it to that person specifically. If you don't, your spouse or children may not know of your intention.

Getting Down to the Nitty Gritty: Specific Assets

Slicing a pie can be a helpful visual tool to give you the big picture, but it's not well-suited to particular items. It's hard to transfer, say, one-third of a car or divvy up a set of golf clubs.

It's often helpful to look at specific assets and think of how you'd like for them to end up, based on whether you die first or your spouse dies first. When thinking about what happens if your spouse doesn't survive you, look at those beneficiaries on your optional list (particularly any whom you have starred) to see whether you may be able to include them. If your spouse survives you, you have two choices: what you want to have happen at your death, and what you want to have happen at your spouse's death.

Roughing Out a Plan

The worksheet shown below takes each of your main assets and asks you to fill in where they should go at your death or your spouse's death.

Leaving Your Property				
	Approx. value	If I pass first, then at my death I wish this to go to:	If I pass first, then at my spouse's death I wish this (or what's left) to go to:	If my spouse passes first, then at my death I wish this to go to:
House				
Retirement plan assets				
Investment accounts				
Life insurance/ annuities				
Any assets or property I have inherited from my parents or grandparents				
Vacation homes/other real estate (list)				
Automobile				
Personal mementos:				
Jewelry				
Family photos				
Furniture				
Artwork				
Other				

EXAMPLE: Caesar wants his wife Cleo to have their house for life if she survives him, but ultimately wants it to go to his children, Caesar, Jr. and Shelly. If Cleo passes away first, he wants it to go directly to Caesar, Jr. and Shelly. But when it comes to the life insurance proceeds, Caesar wants them to go to Cleo, period, for her to spend as she needs to. If there's anything left at her death, how she leaves it is up to her.

Caesar's choices would be as follows:

	Approx. value	If I pass first, then at my death I wish this to go to:	If I pass first, then at my spouse's death I wish this (or what's left) to go to:	If my spouse passes first, then at my death I wish this to go to:
House	$300,000	Cleo	Caesar, Jr. and Shelly	Caesar, Jr. and Shelly
Life insurance/ annuities	$100,000	Cleo	Let Cleo decide	Caesar, Jr. and Shelly

To make sure your item-by-item division doesn't reach an unintended, unequal result, tally up the approximate value of each beneficiary's expected inheritance. Although you don't have to treat everyone identically, you should get a sense now whether your proposed plan looks a bit lopsided so you can correct it if needed. If you've divided your things up, your must-inherit beneficiaries are taken care of, and there's still something left over, look at your maybe-inherit list (particularly any names that are starred) to see whether there's something you might leave to persons or charities on that list.

When planning for things like retirement benefits, life insurance, and any other asset or account that lets you designate a beneficiary to inherit it, that designation will usually—but not always—control. In other words, your will won't affect what happens to the asset. For example, if you designate your spouse as the beneficiary of your life insurance but provide that everything in your will is split between your spouse and children, then your spouse is going to get the life insurance proceeds. Start thinking today about those types of assets, because you're going to want to make sure you get them in line with your overall plan. (Chapter 6 discusses these "nonprobate" assets in detail.)

> ⚠ **CAUTION**
>
> **Don't forget your spouse may have rights to a bigger slice.** As discussed above, some federal and state laws give your spouse certain rights to claim some of your property after your death. That means you might need some additional planning if you wish to make a substantial gift to your children and not leave your spouse a significant portion (one-third to one-half, generally) of your estate. For example, under federal law leaving certain retirement plan assets to someone other than your spouse requires your spouse's written consent. Texas gives a surviving spouse the right to occupy a marital home for life under certain circumstances. Most states give the spouse a right to elect to obtain a share or percentage of the deceased spouse's estate even if the will says something else. (A spouse can, however, waive these rights and other techniques can be used to minimize the likelihood of a claim by your spouse for more than you've specified.)

Bottom line: This is a preliminary, rough division you're making here. Your lawyer will help you get the right structure to obtain the results you want. Just don't be surprised if the process isn't as easy as saying what you wish to have happen in your will or on a beneficiary designation—other documents or agreements might be required.

Young Beneficiaries: When and How Should They Inherit?

When planning for children, stepchildren, or grandchildren, you need to think about whether you want them to receive their full inheritance at your or your spouse's death, or whether it should be spread out over time. Obviously, making that decision starts, at least, with looking at how old they are.

Recent experiments by neuroscientists confirm what parents of teenagers have long known: The adolescent brain is not fully mature. One of the last parts of the brain to develop is the prefrontal cortex or frontal lobe, which is responsible for much of a person's judgment, ability to think ahead, and tendency to weigh risks and benefits. Research shows this key portion of the brain isn't fully formed until the early to mid-20s.

> **RESOURCE**
>
> **More about young adults.** Even though the brain may have finished forming by the mid-20s, a willingness to accept responsibility may not appear until later. That age may be getting longer. Writers have identified what is variously called "extended adolescence" or "emerging adulthood," between ages 18 and 30, in which the young adult's identity continues to be shaped.
>
> "A Challenge for Churches: Adulthood Takes Its Time," by Peter Steinfels (*New York Times*, December 8, 2007)
>
> *Emerging Adulthood: The Winding Road From the Late Teens Through the Twenties*, by Jeffrey Jensen Arnett (Oxford University Press).

Regardless of the cause—biology or environment, video games or too many high-powered energy drinks—many parents conclude that the traditional ages of adulthood, 18 and 21, and even the mid-20s are too early to entrust a child with a substantial inheritance if suitable alternatives are available.

The key is to make the money available when it's really needed, but not so early that it runs a high risk of being squandered. Your main choices are to give money while you're alive or wait until your death, at which time you can leave property with or without strings attached.

Generally, until about age 40, financial need is greater than emotional maturity. Somewhere in the 40s the maturity catches up to the need. (I usually tell my clients that by age 45, their children are likely to be about as mature and responsible as they're going to be.) Finally, the maturity exceeds the need. What does this mean for your planning? To avoid giving too much too soon, you might want to leave amounts in trust for your children during the years in which their financial need exceeds their emotional maturity. That way the trustee you've chosen can dole out the money, following guidelines you've left. Once the beneficiary's maturity level catches up, outright gifts might be more appropriate.

Financial need is higher when the child is starting a family, buying a house, paying for college, and raising children. If you wait too long, then the money may arrive past the time when it could have been most helpful.

How do you know when your child is financially mature? Most parents' definition of financial maturity runs along the lines of the following: "My children are financially mature when they begin spending my money the way I would spend it." But if you're waiting for that moment, your wait may be interminable. Children have different priorities. Modern culture assigns different weights than in your day.

I once talked to a woman who wished to tie up everything in trust for her children until they were in their 70s because she didn't think they'd be mature enough until then! Most people wouldn't intentionally opt for such extremes, but if you are waiting until your death to make any transfers to your children, with today's life expectancies, you may unintentionally be doing the same thing. Your children might not receive their inheritance until they're past the age at which it could be most appreciated and used while they are raising their families.

By encouraging lifetime giving where appropriate, I am not suggesting you transfer more wealth to your children than is prudent given your own projected needs and resources. I suggest you take an honest look at your resources with your financial adviser to see whether your anticipated wealth at retirement, using conservative projections, is more than sufficient to maintain the standard of living you'd like to maintain. If it is, then there may be opportunities for you to begin giving to your children while they're still at an age and stage in life to really appreciate it and use the money wisely. (Making lifetime gifts can also have tax benefits, if you have enough assets to be concerned about federal estate tax; see Chapter 5.)

Trusts Designed to Influence Behavior

Some parents go to great lengths to promote certain behaviors in their children, such as finishing school, getting and staying married, or marrying within a certain religion. They do this by setting up trusts that reward the children who exhibit the desired behaviors.

Such "incentive trusts" can be very attractive to those of us who are high on the control continuum. Something to keep in mind, however, is that these trusts work like government programs and tend to follow the law of unintended consequences. They may give the child an incentive—but the incentive may be to devote time to figure out how to milk the trust dry by complying with its terms, rather than its spirit.

Standard trust language allows not only for distributions to meet basic needs, but also to fund education, a down payment on a home, or a new business or other desirable endeavors by the recipient. At a minimum, trusts do involve some behavior-shaping.

My personal view is that, absent huge wealth, at some point, you've got to hand the keys over. It's like when your children reached the age of 16 and were learning to drive. They were still learning. Still, you trained them as best you could and then you handed them the keys.

SEE AN EXPERT

Get expert help. Unless your financial expertise rivals that of Warren Buffett, don't go this alone—have a trusted adviser assist you in running projections.

Building Relationships With Children and Stepchildren

Your feelings about providing for children and stepchildren will depend to a large extent on the strength of your relationships with them. It is common for parents in blended families to experience strained relationships with children. Moreover, developing relationships with stepchildren requires stores of time and patience.

The principal way to develop good relationships with children and stepchildren is to spend time with them. Time allows for healing, encourages the development of trust, and fosters the creation of shared interests. You can't make it up later—a generous bequest won't make up for 20 years of a miserly spirit.

Many stepparents suggest the following as important to building a good relationship with stepchildren who are still at home (or who split time between your home and their other parent's home):

- **It takes time—lots of time.** If the stepchild is too young to remember the other parent, the relationship may deepen quickly. But often, children resent the new stepparent, and it takes a wealth of patience for the stepparent to hang in there, day in and day out, and absorb the blows without fighting back.

- **It takes a good relationship between the spouses.** You and your spouse must maintain a unified front to avoid getting played off of one another. You can anticipate frustrating times with each of the children and stepchildren. Take time for yourselves to keep your relationship strong.

- **Go slowly.** Let your spouse be the disciplinarian of your spouse's children until you've established a bond with them.

- **Bite your lip.** Don't criticize the other parent in front of the stepchild. Be prepared to feel very defensive about any criticism (real or perceived) your spouse or stepchild may level against your children—and try not to react in a way that escalates tension.

- **Develop your own relationship.** Try to find activities in which you and the stepchild can participate, that are uniquely your own.

Relationships are strengthened by the time you spend together, the intimacy of your discussions, and the frequency with which you talk. You may not have the luxury of seeing your children and stepchildren daily, but you can still spend time with them, take an interest in what's important to them, and participate, in a nonintrusive way, in their activities. And it may be appreciated, even if they don't say so to you directly.

At some point, it's not about anything you've done or haven't done. You do the best you can, you set some boundaries, and hope that time and your sweet sunny disposition will wear them down. You may never realize how much your efforts were truly appreciated.

RESOURCE

More about parenting and stepparenting.

Walking on Eggshells: Navigating the Delicate Relationship between Adult Children and Parents, by Jane Isay (Flying Dolphin Press). In it, the author relies on her own experience and extensive interviews to help parents and stepparents work their way through relationships with their children.

"How I Turned Into a Stepmonster," by Maria Dahvana Headley, *The New York Times,* September 16, 2007, which despite the title has a happy ending.

www.stepfamily.org (collection of articles and other resources)

www.stepfamily.net (links to discussion groups)

www.thestepfamilylife.com (blog and columns with a dose of Christian spirituality written by "real life stepmom" Dawn Miller; includes links to other resources).

You and Your Spouse:
Talking It Through, Working It Out

Talking About the Tough Stuff..58

    Step 1: Prepare 58

    Step 2: Pick the Right Time and Place, Maximize Your Energy and

             Presence..61

Tips for Resolving Differences 63

Common Roadblocks—And How to Get Around Them 65

To get the estate plan you really want, you and your spouse will need to talk about what's important to you. Talking helps you work through the issues and resolve any minor, mildly bothersome differences before they become humongous, paralyzing ones.

You and your spouse have already come up with your Big Five estate planning goals and concerns (Chapter 2). Now it's time to delve into the specifics and think about what you would want to happen if you were to pass away and your spouse and children survived you. How would you want the following to be treated?

- **Your house.** Should it be sold and the proceeds divided among your spouse, children, and/or stepchildren? Or should your spouse inherit it or have the right to live there rent-free for the rest of your spouse's life? If there's a mortgage on the house, who should pay it?

- **Bank accounts, brokerage accounts, and other financial assets.** How much of your estate do you intend to leave to your spouse? How much to your children? Do you want to leave assets to your spouse or children outright (no strings attached) or in trust?

- **Retirement plans and life insurance.** Who should be the beneficiaries? Your spouse? Your children?

- **Personal items.** Should they go to your spouse (for example, with the house) or should all or a portion (especially family heirlooms) go to children?

- **Disposition of your body.** Do you wish to be buried or cremated? Do you want to be an organ donor or have your body donated to science?

Both you and your spouse will need to answer these questions. To begin, each of you should decide what you would want if the other survived you, and then again as if the other passed away first. Your answers will likely change when the scenario does. In addition, each of you should think about how you might answer if you and your spouse were to pass away simultaneously or within a short period of time of one another, or if one of you were to pass away first and the survivor to live many more years.

Let's look at a fairly typical blended family. Kim and Randy are married and live in a house they jointly own. Each has children from a prior relationship and no children together. Randy's total assets are greater than Kim's, and he plans to provide for his children out of his separate assets. He's not as concerned about maximizing his children's inheritance with any assets owned jointly with Kim. For Kim, her interest in jointly owned assets amounts to the bulk of her estate, so she is committed to making sure her interest in those assets passes to her children. Each will provide for his or her children, so neither is worried about providing for stepchildren.

Kim decides that if Randy survives her, she wants him to be able to live in their house rent-free for the rest of his life and then have her half interest in the house pass to her children. She also wants Randy to get what's in their checking account, but wants her children to be the beneficiaries of her retirement plan assets. If Randy dies before Kim, she wants to leave everything to her children.

Randy also wants Kim, if she survives him, to be able to live in their house rent-free for the rest of her life, but Randy is comfortable leaving the house to Kim outright so that she can do what she wishes with it, including selling it or leaving it to her children or whomever she wishes at her death. Randy would like to have a portion of his assets pass to his children, but would leave Kim the checking account and distributions from his retirement plans during her life. Anything left at her death would pass to his children. If Kim didn't survive Randy, he wants to leave his interest in all of his assets to his children.

Once you and your spouse have thought through these issues, you'll want to talk them over. Admittedly, some of this looks a little dreary. But it's not so bad. Estate planning lies somewhere in the middle between picking a vacation spot and being called to your child's school for a parent/teacher conference to "discuss certain behavioral issues."

Talking About the Tough Stuff

As you and your spouse were going through the worksheets in Chapter 2 or otherwise fleshing out your goals and concerns, you likely found a handful of items that you need to discuss further or about which you have different opinions. That's to be expected.

It's natural to be a little hesitant before broaching issues and differences with your spouse. I'm going to offer some tips on communicating and resolving variances, but remember: You know your particular situation better than anyone else. You probably have a sense of what works with your spouse and what doesn't. So use the knowledge you already have; you'll be way ahead.

I should begin by pointing out what may be obvious: I am not a trained psychologist or mediator. I am, however, on my very best days, a fairly well-trained husband. And I've helped lots of couples talk through these very issues. The key is to avoid launching or lapsing into a full-blown discussion just because something is on your mind, when if you had plotted it out beforehand you would have picked another time.

Speed Bump or Pothole?

Try to think of issues and any disagreements over your estate planning as speed bumps. Slow down a bit, proceed over the bumps, and then continue without straying from your course. Don't let problems come at you like unexpected potholes—you'll end up veering back and forth straining to avoid them and may stray off course in the process. And like ignored potholes, your problems will only get deeper.

Step 1: Prepare

Preparation lays the foundation for a successful conversation. The good news is, you began your prep work when you worked through Chapter 2. Now, you need to winnow your to-be-discussed list to a manageable number of issues and think about what you'll say—and what your spouse might say in response.

For example, Alicia is planning to talk with her husband, Justin. Her unedited list of things might look as follows:

- deciding what to do with the house when one of us passes
- making sure that Justin can tap into my retirement plan if I pass first
- making sure that I can tap into Justin's retirement plan if I survive him
- making sure that my children—and not Justin's kids—get my stuff
- leaving my mother's china to my daughter
- deciding whether we should be buried or cremated
- deciding where we should we be buried
- deciding who should conduct the services.

After thinking about it, Alicia decides to narrow her list to the following:

- deciding what to do with the house
- talking about sharing retirement benefits
- agreeing that personal property (not essential furniture) pass to each one's children at death
- telling she would like to be buried where she grew up, and asking him for his preference.

I would try to hit no more than five to seven key areas, and make it a mix of hard and easy questions. Anything more than that might prove overwhelming. I don't recommend raising only the likely points of contention, because you want to emphasize your agreements over any disagreements.

How should you order your list? There are two schools of thought. Some folks like to hit the tough stuff up front, putting off the easy issues because they can be resolved quickly; others like to tackle the easy issues first and build a momentum of consensus before moving on to the tough issues. You know yourself and your spouse better than anyone else, and whether it's better to lead with the tough items or ease into them.

Don't dread the conversation; in my experience, people are able to work things out. Most people don't spend a lot of time thinking about these issues or talking them over with their spouses. By having the conversation, you're way ahead. Don't be surprised if your spouse responds to something you thought was going to be a huge sticking point with, "Hmm … I never thought about that" or "Now that you mention it, I think you're right." You want a flexible, back-and-forth discussion to avoid entrenched positions where someone who initially responded a certain way feels obligated to hold firm.

A little discernment goes a long way. You want to have thought about what you're going to say before the words come cascading out, but you need to be yourself and not overly scripted.

If you have some nervousness or are unsure about how your points may come across (both perfectly normal), you may want to bounce your issues list off a trusted, honest friend first. Pick a friend who won't just commiserate with you, but can point out where you might need to think further before going to your spouse. You also might try beefing up your list, writing out points and subpoints if that helps crystallize your thoughts.

If you keep a journal or find that writing things out in a complete narrative (as opposed to a list) gives you clarity, you might try journaling or stream-of-consciousness writing, where you just let yourself and your pen go without trying to edit as you write what pops into your head.

How will you know when you're prepared? Well, if you get fully, fully, fully, fully, fully, fully prepared, you've probably waited too long. This is more like preparing for a midterm test in school as opposed to a graduation exam where everything's riding on your performance. Thankfully, you and your spouse will have numerous chances to talk this through and reach agreement on what's really important to you. Both of you will probably make a few flubs along the way, but it will still work out.

Step 2: Pick the Right Time and Place, Maximize Your Energy and Presence

The second step to a successful discussion is carefully integrating four components: time, place, energy, and presence. Get these four things working for you, and all of your preparation will be put to good use. Take heart: It's not like you're waiting on some celestial alignment that only comes around every 100 years. If you miss a chance, a better one may be right behind it.

Time

For the time to be right, it has to be somewhere between a mad dash to the airport and the middle of a long-awaited vacation. You may want to compare calendars with your spouse to pick a mutually convenient time to discuss these issues. Scheduling may help keep the conversation from getting put off, and it can make sure your spouse doesn't get blindsided by a heavy discussion. Probably the best way to show how to pick the timing for a talk is to show when it might not be the best idea.

> EXAMPLE 1: The school bus will be here in five minutes, Junior's breakfast is in the microwave, and the components for his lunch are scattered throughout the kitchen. The only pair of shoes he has that fits is currently a single, its match having been seen most recently in the mouth of the Labrador who likes to dig. There's a teacher's note to be signed, a fundraiser that's due, a class pet that's gone missing, and how are you going to pack that poster on the history of the avocado without destroying all of the hard work you put in as you "helped" him with it? Not now.

> EXAMPLE 2: It's your first time alone in weeks. Candles are softly flickering, glasses are quietly clinking. A smile is curling across your spouse's face. Van Morrison plays in the background. The takeout's terrific. You've locked the cat in the basement, and the kids are at your mother's. Not now.

Place

Think about where you and your spouse have your best talks. For my wife and me, it's a handful of places: walking on the beach, boating around the lake, or taking long car trips. Removed from the daily grind, we tend to let the workweek barriers come down, and the conversation flows more readily and easily.

Your ideal place should be one where you can be alone without distractions. Turn off the TV. Your computer and cell phone, too. Personally, my attention span leaves something to be desired. Your or your spouse's may, too, so make sure there are not a lot of other things going on to sap your attention.

Energy

My wife and I both have stressful jobs. If she's been charging hard 18 out of the last 19 days, I'm likely not going to get a good response if I catch her before she has a chance to recover and revive. Similarly, if I have a big project due at work or a book chapter deadline looming, I tend to get a little wild-eyed. Physically and mentally, I'm at a low ebb. Talking about the serious family and financial issues is stressful; it does take energy. And if your batteries are running low, you don't need to deplete them further by having a serious discussion when your partner would prefer to have some serious TV or tub time. If it's been crisis central at your house or work for a couple of weeks, give it a rest until you both feel better.

Presence

If you're going to have this discussion, be fully present for it. Don't think about the hundred other things you need to do. Be a good listener—make eye contact, stop fiddling with stuff, don't gaze longingly at the newspaper, cell phone, computer, or magazine while your spouse is speaking. Your goal is to create an environment where you can be honest about what's on your mind and trust your spouse to hear your truth while allowing your spouse the opportunity to do the same.

Let your spouse finish before formulating a response in your mind. This one is difficult for me, so I have to try hard to focus on what the other person is saying and trust I'll have something to say when it's time.

Be accepting. Be supportive. Be nonjudgmental. This isn't about you or your relationship, it's about hearing your spouse's views on issues near and dear to your spouse, views that were likely formulated long before you came into the picture. Remind yourself, "This is not about me. This is not about US."

If despite your preparation you forget something, come back to it. If you goof up, apologize and move on. Rely on the strength of your relationship and your love for one another to get you through this.

Tips for Resolving Differences

Before long, your discussions will probably resolve some of the disagreements and lay to rest some uncertainties. Still, you might be left with a few key areas over which you and your spouse have some differences. What should you do next? Here are five ideas.

Keep talking. Many of these issues are deeply felt, coming from the heart. Often, people have a great deal of difficulty communicating what is truly on their mind. What we say initially may not reflect our real feelings. It's hard to say something you think the other person doesn't want to hear. By continuing the dialogue you may find out what is really going on, not just the surface, and see a key to resolution.

Quit talking, do something. Hours or minutes into the discussion over the disagreement, your spouse is fidgeting. You know that rehashing feelings, reasons, concerns, and goals is the last thing your spouse wants to do at this point. You can almost see the muscle fibers twitching. So, do what is done in business meetings all the time: Assign the disagreement as an action item for which your spouse is to follow up and suggest solutions. Agree to take some items of your own. That way, you're not saddling one spouse with all the chores, but acknowledging that these issues take time to resolve. Trust one another to come up with solutions. Solutions may surface as you read more about estate planning techniques in this book, talk with friends who have been in the same boat, meet with the lawyer that you pick to handle your estate planning, or just take a step back to reflect.

Horse trade. Here, you can do what married couples do all the time—you can bargain. Not sure about something? Tell your spouse you'll do X (what he or she wants) if you can have Y (what you want).

Select the third way. If compromise is impossible (you both want to be buried together, but he wants to be in Houston and you want to be in Seattle), then pick a third choice. "Okay, if we can't be in two places at the same time, how about if we get buried in Key West since we've always enjoyed visiting there and we hope to retire there someday anyway?"

Be creative. See if there's a different way to accomplish the same thing. There's more than one way to skin a cat, keep assets out of the hands of an ex-spouse, or make sure the survivor of the two of you has a place to live. See if you can address what you both want by looking at a different technique. This book can help you, because I'll talk about multiple ways to handle things as we go along. Your lawyer can help as well.

Okay, you've done your homework. You've picked the right time and place. You and your spouse have the energy. You're fully committed and present. The cell phones are off, the TV remote is hidden under the cushions. It's quiet enough to hear the burbles in the fish tank—and you don't even have a fish tank.

If you still don't agree—even after each of you has articulated your goals and concerns beautifully, sensitively, and stirringly—don't give up. Lots of people find this part of the planning challenging, but they get it done anyway. You and your spouse can, too.

What to do? Well, if your partner is the dominant one in the relationship, you could cave. That doesn't feel too good. Or you could pout and throw things. That feels better, but doesn't really resolve anything except perhaps get rid of a few unwanted wedding gifts.

Here's my three-part plan for when you hit an impasse.

First, give it a day or two or a week. Perhaps your spouse will come to his senses. Perhaps you will come to yours. People do change their minds after having time to think things over.

Second, if a little R&R (rest and removal) don't cure it, save the point for when you meet with your lawyer. Your lawyer is independent and has experience in resolving differences. Your lawyer may be able to help you.

Third, if cooling off and chilling with your lawyer don't fix it, then agree with your spouse to disagree. That's it. You do it your way in your plan; your spouse does it his or her way. For example, say you believe strongly that children shouldn't get a lot of money outright at a young age, so you want to set up trusts for your children. Your spouse thinks if the children are old enough to be drafted, they're old enough to handle money. So you create a trust in your will and your spouse doesn't. Not perfect, but you move on. Who knows? The next time you get together to review your plans, things will likely have changed and the differences that seem to define you now may largely have receded.

How you feel now is not how you may feel forever. Second marriages, like any relationship, have seasons. As you and your spouse grow together, your feelings may change. When school-age children complete their education and get out on their own, their needs change. Life is constantly tumbling you and your loved ones around. The crash-prone child you shuddered to lend the car to at age 16 may become the most responsible person of the bunch at age 25.

Common Roadblocks—And How to Get Around Them

Because estate planning can touch on such core emotions, it has the ability to resurrect a few demons here and there that can throw you off track. If you get stuck and you're not sure whether it's because you and your spouse disagree at a rational level or there's something going on inside your subconscious, then you need to take a step back. To get to the root of what's holding you back, you may need to spend some time alone looking inward, journaling, or talking with a trusted and honest friend, counselor, or spiritual adviser. Here are some of the things I see often in my practice that can trip up your planning, and some ideas to keep you moving.

Unresolved emotional issues from a previous relationship. Negative feelings from a relationship loss can linger for years, and many people remarry without fully putting to rest issues from the previous relationship. You could still be harboring feelings of fear, anger, resentment, self-doubt, guilt, or lack of trust, any of which can impede your planning. Plus, the experience of talking with your spouse about the division of wealth and treatment of children may seem eerily similar to your negotiating a property settlement during divorce and bring up bad memories, if not old wounds.

Thankfully, there are a number of resources out there for coping with and moving on from a relationship loss. Among these include the widely used *Rebuilding: When Your Relationship Ends,* by Bruce Fisher and Robert Alberti (Impact Publishing). First published in 1981 and later revised, this work is a standard text in recovery workshops. It illustrates with empathy the stages and emotional changes of recovery and provides exercises for completing one's recovery. Depending on the severity of the issue, you or your spouse may want to consider counseling.

Unresolved emotional issues from a previous negative experience. For many people, the loss of a parent or close relative, and the feelings and experiences surrounding that loss, affect them years later. If your spouse, for example, experienced ill treatment at the hands of a sibling or stepparent following the loss of a parent, those bad feelings can negatively affect your spouse's current planning. Your spouse's unresolved anger at the sibling or stepparent may rob your spouse of the energy and focus needed to continue your present planning.

If the pain is present, but not overwhelming, it may be helpful to keep in mind that that was then/this is now. You're dealing with an entirely different set of people and situations. Use the negative experience as motivation to avoid making some of the same mistakes in your own planning. For example, if your spouse feels (as many do) that a previous executor enriched himself at the expense of other beneficiaries, suggest that you both take great pains to select independent, impartial executors or trustees in your plan so that your children don't suffer as you did. Still stuck? Counseling may be advisable.

Current issues interfering with your decision making. Addictions, depression, insecurity, or a host of other conditions can affect planning. Someone who is actively battling addiction may not have the emotional reserve to deal with a weighty issue such as estate planning. Depending on the severity, treatment, rehabilitation, or counseling may be needed before you can move forward.

Frustration with the length, difficulty, or expense of the process. Estate planning is hard stuff when done correctly. It can take from one to six months to get it right. It can take a lot of money, too. People have a tendency to throw up their hands when the going gets tough and the bills are adding up. My advice: Don't quit! Keep going! You'll get there! Review your estate planning goals and concerns. If you don't finish, those goals will go unfulfilled and your concerns will remain unaddressed. If cost is an issue, remember that failing to plan or resuming your planning down the road with someone else will likely be more expensive than sticking with it now. Plus, valuable planning opportunities can be lost the longer you wait. For example, if you have a taxable estate, the sooner you can begin making gifts to your children, the sooner you can begin making a meaningful dent in your ultimate estate tax bill. There's an annual limit on such gifts ($13,000 in 2009), and you don't get to make up for lost years.

Not nearly enough time to devote to estate planning. On paper, it seems like you should be able to get everything done. In actuality, it's not going to happen, not now, unless you cut out something else. So either simplify or wait until things lighten up. There's a bit of a trap with putting things off, because waiting for the best time often means that nothing gets done. If you are truly overwhelmed and the cause will be short-lived (big project at work nearing completion, son's traveling soccer schedule soon over), then perhaps it's a good idea to postpone the process until you can deal with the complicating person, plan, or situation in your life. If you're overwhelmed and there's no end in sight, you need to carve out time for your estate planning, because there may never be an ideal time. Again, focus on your reasons for completing your estate planning—without an unfinished plan hanging over you, you'll have one less stressor in your life. Think of how great it will feel to cross this off the list!

Too much information or too many options. Estate planning presents a myriad of choices, new terminology, and unfamiliar techniques. These can be overwhelming. I think of it as being paralyzed by the infinity of the possible. Most of us like to keep our options open, which can impede our ability to focus on the choice that's right for us. To get over this, focus on your goals and concerns and use your lawyer, spouse, and trusted friends as filters to shut out the noise. Let them help you home in on what is most important to you. For example, this may be the first time you've ever done estate planning. Your lawyer may have done 50 plans this year. If you get stuck by all the choices, ask your lawyer's recommendation. Many lawyers prefer to lay the options on the table and let the client decide, but will, if asked, offer their opinion on what is best for you. Or if the issue is whether a child is ready to take on a certain responsibility, ask an older friend who's been there or knows your child well.

Taxes

Federal Estate Tax 73

    The Applicable Exclusion Amount..74

    The Unlimited Marital Deduction..75

    Why Planning Is So Important...78

    Stepped-Up Basis vs. Carryover Basis.. 80

    Calculating the Estate Tax...82

    Who Pays the Estate Tax?...85

State Estate Taxes..87

The Federal Gift Tax..87

    Annual Exclusion Gifts.. 88

    The Lifetime Credit..89

    Neat Planning Opportunities With the Gift Tax 90

Gift Tax vs. Estate Tax: Why It's Better to Give Now Than Later.....................92

The Generation-Skipping Transfer Tax...95

Estate and gift and generation skipping
Taxes like these keep my stomach flipping
I'll pay my fair share, but won't you see
If we can just try for none out of three?

When most of us think about taxes, we think of income or capital gains taxes that we dutifully hand over to the federal government each year based on how much money we made or how much profit we had after selling property or shares of stock.

But when you're doing estate planning, you need to think about a different kind of taxes, known as transfer taxes. Transfer taxes are taxes you or your estate may pay when property goes from you to a loved one. Taxable transfers can occur during your life, as when you give property to a child or grandchild or place property into an irrevocable trust. These transfers can also occur after your death, either when property is transferred out of your name into that of your loved ones, or when distributions are made from certain trusts. Not all transfers are taxable, and many people never have to concern themselves with these taxes. But when they do apply, transfer taxes are at some of the highest rates for all federal taxes.

The three federal transfer taxes are:

- estate tax
- gift tax, and
- generation-skipping tax.

Some states have their own versions of these taxes.

The transfer tax laws don't care whether this is your first, second, or other marriage. But of course, couples in blended families have special concerns. You ultimately may want "your stuff" going to your children after your spouse is provided for; your spouse may want the same for his or her children. The good news is that tax planning lends itself well to your situation if you want to provide for your children and your spouse wants to provide for his or her children. Through the use of tax-planning trusts (more on that in Chapter 6), you'll be able to provide

for your spouse and your children and still take full advantage of tax
law provisions that let you leave large amounts of assets, tax-free, to your
spouse and others. So don't be concerned that the tax planning is going
to disturb your primary goals of providing for your spouse and your
children.

The Big Three Federal Transfer Taxes: A Summary		
Estate Tax	**Gift Tax**	**Generation-Skipping Transfer Tax**
• Applies to fewer than 1% of estates • Rates are high: 45% to 55% • Fairly easy to reduce tax owed if you plan now • Can be reduced by making nontaxable gifts during life	• Applies to many transfers of more than $13,000 per recipient • Usually easy to avoid	• Applies to certain transfers from grandparents to grandchildren and later generations • Rarely imposed because transfers must be very large before they are taxed • Rate is high: 45% • Imposed *in addition to* any estate tax owed • Extremely complex

Tax laws are complicated—and changing. The discussion here is greatly
simplified and is intended only to give you an introduction to some tax
terms and concepts. It may even be out of date by the time you read
it, because tax laws are expected to change quickly. For updates, go to
www.nolo.com. Don't rely on this discussion alone for your planning!
Go see a tax accountant or tax lawyer. As they say on the commercials,
your mileage may vary. Trained professionals on a closed course. This
bag is not a toy. Contents are packaged according to weight, not volume.
Bags may have shifted during flight. Do not read this chapter while
driving or operating heavy machinery. You get the idea.

Top Five Estate Tax Mistakes Blended Families Make (for Taxable Estates)

1. Failing to take advantage of each spouse's applicable exclusion amount.

2. Failing to specify from which assets or whose inheritance any estate tax should be paid.

3. Failing to take full advantage of lifetime giving opportunities and other estate reduction techniques.

4. Failing to use irrevocable life insurance trusts as a way to provide an income and estate tax-free source of cash. (See Chapter 6.)

5. Failing to adequately plan for the generation-skipping transfer tax, which is in addition to any estate tax that may be due.

RESOURCE

More information on taxes.

The IRS (www.irs.gov) provides a number of publications and information, including IRS Publication 950, *Introduction to Estate and Gift Taxes*. The IRS's publications offer examples and helpful information for consumers, although navigating the website can sometimes be frustrating.

The American Institute of Certified Public Accountants (www.aicpa.org) has information on gift and estate taxes under Consumer Resources.

Motley Fool (www.fool.com) has estate tax planning information under its Retirement section.

Smart Money (www.smartmoney.com) has estate tax planning information in its Personal Finance section.

Kiplinger's (www.kiplinger.com) has estate tax planning information in its Your Retirement section.

Worth Magazine (www.worth.com) has estate tax planning information in its Wealth Management section.

Be careful when you use online search engines to research taxes. A lot of the random information on the Web is out of date, misleading, trying to sell you something you may not need, inapplicable to your state, or just plain wrong.

Federal Estate Tax

The federal estate tax applies to individuals who die leaving large sums of money or property to persons other than their spouses or charities. Right away, we see two components that trigger the estate tax:

- you have to leave a lot of money or property, and
- you have to leave it to someone other than your spouse or a charity.

If the tax applies, the bite can be severe. The rate for estates of people dying in 2009 is 45%; that is, 45¢ of every dollar (over the threshold amount) you're trying to leave to someone other than your spouse or charity goes to the IRS. Estate tax is paid out of property in the estate before the recipients get anything; inheriting property doesn't subject the recipient to tax.

> **EXAMPLE:** Ted dies, leaving an estate of $10 million, including a $2 million bequest to his son, Teddy. The estate tax attributable to the bequest to Teddy is $900,000 (45% of $2 million). Teddy's not responsible for paying the $900,000 out of his inheritance—it will probably be paid out of the assets left in Ted's estate after the $2 million to Teddy and other specific bequests in the will are made.

The good news is that the thresholds are high. Because of that, estate tax applies to only a very small portion of the population. In 2005 more than 1.5 million Americans died, but only 18,431 estates filed returns that showed a federal estate tax liability. And since then, the amount excluded from tax has gone way up (more on this below).

Why did 18,000+ people have to pay estate tax in 2005? Well, some had too much money and didn't have a spouse to leave it to or didn't want to leave the taxable portion to charity instead of their kids. Others didn't do the right planning.

If your estate will probably owe estate tax, making gifts and doing some good estate planning now can probably greatly reduce the impact of estate tax. Let me say that again: *If you have a potentially taxable estate and do some planning, you can save taxes and leave more to your loved ones. If you don't do the planning, you're making the federal government an unnecessary beneficiary of your estate.*

To speak the language of estate tax (I know, scary concept), you need a working knowledge of the following key concepts:

- the **applicable exclusion amount,** which lets you leave a certain amount tax-free to anyone
- the **unlimited marital deduction,** which lets you leave any amount, tax-free, to your spouse (as long as your spouse is a U.S. citizen), and
- **stepped-up and carryover basis,** which affect what recipients are considered to have "paid" for assets for tax purposes should they sell them.

The Applicable Exclusion Amount

The applicable exclusion amount is the amount you can leave, free of federal estate tax, to someone other than a spouse or a qualifying charity. This is the threshold I mentioned above.

The applicable exclusion amount has increased greatly in the past few years. For 2009, it's $3.5 million. This means that people dying in 2009 can leave, estate tax free, $3.5 million to someone other than their spouse or a charity (children, stepchildren, and grandchildren, for example). That's in addition to anything they do leave their spouse or a charity.

In 2010, the federal estate tax is scheduled to take a vacation. *For that year only,* estate tax has been repealed, and the applicable exclusion amount is unlimited. Under current law, Bill Gates could die in 2010 and leave his entire fortune to you, and there wouldn't be a dime of federal estate tax due.

However, unless federal estate tax repeal is made permanent or unless the federal estate tax laws are otherwise modified, in 2011 the applicable exclusion amount will revert to $1 million. Not only that, in 2011 the rates are scheduled to go back up: the top estate tax rate would be 55%.

The Future of the Estate Tax?		
Year of Death	Applicable Exclusion Amount	Estate Tax Rate
2009	$3.5 million	45%
2010	Unlimited	0
2011	$1 million	55% (top rate)

Most practitioners (including me) don't really believe that the applicable exclusion amount will revert to $1 million in 2011. They expect Congress to act before then to prevent the one-year repeal in 2010 and to keep the estate tax at about the 2009 level: $3.5 million exclusion and 45% tax rate. Although it's ultimately in the hands of the U.S. Senate and House of Representatives, President Obama has proposed keeping the estate tax at its 2009 levels. You'll want to keep a close eye on this if the estate tax may apply to you. (Check www.nolo.com for updates.)

The Unlimited Marital Deduction

The unlimited marital deduction refers to the unlimited deduction an estate gets for amounts left to a surviving spouse. In English, that means that there's no estate tax on anything you leave to your spouse. You have to meet a couple of requirements: your spouse must receive a "qualifying interest" and must be a citizen of the United States. (A noncitizen spouse can receive up to $133,000 free of tax.) A "qualifying interest" means the property is transferred outright—that is, no strings attached—or placed in a trust that meets certain technical IRS requirements.

> EXAMPLE: David and Martha have a joint net worth of $5 million, divided equally between them. David dies in 2009 and leaves everything outright to Martha. There is no estate tax payable at David's death.

At the death of the first spouse, because of the unlimited marital deduction, it doesn't matter how much you have. If you leave it all to the surviving spouse, then there's no estate tax. The tax issue comes up at the second spouse's death.

> EXAMPLE: Same as above, but then Martha dies in 2011 with an estate of $5 million and leaves everything to her children. Under current law, estate tax would be payable at Martha's death because her estate would exceed the 2011 applicable exclusion amount of $1 million. How much tax? Over $2 million!

Most estate tax planning is designed to use each spouse's applicable exclusion amount to avoid a larger than necessary tax bill at the second spouse's death. Under current law, it's "use it or lose it." Failing to use the first-to-die spouse's applicable exclusion amount can result in a much higher tax paid at the second spouse's death (as in the second example above). Because you don't know who's going to go first, you want to make sure the estate tax plan works either way.

> EXAMPLE 1: Rena and George have a combined $7 million estate, divided equally between them. If either dies in 2009, the full amount of $3.5 million can be protected from federal estate tax.

> EXAMPLE 2: Same as above, but $5 million is Rena's separate property, and $2 million is George's separate property. If Rena dies in 2009, then she can leave $3.5 million to her children (or put $3.5 million in a trust for George and her children) and leave the rest to George without incurring an estate tax. Then, if George dies later in 2009, he could protect the full amount of $3.5 million (his $2 million plus the $1.5 million he inherited from Rena). But if George dies first in 2009, he wouldn't be able to use his full $3.5 million exclusion, because he has only $2 million. If Rena then died with the $5 million in her name, $1.5 million would be subject to an estate tax of 45%, or $675,000. Because George did not fully use his applicable exclusion amount, his and Rena's heirs would get $675,000 less.

Same-Sex Spouses

Even if your state allows same-sex marriage, you and your spouse are still not entitled to use the unlimited marital deduction for federal estate tax purposes. The federal government doesn't recognize same-sex marriages, even though they're valid in some states. Other, specialized techniques may be available to lessen the tax bite, so be sure to consult an experienced practitioner.

The Applicable Exclusion Amount—Coming Soon in a Handy "To Go" Container?

You may have read in the news about government proposals to make the applicable exclusion amount "portable." Basically, that means that a couple would get one—larger—exclusion amount, which could be used by either or both spouses.

Under current law, each spouse has an applicable exclusion amount of $3.5 million—she has $3.5 million she can shield, he has $3.5 million. That's not the same thing as saying that the couple has a combined exclusion of $7 million.

Right now, if the husband passes away and leaves everything outright to his wife, then his $3.5 million exclusion has been wasted. Or, if the wife dies first, but doesn't have $3.5 million in her name (even though the couple's combined net worth is $7 million), then her $3.5 million shield has been lost. That's a big reason why estate planning for wealthy individuals is so important. Estate tax portability would reduce some of the sting from not planning by allowing the second-to-die spouse to use the unused portion of the first-to-die spouse's applicable exclusion amount.

Tax laws favor those who plan. One of the negatives cited by the government in adopting portability is that a sizable chunk of revenue would be lost—meaning that the current structure counts on a number of people not doing the planning necessary to use their applicable exclusion amount.

Why Planning Is So Important

Assume a couple has a joint net worth of $7 million. Five million is in the husband's name, $2 million in the wife's. If the husband passes first and leaves everything to the wife, there's no federal estate tax payable because of the unlimited marital deduction. However, if the wife dies in 2009, she can leave only $3.5 million to the children tax-free.

Without tax planning

At husband's death in 2009 ($5 million estate)

      All to spouse: $5 million
      Federal estate tax: $0

  At wife's death in 2009 ($7 million estate comprising $2 million of her own, $5 million inherited from husband)

      $ 7 million
      − $ 3.5 million (applicable exclusion amount)
      = $ 3.5 million

      Federal estate tax: $ 1,575,000 (45% of $3.5 million)
      To kids: $ 5,425,000

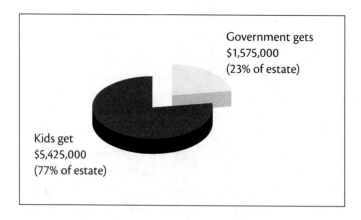

Government gets
$1,575,000
(23% of estate)

Kids get
$5,425,000
(77% of estate)

But if we use the husband's $3.5 million applicable exclusion amount at his death (this can be done by placing it in trust for the wife during her lifetime, then to the kids—see Chapter 6), we can completely eliminate the estate tax at the wife's death. Here's how it works.

With tax planning

At husband's death in 2009 ($5 million estate)

To trust for wife and kids:	$3.5 million
Directly to spouse:	1.5 million
Federal estate tax:	$ 0

Wife's death in 2009 ($3.5 million estate comprising $2 million of her own, $1.5 million inherited from husband)

To kids:	$3.5 million
Plus amount from husband's trust:	+ 3.5 million
Federal estate tax:	$ 0

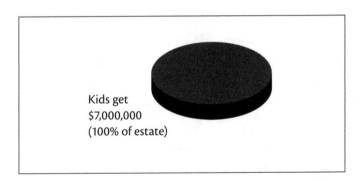

Kids get
$7,000,000
(100% of estate)

With some fairly simple planning, this couple can save $1,575,000 in estate tax, make sure the surviving spouse is provided for, and leave the entire $7 million to the children. Not a bad day's work!

Stepped-Up Basis vs. Carryover Basis

The third basic concept in understanding estate tax is the difference between a stepped-up basis and a carryover basis. Basis doesn't affect the taxes your estate pays, but it affects the income or capital gains taxes your beneficiaries will ultimately pay if they later sell something they inherit from you.

Here's how it works. Let's say you paid $4,000 for a vintage Corvette. You sell it for $10,000 to pay for your child's braces. You would owe taxes based on $6,000 of gain; that is, the profit you made on the car.

$10,000 sales price
– $ 4,000 your basis
= $ 6,000 your gain

Now, let's say you inherited a Corvette that's worth $10,000 from your late father, who paid $4,000 for it. Remember, inheriting the property doesn't subject you to tax—we're talking about the tax that will be due when you sell it. If you sell the Corvette for $10,000, what would your taxable gain be?

Your dad's basis was $4,000—the amount he paid for the car. If his basis carried over to you (carryover basis), you'd be deemed to have paid for the car what your dad did; that is, $4,000. Your taxable gain would be $6,000, just as if you'd bought the car yourself.

$10,000 sales price
– $ 4,000 your basis (carryover basis)
= $ 6,000 your taxable gain

But the good news is that when you inherit property, the basis is not carried over from the previous owner. Instead, your basis is the value of the property as of the date of death of the person you inherit it from. Assuming the value has gone up, the basis is "stepped up" to the current value. This usually means you will pay less in taxes down the road if you sell what you've inherited.

Let's go back to the Corvette. If you get a stepped-up basis, then your basis is what the car was worth on the date of your dad's death; that is, $10,000. If you sold it for $10,000, your taxable gain would be $0.

$10,000 sales price
− $10,000 your basis (fair market value at dad's death)
= $ 0 your taxable gain

Key Terms

Carryover basis: Your basis is the basis of the person who gave it to you.

Stepped-up basis: Your basis is the fair market value as of the date of death of the person you inherited it from.

Will Basis Rules Change in 2010?

As with the estate tax generally, there is lots of uncertainty about basis. Remember how the estate tax is repealed in 2010? Well, the government is going to get its money some way, and the way it's going to get it for those dying in 2010 is to give some people a carryover basis in what they inherit that year. For 2010 only, if you inherit property, up to $1.3 million of the estate's assets will get stepped-up basis, and the rest will get carryover basis. That, anyway, is what's supposed to happen under current law. Congress will probably change this provision before 2010, along with the rest of the estate tax.

Here's what causes some concern about carryover basis: Who knows what your dad paid for the Corvette 20 years ago? Who keeps those kinds of records? How are you going to know what the basis is?

When you *inherit* property, as I've said above, you generally get a stepped-up basis; when a living person *gives* you property, you get carryover basis. We'll talk about that more in "The Federal Gift Tax," below, but it's an important distinction. Remember:

- Inherited property (except in 2010): stepped-up basis
- Gifts (and certain property inherited in 2010): carryover basis.

How might this affect your planning? If you have two assets worth the same amount, but one has a high basis and the other a low basis, you can save your beneficiaries some gain pain. *Give* the high-basis asset (because your recipient gets your basis) and *leave by will* the low-basis asset (because your recipient will get a stepped-up basis).

> **EXAMPLE:** Joe has a vintage flat-bed truck with a fair market value of $10,000 and a basis of $500. He also has a vintage John Deere model 3320 (worth $10,000) that he recently bought for $10,000. If Joe wants to make a gift of $10,000 to Cameron, and leave $10,000 to Jessica in his will, he'd be better off giving the tractor to Cameron and leaving the truck to Jessica. Both Cameron and Jessica would have a basis of $10,000 should they wish to part with the truck or the tractor.

Either way, whether you give something away during your life or leave it at your death, the recipient is getting something good. The only difference is that if it's a stepped-up basis it is, as my son used to say, "more gooder."

When is basis not important? When you leave cash, such as cash in a checking or savings account, to a beneficiary. The basis of one dollar is one dollar.

Calculating the Estate Tax

If your net worth is over $1 million, you'll want to look at whether your estate might owe federal estate tax. The tax is calculated based on a number of factors:

- the applicable exclusion amount in the year you die
- the value of all your stuff at your death (your gross estate)

- the amount of debts you have and expenses paid in settling your estate
- how much you leave to charity
- how much you leave to your spouse, and
- how much you leave to everyone else.

Here's how it works, on a vastly simplified basis. (The worksheet below shows you more detail.) Start by making a rough calculation based on what would happen if you died this year, just to see what the tax would be.

First, look at your assets. (This is what you added up for yourself in Chapter 3.) In essence, this consists of everything in which you have an interest at your death, *plus* life insurance proceeds and annuities payable to your estate or (if you own them) your heirs, *plus* the value of certain gifts that you've made within the last three years. In short, include:

- houses and other real estate
- cars, personal property, jewelry, and artwork
- cash and investment accounts
- life insurance proceeds paid on life insurance owned by you or paid to your estate
- retirement plan assets, and
- the value of gifts you made within the last three years for which you filed a federal gift tax return (meaning large gifts).

Then, subtract from that amount certain deductions that are used to determine the amount against which tax is owed. These include amounts left to your spouse (the unlimited marital deduction), the value of gifts to charities, estimated funeral expenses, mortgages, debts, and any state estate tax paid.

The applicable exclusion amount operates as an additional deduction against the value of your estate, so that the estate pays tax only on what is left to nonspouses/noncharities over the applicable exclusion amount in the year of death. For most people, this means they won't owe any federal estate tax. But if you leave a lot of assets, you'll take the remainder and multiply it by the applicable federal estate tax rate.

If you want to get a rough idea of the tax you or your spouse might owe, here's a fairly simple worksheet. I adapted it from one contained in a Congressional Research Service Report entitled "Calculating Estate Tax Liability: 2001 to 2011 and Beyond" (November 3, 2006), available at www.nationalaglawcenter.org/assets/crs/RL33718.pdf.

To illustrate, here's how a $7 million estate might look for someone who dies in 2009 and leaves $2 million to his spouse and the rest to his children. For simplicity, I've assumed the person is debt-free and has no funeral or administrative expenses.

Sample Worksheet: Estimating the Estate Tax Bill	
Instruction	
1. Enter value of all assets.	*$7,000,000*
2. Enter cost of debts, funeral, and administrative expenses.	*0*
3. Enter the amount passing to the surviving spouse or charity.	*$2,000,000*
4. Subtract lines 2 and 3 from line 1 and enter here. This is the taxable estate.	*$5,000,000*
5. Enter applicable exclusion amount for year of death.	*$3,500,000*
6. Subtract line 4 from line 5 and enter here. Do not enter a negative number.	*$1,500,000*
7. Enter the marginal rate for the year of death.	*45%*
8. Calculate the estate tax liability (line 6 times line 7).	*$675,000*
9. Calculate remainder passing to persons other than a spouse or charity (line 4 minus line 8).	*$4,325,000*

In this example, out of the $7 million estate, the spouse gets $2 million, the IRS gets $675,000, and the other beneficiaries get $4,325,000.

Who Pays the Estate Tax?

If there will be an estate tax owing at the second spouse's death, who is going to pay it? Most estate plans defer paying any estate tax until the surviving spouse's death. What's left in the second-to-die spouse's estate is used to pay the estate tax. The beneficiaries of the second spouse inherit less because they get their inheritance after the taxes are paid.

In a first marriage, this arrangement generally doesn't cause problems, because the beneficiaries of both spouses are usually the same. But in a second marriage, it's common for one set of children to inherit when the first spouse dies, and a wholly different set to inherit when the second spouse dies. This can cause major tension. If the estate tax isn't paid until the second spouse's death, his or her children might not get their full inheritance, while the first spouse's children received theirs.

> EXAMPLE: Noah and Rachel have a combined estate worth $10 million. Noah has three sons from a previous marriage; Rachel has a son and a daughter. Noah and Rachel wish to split their estates equally. Noah leaves $3.5 million to his sons and puts $1.5 million in a trust for Rachel to pay income to her for life, with instructions that the trust funds be distributed to his sons after her death.
>
> At Noah's death:
>
> $~~~~$ $ 3.5 millon to sons
> $+$ $ 1.5 millon in trust for Rachel (eventually going to sons)
> $=$ $ ~~~5 millon your taxable gain
>
> Estate tax: $0
>
> Why is there no federal estate tax due at Noah's death? The gift to his sons isn't taxed because Noah has $3.5 million he can leave tax-free to his sons. The $1.5 million that goes into the trust for Rachel isn't taxed because it qualifies for the unlimited marital deduction. However, the $1.5 million trust becomes part of her estate and increases the tax that will be paid at her death.

When Rachel dies, her estate is $6.5 million (her $5 million plus the $1.5 million in the trust set up by Noah). Under Noah's plan, the trust pays $1.5 million to Noah's sons. So, Noah's sons receive a full $5 million. Rachel's children, on the other hand, receive $1,350,000 less, or $3,650,000. Why? Because Rachel's children effectively pay the estate tax on the $1.5 million passing to Noah's children. They still get a lot of money, but they don't get as much as Noah's children because of the estate tax.

$6,500,000 Rachel's estate
+ $3,500,000 applicable exclusion amount
= $3,000,000 taxable estate

$1,350,000 estate tax ($3 million x 45%) due

At the end of the day, here's how it stands: Noah's children: $5 million and happy; Rachel's children: $1,350,000 less and angry at the unfairness.

You don't have to understand the hows or whys, but you do need to make sure that you are aware (and that your attorney has taken into account) whether estate taxes will be paid upon the death of either spouse. You also want to understand how and from whose inheritance any estate tax is going to get paid. Most blended families don't want one set of children inheriting all of the property and the other set getting less because they got hit with all of the taxes.

The estate tax is payable within nine months following the date of death, so your survivors don't have a lot of time to raise funds to pay it unless they apply for an extension. The person you've named to represent your estate could request an extension of time to file for up to six months from the due date of the return. But the estate tax is still due on the original due date (nine months after death), and interest accrues on any amount owed then that isn't paid until later.

State Estate Taxes

So far, I have focused on federal estate tax because it's applicable to every state. The majority of states don't currently have an estate tax. For those that do, however, the tax may apply to people who wouldn't be subject to a federal estate tax, because many state estate tax thresholds are lower than the federal one. States are likely to revisit their estate tax to raise more funds in the future.

State estate tax rates tend to be much lower than the federal rate—commonly around the 15% range. Still, combined federal and state estate tax rates easily could exceed 50%. State estate tax structures vary widely, so it's best to consult with a practitioner in your state to see whether there's a potential estate tax issue.

Some states also impose an inheritance tax, which is different from estate tax in that property is distributed before the tax is paid. It's the inheritor's responsibility to pay the tax. The rate depends on the recipient's relationship to the person who left the assets. Surviving spouses generally pay no inheritance tax, while unrelated people pay the maximum rate.

The Federal Gift Tax

Estate tax applies to transfers at death; gift tax may arise for transfers made during life. The federal gift tax, if applicable, is the responsibility of the giver, not the recipient. Most people, even very wealthy people, don't pay gift tax during their lifetimes, yet they are able to transfer a lot of money and property to their loved ones. You can too, with just a little planning and patience.

Like estate tax, gift tax applies to individuals who give large sums of money or property to persons other than their spouses or charities.

> **EXAMPLE 1:** Bipin gives $100,000 to his spouse, Gita, a U.S. citizen. No gift tax, because outright transfers to a spouse who's a citizen don't trigger the tax.

EXAMPLE 2: Bipin gives $100,000 to the American Cancer Society. No gift tax, because it's a charity.

EXAMPLE 3: Bipin gives $100,000 to his son, Sanjay. Potential gift tax, unless Bipin makes the gift over a period of years of not more than the annual exclusion gift amount (currently $13,000 per year) or consumes some of his lifetime credit of $1 million. The annual exclusion gift amount and lifetime credit are discussed in detail below.

Annual Exclusion Gifts

Annual exclusion gifts are gifts that may be made without the giver (donor) incurring a gift tax. They are called annual exclusion gifts because in any one year there is a maximum amount that may be given to any one person that can be excluded from gift tax. Currently, that amount is $13,000 per year, or $26,000 for couples making joint gifts. (The amount is adjusted each year for inflation.)

When couples make gifts, the IRS calls them split gifts. To exempt the full $26,000, the spouses don't each have to transfer the amount of $13,000 to the recipient—it can come from one spouse's separate money. The couple just has to elect to make joint gifts on a gift tax return filed for that year. They won't owe any gift tax if it's at or under $26,000 per recipient.

EXAMPLE: Arturo wants to give $26,000 to his son, Reynard. If Arturo and his wife, Wylene, split gifts, Arturo can give the full amount of $26,000 in 2009. Arturo and Wylene need to file a gift tax return showing their decision to split gifts and a gift tax liability of $0.

Each year you get a new annual exclusion gift amount. Generally, these gifts may be made for any purpose to any person. In other words, anyone, not just your child or other relative, can be a recipient. When you give property, the value of the property on the date of gift is what determines the value for gift tax purposes. The recipient receives a carryover basis in the property. (See "Stepped-Up Basis vs. Carryover Basis," above.)

Theoretically, you and your spouse could give away $26,000 to everyone you know every year and still wouldn't owe gift tax. The need for tax planning arises when you want to give more than $26,000 to any one person, or if you're trying to get big assets out of your estate and you want to dribble out fractional interests over time.

> **EXAMPLE:** Bob wishes to give Randolph $100,000. If Bob and his wife, Mary, elect to make joint gifts and file gift tax returns each year, then in just four years, Bob can transfer the full amount to young Randolph and not have a gift tax liability.

What if Randolph is in a tight spot and needs the $100,000 *today?* Then, in order to give the money gift-tax free, Bob will have to consume some of his lifetime credit. That's discussed next.

The Lifetime Credit

The lifetime credit is the aggregate amount of otherwise taxable gifts you can make during your life without having to pay federal gift tax. Currently, the lifetime credit is $1 million. The lifetime credit gets used only when you're making gifts in excess of the annual exclusion gift amount. You get to exempt any number of $13,000 ($26,000 for split gifts) gifts without affecting the lifetime credit. You chip away at your lifetime credit only when you go over the annual exclusion gift amount in any one year. Annual exclusion gifts don't count against the lifetime credit.

Unlike annual exclusion gifts, where a new exclusion arises each year, you get only one lifetime credit. Once you use any portion of your lifetime credit, it reduces the amount you have left. At your death, the amount of lifetime credit you've used counts, dollar for dollar, against the amount you can leave free of federal estate tax.

> **EXAMPLE:** In 2003, Simone gave her daughter, Giselle, $100,000 more than the annual exclusion gift amount for that year. In doing so, Simone used up $100,000 of her lifetime credit. When Simone dies in 2009, the estate tax threshold is $3.5 million. Because of the taxable gift, only $3.4 million ($3.5 million less the $100,000 gift) of Simone's estate is excluded from estate tax.

When calculating how much you can exclude from federal estate tax, start with the maximum amount for the year of death and then reduce it by the amount of lifetime credit you have already used. Although the applicable exclusion amount is $3.5 million, the lifetime credit is only $1 million. You can, therefore, consume up to $1 million of your applicable exclusion amount through lifetime giving, leaving $2.5 million of available applicable exclusion amount.

Neat Planning Opportunities With the Gift Tax

The gift tax laws give blended families some nifty planning opportunities.

First, if you and your spouse have a potentially taxable estate, then with a little patience, both of you can get a large amount out of your estate by making annual, nontaxable gifts. You can give money to your kids, their spouses, your stepchildren, and your grandkids and transfer a great deal of wealth out of your estate without requiring anything more than a checkbook and money in your account.

You can also transfer stocks, business interests, and partial shares in real estate. Giving assets away before they increase in value gets that increase in value (appreciation) out of your estate, so it won't be taxed later. There are a number of techniques that take advantage of your ability to give away appreciation to your children so they'll get the benefit and you'll get the appreciation out of your estate.

> **EXAMPLE:** Ben gives his daughter $13,000 of stock. There's no gift tax on the gift because it doesn't exceed the annual exclusion amount. Five years later, the stock is worth $113,000 (it's gone up $100,000). The $100,000 increase is out of Ben's taxable estate.

If he had waited to leave the stock at his death, the full $113,000 would be subject to tax. Now it's all out of his estate, he hasn't had to pay any tax, and his daughter gets the use of the stock while he's alive.

For folks whose finances permit them to make gifts while still meeting their needs, annual nontaxable gifts can be a great start toward reducing a potential estate tax burden. The recipient doesn't have to be biologically related to or adopted by you, so you can benefit your stepchildren and achieve estate tax savings at the same time. By splitting gifts, you can get twice as much out of your estate each year tax-free than if you weren't married.

Second, if you're saving for a child's, stepchild's, or grandchild's college education and you want to establish a Section 529 plan for the student (discussed in Chapter 6), you can front-load the contributions to the plan. Contributions to Section 529 plans count against your annual gift tax amount, but you and your spouse can use five years up front. So, you could take $65,000 (5 x $13,000) and put it in a qualifying Section 529 plan. Together, you and your spouse could give $130,000 (5 x $26,000 = $130,000).

> **EXAMPLE:** Wilma and Lowell have a potentially taxable estate and wish to provide for Wilma's daughter's education. Wilma and Lowell can establish a Section 529 account for the child in the amount of $65,000, and still have room over the next five years to make another $65,000 in annual exclusion gifts to her—even if all the money comes from Wilma. They still have to file a gift tax return, but they won't owe any gift tax on these gifts.

Third, you can make some payments that aren't subject to the federal gift tax, don't count against the annual exclusion gift amount, and don't eat up any of your lifetime credit. Federal tax law (IRC § 2503(e)) provides that amounts paid on behalf of an individual as tuition to an educational organization for education or training or to any medical care provider with respect to an individual are not taxable. (For more on this, see "Paying Tuition or Medical Expenses" in Chapter 6.)

In 2010, the gift tax does not go away with the federal estate tax. The gift tax remains in effect, with a $1 million exemption amount and a rate of 35%.

Gift Tax Basics

- Generally, married couples can give up to $26,000 per year to any one person in any one year without gift tax consequences.
- Each spouse can give an unlimited amount to the other spouse (or, if the recipient spouse isn't a U.S. citizen, $133,000).
- Each person has a lifetime credit of $1 million.
- Certain payments for education or medical expenses can be made without counting against the annual exclusion amount or the lifetime credit if made directly to the school, hospital, or medical provider.

Gift Tax vs. Estate Tax: Why It's Better to Give Now Than Later

Sometimes you'll hear that the estate tax is tax-inclusive, but that the gift tax is tax-exclusive. What does this mean?

It means that if you leave someone $100,000 in your will, and your estate is subject to estate tax, the full $100,000 is subject to the tax. Your beneficiary may end up with only $55,000 once the tax is paid. The amount that will be paid as tax is included in the total amount subject to tax: There's a tax on the tax.

By contrast, gift tax is imposed only on the amount the beneficiary actually receives. If the gift is $100,000, the tax is in addition to the gift. The beneficiary still receives the full amount. There's no tax on the tax with a gift tax (say that three times fast). All other things being equal, more money ends up in the hands of the beneficiary with a gift tax than with an estate tax.

That's why gift tax paid within three years of death is pulled back into the estate: The government doesn't want to encourage large deathbed gifts that would otherwise remove the gift tax from what is subject to the estate tax.

> **EXAMPLE:** Ramon has an estate of $5 million. He would like to make a gift of $2 million to his son, Fortunato. He is willing to give the money away today or leave it to Fortunato in his will. Ramon has already used his annual exclusion for the year by giving Fortunato $13,000. What are the consequences of each strategy?

Gift (Ramon gives $2 million to Fortunato now)

- Upon making the gift, Ramon would incur a gift tax of $450,000. Because Ramon would use his lifetime gift tax credit of $1 million, only the other $1 million of the gift would be subject to tax (45% x $1 million = $450,000).
- If Ramon died more than three years later, in a year when the applicable exclusion amount was $3.5 million and the tax rate 45%, his estate would be subject to estate tax as follows:

Estate before gift	$ 5,000,000	
Gift	− 2,000,000	
Gift taxes paid	− 450,000	
Estate at Ramon's death		$ 2,550,000
Applicable exclusion	$ 3,500,000	
Exclusion already used	− $ 1,000,000	
Available exclusion		− 2,500,000
Taxable estate		50,000
Estate tax rate	x	45%
Estate tax due		$ 22,500
Gift taxes paid	+	450,000
Total taxes paid		$ 472,500

At death (Ramon doesn't make a lifetime gift, but leaves $2 million to Fortunato in his will)

- If Ramon dies in a year when the applicable exclusion amount is $3.5 million, and
- The rate is 45%, then Ramon's estate would be subject to estate tax as follows:

Estate at Ramon's death	$ 5,000,000	
Available exclusion	3,500,000	
Taxable estate	1,500,000	
Estate tax rate	x 45%	
Estate tax due		$ 675,000
Total estate tax if gift had been made		– $ 472,500
Cost of waiting		$ 202,500

Put another way, the cost of waiting is 45% of the gift tax paid (0.45 x $450,000 = $202,500) because the amount of gift tax you already paid is no longer in your estate.

If all you're doing is looking at the ultimate tax bill, it's better to go on and make gifts, even if you have to pay a gift tax, because you may pay less in total taxes. Of course, you have to factor in the time value of money (a dollar spent three years from now costs you less than the dollar you spend today because you get to keep it and invest it for the additional period of time) and the fact that most people are reluctant to pay a gift tax today to save on estate tax tomorrow. The catch is that you have to live for three years after making the gift so that the gift isn't pulled back into your estate for estate tax purposes.

Another good reason to make gifts today is that you get the appreciation on those assets out of your estate. In the example above, we're assuming that if Ramon doesn't make the gift today, the $2 million is still worth $2 million years from now. But that $2 million could have appreciated to $3 million. If so, Ramon's estate would incur an additional estate tax of $450,000 on the appreciation that could have been avoided by making the gift.

The Generation-Skipping Transfer Tax

The generation-skipping transfer tax (the GST tax) may be imposed when you are trying to leave more than a threshold amount to a grandchild or great-grandchild. The GST tax applies to wealthy people who can afford to provide amply for themselves and their children and still have enough left over to make substantial gifts to grandchildren. It is in addition to any estate tax that may be owed.

The tax is there to keep you and your children from avoiding the gift and estate tax that would otherwise be assessed when your children passed these assets to your grandchildren. (In GST tax lingo, grandchildren and on down are referred to as "skip persons." It's not a sentiment you find often on holiday cards: "To my favorite skip person on his 1st birthday.")

The GST tax can apply to transfers made during life or at death. It's kind of like a combination of the gift and estate taxes: It has a threshold that tracks (for now) the estate tax applicable exclusion amount, and annual exclusions that track the annual exclusion gift amounts. So, in 2009, you would have to leave a lot—over $3.5 million—to grandchildren to trigger the GST tax if you took advantage of all of the exemptions and exclusions. (The GST tax runs away with the estate tax in 2010, only to return with a bad attitude and lower exemptions and exclusions in 2011.)

To see why there's a need for the GST tax, look at five generations of the wealthy Kettle family. By the time Justin and Caitlyn receive their inheritance, the family wealth would have been subject to estate tax four times.

What if the enterprising Kettles figured out that entire generations could avoid the estate tax if they were to skip generations when making their gifts?

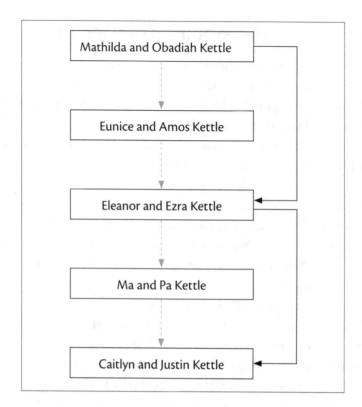

In this scenario, without the GST tax, much of the family's wealth would be taxed only twice instead of four times. Needless to say, the government doesn't like missing out on one or more generations' worth of tax, so it adopted the GST tax.

In practice, the GST tax is extremely complex and can arise to bite the unwary. If you have a taxable estate and are trying to pass wealth down to your grandchildren or future generations (or leave property in a trust that might ultimately benefit future generations), you need an expert in the field to avoid surprises. It really is tough stuff left best to experts who know the dance. (Cable's lowest-rated program: Dancing With the GST Stars!)

Tools and Techniques for Blended Families

Understanding Probate and Nonprobate Assets..99

Will or Trust? Get This Right and Things Start to Fall Into Place 104

   Comparing Wills and Trusts... 105

   How Does a Will Work?.. 109

   How Does an RLT Work? 113

   What's So Bad About Probate?... 114

Providing for Your Spouse but Making Sure Your
  Children Ultimately Get Your Stuff...117

   Leaving Everything Outright to Your Spouse:
     Probably Not a Good Idea 117

   Prenups and Postnups, Contracts to Make a Will, and Joint Wills.......... 120

   Life Estates: An Oldie But a Goodie.. 124

   QTIP and Credit Shelter Trusts: Estate Planning Workhorses 127

Providing Cash for Loved Ones With Life Insurance........................... 136

   Buying Life Insurance 137

   Special Life Insurance Considerations in Community Property States...... 138

Sharing the Wealth Now: Making Gifts During Your Life 139

   Making Tax-Free "Annual Exclusion" Gifts 140

   Giving to Meet a Need: Section 529 Plans 140

   Paying Tuition or Medical Expenses 141

Other Tax-Saving Tools... 142

   Joint Revocable Trusts 142

   Lifetime QTIP Trusts 143

   Life Insurance Owned by Children 145

   Irrevocable Life Insurance Trusts 146

   Qualified Personal Residence Trusts... 147

A journey of a thousand miles
Succeeds if you'll first search the aisles
For tools, techniques and stratagems
To satisfy your needs and whims

Successful estate planning is all about choices—your choices—making them and bringing them to life. With planning, you get to decide what's best for you and your loved ones. You get to choose who receives your money and prized possessions. You get to pick when and how best to distribute your property.

Yet, year after year, people in blended families die and they don't get their choices. Instead:

- their property ends up in the hands of someone they didn't want to have it
- taxes that they could have avoided are paid to the government, or
- property passes to a child all at once and is squandered rather than being used responsibly for education, buying a house, or living modestly.

How does this happen?

Sometimes, it's because they didn't *communicate* their current choice. They might have failed to update the beneficiary designation on a life insurance policy, so a former spouse received the benefits, rather than their current spouse or children. Or maybe they didn't *coordinate* their choices with the rest of the plan. For example, they left life insurance proceeds directly to a child rather than arranging for the money to go into a trust to be used for the child's benefit over a number of years. Still other times, they *chose the wrong legal tool*, a tool that might have been appropriate for a first marriage but didn't meet the needs of their blended family.

This chapter is about communicating, coordinating, and choosing the right tools so that your choices will be respected. It lays out accepted tools and techniques based on common goals of individuals in blended families. These include:

- providing for your spouse at your death but ensuring that your children ultimately end up with your stuff
- saving on estate tax
- providing for your children, grandchildren, and stepchildren during your life, and
- keeping your and your spouse's plans in sync, so that you don't unintentionally frustrate each other's goals.

Understanding Probate and Nonprobate Assets

Ask people who claim to be up to date on their estate planning, and they'll point proudly to a signed will or trust agreement. And that's good, given that many people haven't done even that much. But in actuality, signing the will or trust only got them halfway there at most, if they neglected to look at their nonprobate assets. What are nonprobate assets? They're the assets that pass outside your will or trust because they have beneficiary designations or you own them jointly with someone else and hold title in a way that gives the survivor the asset at death.

It used to be that a will or trust was sufficient to dispose of most people's wealth. Nowadays, nonprobate assets are likely to form the bulk of your estate. Common nonprobate assets include:

- property that you and another own where the title says the survivor takes all at the first person's death (joint tenancy with right of survivorship, community property with right of survivorship, or tenancy by the entirety)
- 401(k)s and similar retirement plans
- Keogh and other retirement plans
- Individual Retirement Accounts
- life insurance policies
- annuities
- payable-on-death or transfer-on-death accounts.

Nonprobate assets go to the person you've designated as the beneficiary or to the survivor on joint accounts. Nonprobate assets (and the companies that distribute them) don't care whom you're married to at your death, what's best for the child, what you wanted to do with your planning, or even what you said in your will or trust—they just go to the person or persons you've named at your death.

> EXAMPLE: Andrea participates in a 401(k) retirement plan at work. She designates her husband, Darren, as her beneficiary. Andrea later drafts a will splitting her estate equally among Darren and her children from her previous marriage. Darren will receive all of the proceeds of the 401(k) account, because 401(k) plans are nonprobate assets and they don't pass according to what the will says.

It's a Bird! It's a Plane! It's 35 Pages of Paper Dictating Where Your Retirement Benefits Go!

In response to the immense amount of wealth controlled by nonprobate assets and the public's understandable confusion about whether or not wills affect the disposition of these assets, some states have considered the concept of "superwills." Superwills would override the terms of a beneficiary designation in a nonprobate asset and let the will control what happens to the asset. Superwill legislation hasn't been widely adopted, but the state of Washington has a superwill statute that in some circumstances lets a will override a beneficiary designation.

Life insurance is another very common nonprobate asset, and even if you set up a trust for your children, the proceeds won't pass according to what the trust says unless you make specific arrangements. If you simply name young children as beneficiaries and they are minors at your death, a court would need to appoint a guardian, and the life insurance proceeds could pass outright to the children immediately when they become 18 or 21.

EXAMPLE: Andrea buys a life insurance policy on her life. On the form she submits to the insurance company, she designates her two children as beneficiaries of the policy. Later she becomes concerned about her children receiving their entire inheritance in a lump sum at her death, so she sets up a trust for the children to receive their inheritance over a number of years. She doesn't change the beneficiary designations on her life insurance policy. At Andrea's death, all of the life insurance proceeds pass immediately to her children.

There are two "must dos" when planning for nonprobate assets in blended families. The first is to coordinate your beneficiary designations with your will or trust. If you don't, the nonprobate asset may frustrate your overall plan.

You will spend a lot of time carefully deciding how to split your estate among your spouse, children, and grandchildren when setting up your will or trust. (We'll talk about wills and trusts later in this chapter.) If your beneficiary designations aren't in sync with your will or trust, then you won't get the results you want.

The second must-do is to make sure that your former spouse or partner is not still listed as a beneficiary on a nonprobate asset. This happens more often than you might think. Under the laws of many states, when you die, that nonprobate asset will go to your ex-spouse unless you update the beneficiary designation. Of course, if your divorce decree requires you to maintain life insurance or otherwise provide for your ex-spouse, then do so. Here's what I want you to avoid: forgetting about a beneficiary designation you've signed on a nonprobate asset that will pass to your ex-spouse if you don't fix it.

Most states treat wills and trusts differently than nonprobate assets upon divorce. Virtually every state provides that divorce terminates an ex-spouse's rights under a will. Some state statutes extend this rule to revocable trusts.

EXAMPLE: Kendrick executes a will in which he leaves half of his estate to Kayesha and half to his two sons, William and Andrew. Kendrick and Kayesha later divorce. Under most state's laws, when Kendrick dies, Kayesha would not inherit under his will even if Kendrick had never gotten around to revoking his will or executing a new one before his death. William and Andrew would get Kendrick's entire estate.

By contrast, only a handful of states will override beneficiary designations on nonprobate assets following divorce. In a majority of states, the ex-spouse still will inherit the asset if the beneficiary designation doesn't change. This can lead to some harsh results.

EXAMPLE: Tony designates his wife Lisa as the beneficiary of his life insurance. Tony and Lisa have no children together and later divorce. Tony doesn't update his life insurance designation after the divorce. Tony then marries Lacey, and together they have twins, Ryan and Logan. Tony is killed in a car accident when the twins are two. Under the laws of most states, first wife Lisa gets all of the life insurance—Lacey, Ryan, and Logan do not get any of the life insurance proceeds even if Tony's will leaves everything to them.

Some states' laws do revoke beneficiary designations of a spouse on divorce, but there are exceptions and uncertainties. Don't rely on those laws. Even if a state law eliminates the ex-spouse's rights, a court might disregard the state law and give the benefits to the ex-spouse. In a famous case, a Washington court held (and the U.S. Supreme Court affirmed) that federal law overrode the state law attempt to revoke benefits passing to an ex-wife, so the ex-wife got the assets even though the state laws and the person's intentions clearly said otherwise. What was the benefit at issue in that case? Employer-provided life insurance, which the employee may have chosen on his first day on the job and then forgotten about.

The bottom line: As part of your planning, it's vitally important for you to collect all of your beneficiary designations and change them

Special Considerations for Retirement Plans in Community Property States

Retirement benefits are generally part separate and part community property, based on when the contributions occurred. Contributions made before marriage are separate property; contributions made during the marriage are community property. It depends on the state as to whether the actual contribution to the plan in both periods will be reviewed, or whether it will be determined by the length of time before versus the time in the marriage. Usually, if the nonparticipating spouse dies before the participating spouse, then the community property rights of the non-participating spouse terminate at death.

EXAMPLE 1: Elaine and Warren are married and live in a community property state. Warren participates in his employer-sponsored retirement plan. All of his contributions were made while Elaine and Warren were married and living in the community property state. Elaine has a half interest in the retirement plan, plus any interest Warren may leave her. If Elaine dies first, she will lose her half interest in Warren's retirement plan.

EXAMPLE 2: Same situation, except that Warren made half of his contributions before he and Elaine were married and the other half during their marriage. Elaine has a half interest only in half of Warren's retirement plan (so her interest comes to a quarter of the plan), plus whatever Warren may leave her.

If you are or were a resident of a community property state, consult your attorney if you wish to leave retirement plan benefits to someone other than your spouse. Otherwise, your beneficiaries might receive only a fraction of what you intend because your spouse may be entitled to a significant share based on community property laws.

to what you want. In my experience, most folks remember to take the former spouse off an old joint checking account and even an old will. But old beneficiary designations may lie forgotten at the bottom of your desk. Your beneficiary designations may not appear on any of the regular statements you get from your insurance company or retirement plan provider on a regular basis. Think about all the beneficiary designations you've signed when:

- applying for life insurance
- filling out forms at a new job, or
- closing on the purchase of your house.

Together, these documents may control more property than your will does, so you need to go back and check them carefully to make sure they're consistent with your current wishes. Don't rely on your memory. Take the time to find each designation. If you can't find it, the insurer or plan administrator or your lawyer may help you locate it.

Will or Trust? Get This Right and Things Start to Fall Into Place

How many times have you been in the middle of a home repair project when you couldn't find the right tool? When you need a straight-blade screwdriver, all you see in the junk drawer is a Phillips-head. You want to hang a small picture, and the only nails you can put your hands on could have held the Titanic together. A tool that's perfect for one job can be ineffective or even dangerous for another.

A lot of estate planning tools were originally developed for first marriages and haven't changed much since then. A big reason why people don't get their choices respected in blended families is because they choose the wrong tool. You want to make sure you get the right one for your situation.

One of the first decisions you and your attorney will discuss is whether a will or a revocable living trust (RLT) will be your primary estate planning device. This device provides the infrastructure for the rest of your estate plan. Each has benefits and limitations, and what's right for you will depend on a variety of factors—neither is inherently better than the other for blended families.

Your attorney may have a preference for one or the other based on local custom, concerns over probate costs in your state, and the type of disability planning you're doing. In some states, the will is the preferred device; in others, the RLT is the dominant tool. Regardless of which is more common in your area, you'll want to learn about both wills and trusts before meeting with your attorney to get a sense of what may be appropriate for you based on what you're trying to accomplish.

The will or RLT is the tool box holding all of your choices that you make. Into the will or RLT may go other trusts, gifts to children, spouse, and charity, and the names of the people responsible for holding and distributing your assets and taking care of your minor children. So even though you may have a will, it may contain one or more trusts. Similarly, with an RLT, at your death or before, the trust's assets may go into one or more trusts with varying provisions.

You may also have other, separate documents, such as a financial power of attorney (which grants a trusted individual power to handle your financial affairs if necessary), an irrevocable trust (such as a life insurance trust designed to hold one or more policies) or a living will (which specifies your wishes regarding treatment and end-of-life decisions if you are unable to speak for yourself). These documents will be integrated with your primary device, but they don't go into the will or RLT.

Comparing Wills and Trusts

Before we talk about the differences between wills and RLTs, let's look at what they have in common. Most important, either a will or RLT will accomplish the important goals of making sure that your property will go to the people or charities you choose, in the way you want them to get it. It turns out that they share a lot of other features as well, such as:

Flexibility. As long as you are mentally competent, you can change your will or RLT. Unless you have a binding agreement with a spouse to the contrary (such as a prenuptial, postnuptial, or community property agreement), changing your will or RLT generally won't require anyone's consent, won't require that you notify any of the beneficiaries, and won't mean that anyone will ever see the prior plan.

> **EXAMPLE:** Bertha executes a will leaving half of her estate to her new husband, Jack, and half to her children, Kendall and A.J. A month later, A.J. elopes with her high school boyfriend and announces plans to start a family. Bertha can revise her will to put A.J.'s inheritance in a trust to provide for A.J.'s support and education and give her an incentive to complete her education. Bertha won't have to breathe a word about the change or notify Jack, Kendall, or A.J.

Versatility. Wills and RLTs are extremely versatile. You can treat beneficiaries differently, you can include trusts to take effect at your death (these are different kinds of trusts, not RLTs), and you can provide for children and for charities, pets, and properties.

> **EXAMPLE:** Same as above, but now A.J. has a baby. Bertha revises her will to split A.J.'s portion into two trusts, one for A.J. and one for her baby. She keeps the portion that's going to her spouse and other daughter outside of a trust.

Acceptability. Wills and RLTs are accepted throughout the United States. Using either as your primary estate planning device means you've chosen a technique with which courts, financial institutions, beneficiaries, accountants, and lawyers will be familiar.

A will differs from an RLT in these ways:

Court scrutiny. If you use a will, then after you pass away, there will be a court proceeding (called probate) to confirm that you (and not a greedy cousin) signed your name to your will, that you did so without undue influence by any person, and that you were competent when you signed the will.

As part of the process, a copy of your will is given to your spouse and each child. If your spouse and children consent after reading the will, the court won't look closely at the will. But if anyone challenges the will, the court will examine it and listen to the testimony of the witnesses very carefully. So, if you sign your will very late in life in the midst of a debilitating illness and leave everything to your spouse and his children rather than to your children, your children may be able to challenge the will when it's presented for probate.

They may not have the same opportunity with an RLT, which doesn't always have to be circulated like a will and won't be part of a separate court proceeding unless someone files a lawsuit to contest it. As people live longer, there may be greater opportunities for senior citizens to be taken advantage of, and a will provides an independent forum for challenging improperly influenced wills following death. A court provides a disinterested third party to resolve that your will truly represents your last wishes, unaffected by the undue influence of other people. RLTs don't get this same level of scrutiny; under the laws of some states your children and grandchildren might not be entitled even to get a copy of an RLT that doesn't name them as a beneficiary. Other states require trustees to notify heirs (the people entitled to inherit from you by law if there's no will) of a trust and provide a copy on request.

> **EXAMPLE 1:** Henrietta, a widow, signs a will disinheriting her family and children and leaving everything to her gardener, Hunko. Hunko had gotten her out of bed to drive her to her lawyer's office to change her will five days before she died. Henrietta's family will have the opportunity to challenge the will during the probate process on the grounds that Hunko exerted undue influence over Henrietta in getting her to change her will.

> **EXAMPLE 2:** Same situation, but instead of signing a will, Henrietta signs an RLT, names Hunko her trustee and dies five days after the bulk of her assets are put in the trust. By the time Henrietta's family finds out about the RLT and files suit to challenge the RLT, Hunko may have taken everything out of the RLT and moved to a new city.

Features of Wills and RLTs		
	Will	**Revocable Living Trust**
Lets you leave property as you wish	Yes	Yes
Provides for you and protects your assets should you become disabled	No	Yes (for assets you've placed in trust)
Lets your loved ones avoid probate	No	Yes, though probate might not be avoided entirely
Takes effect	At your death	When you sign it. Revocable during life; irrevocable at death or during disability
Changeable	Yes	Yes
Flexible	Yes	Yes
Keeps assets out of the reach of creditors or claims of lawsuits	No	No
Affects the amount of taxes you pay or can avoid during your life	No	No

Simplicity. To get the benefits of an RLT, there's more paperwork; you have to transfer title in your assets to the RLT. A will doesn't require that.

Privacy. What you leave and to whom is generally not a matter of public record with an RLT, but it is with a will. Have you ever seen those copies of wills from famous people? That's because generally anyone can get a copy of a will once it's been filed in court. If privacy is a big concern, an RLT may be more attractive to you. (But remember that ownership of real estate is always a matter of public record.)

Possibility of joint trusts. You and your spouse can have a joint trust, which is one way to have a coordinated estate plan. Most wills, on the other hand, are individual.

Lifetime effectiveness. RLTs can be designed so that if during your lifetime you become unable to care for yourself, your trustee can manage trust assets to provide for you (pay bills, costs of health care, and other expenses). Wills take effect only at death. If you have a family history or risk factor for dementia, an RLT can be a good tool. Like a will, you can revise it up to the point of your incapacity; unlike a will, it can be helpful during your life.

> **EXAMPLE:** Maria creates an RLT and transfers her money and other property to it. If she becomes disabled, the money and property she's put in the trust can be used to support her and pay her expenses.

It's a Will! It's a Trust! No, It's Both!

An RLT typically contains at least two trusts: one that takes effect upon signing and lasts until your death or incompetency and one that takes effect at your death or incompetency. Because an RLT takes effect during your life, it is a type of living trust (or inter vivos trust if you're a lover of Latin).

Wills also may contain one or more trusts. A will might include one trust for your children and another for your spouse. Neither of these, however, takes effect during your life. They come into being only at your death. Trusts that take effect at your death are called testamentary trusts.

How Does a Will Work?

Your will provides for how you would like your probate assets distributed at death. Assets left directly to a beneficiary are called outright bequests; assets left to a trustee to be held for the benefit of another are called bequests in trust.

While you're alive, the will has no legal effect. It's as if the will is a hibernating animal that awakens from its slumber only once you have passed away.

Once you've passed away, a will acts as the guide to your final intentions for everything, from whom you want to raise your young children to whom you'd like to inherit your car. You can change your will at any point up until your death, as long as you have the mental capacity to understand what you are doing. A will governs only the distribution of probate assets; nonprobate assets (discussed above) pass outside of the will.

So, what does a will look like? Because wills have been around for so long, there are certain customary ways to organize them. There's also a formal procedure, required by law, to follow when you sign your will in front of witnesses. Reading a will can be a challenge if you're not used to the kind of language that's often used, but it might get easier if you think of a will as a three-course meal with an appetizer, main course, and dessert.

The Language of Wills

Wills have their own language that's evolved glacially (that is, not much) over centuries. At the beginning of a will, you typically find a formal recital, such as: "I, Fabio, of the Fabulous Hair, being of sound mind and impressive body, do make and publish this my Last Will and Testament, hereby revoking all wills and codicils heretofore made by me."

Appetizer

The first part of the document states where you live, identifies your spouse and children, names your executor (the person charged with settling your estate once you're gone), any alternates, and any trustees, if you're using trusts in your planning, and authorizes your executor to pay your debts and settle your estate.

In some states, it's common for the introduction to your will to specify whether you wish to be buried or cremated. Whether or not you cover this issue in your will, you should definitely communicate your desires to your loved ones outside your will, because your will likely won't be read until after your loved ones have already provided for your burial or cremation. You don't want them to make a decision, then read your will and find they made a choice you didn't want.

Main Course

Next comes the substance of your will. It establishes who gets your personal belongings and other probate assets. It also commonly establishes who gets your house if it's in your name alone. This section also creates any trusts that are part of your planning. For example, you might include a trust for a child and set out how distributions will be made from the trust and at what ages.

You may also specify here who will be the guardian of your minor children should both you and the child's other biological parent die before the children turn 18. When you're naming a guardian for a minor child, keep in mind that if the other legal parent is alive and still has parental rights (they haven't been terminated by an adoption or other proceeding), that parent would get custody even if you name someone else to be guardian. The personal guardian would look after and raise your child. This person wouldn't necessarily have access to the money you're leaving for the child—that money can be left in a trust or to another person.

What's a Codicil?

A codicil is an amendment to a will. Back when wills were typed or hand-written, people didn't want to retype or rewrite the whole will to change a paragraph or two, so they used codicils. For example, if you left Mama's china in your will to your sister-in-law and later changed your mind, you might execute a codicil to change who gets the china.

A codicil must be signed in front of witnesses, just like a will. Nowadays, printing out a whole will with changes is often easier than typing a separate codicil. Codicils are still used, just not as regularly as before.

Dessert

Ah, dessert. In this portion of the will, you'll find pages of boilerplate, the ever-increasing list of provisions that have been added over the years as new questions have come up and new challenges have been made to wills. It's a good idea to at least skim the boilerplate, and of course you should feel free to ask questions, but don't wear yourself out trying to slog through and understand all of it. The boilerplate gives power to the people you've named to carry out your wishes with a minimum of hassle and fuss, and discusses how and from what assets taxes will be paid.

No-Contest Clauses

If you're planning to treat one of your children more favorably than the others or trying to substantially limit what your spouse is to inherit from your estate, your lawyer may recommend inserting a no-contest clause in your will.

Also known by the vivid Latin phrase "in terrorem clause," a no-contest clause penalizes someone who would challenge your will by providing that anyone who sues loses his or her inheritance. A no-contest clause is designed to keep disappointed beneficiaries from trying to have a court throw out your will (say, on the grounds that the person to whom you left more money improperly influenced you to make the will).

Here's how it works. You state in your will that if a beneficiary sues over the will, then they lose the inheritance you've left them. You leave Bob $1,000 in your will, but say in the will that if he challenges the will, he gets nothing.

To make the clause effective, the disgruntled beneficiary must have something to lose. If you leave someone nothing in your will, then the no-contest clause won't be a disincentive to challenging the will.

Some states and courts don't like no-contest clauses very much and are very reluctant to enforce them. They argue on public policy grounds that people should be able to challenge a will without facing the threat of losing it all. So they're not a slam dunk, but if you think someone might challenge your will, you may want to discuss a no-contest clause with your lawyer.

How Does an RLT Work?

Revocable living trusts are popular in many states, particularly where the probate process is especially costly or drawn-out, and people want to avoid if at all possible.

With an RLT, you create the trust and transfer assets to it during your lifetime. While you're living, you have the right to change or undo the RLT—that's why it's a "revocable" trust. You can use what's in the trust and keep what it earns or give it away. Basically, you can do anything with the trust assets that you could have done before creating the trust. Because you reserve all these powers, RLTs generally don't affect your taxes during your life. You're taxed on trust income just as if you owned the trust assets, and you don't have to file a separate tax return for the trust. By setting up the RLT, you haven't made a taxable gift.

For most RLTs, you would be the trustee during your life, and you would appoint a third party to act as trustee at your death or disability. The person who takes over is called the successor trustee.

Even if you have an RLT as your primary estate planning device, you ordinarily will sign a will as well. The will has provisions designed to catch anything that wasn't transferred to the RLT during life and dump it into the trust. Because the will pours these isolated assets into the trust, it is commonly called a pour-over will. The will acts like a cowboy rounding up the last of the stragglers (in this case, assets) and herding them into the RLT pen for distribution according to the RLT's terms. In most states, you can also make a plain old backup will and take advantage of your state's simplified procedure for transferring leftover assets less than a certain value.

One advantage of an RLT over a will is that it offers some protection for you should you become disabled. The successor trustee you name in the trust—an individual or institution in whom you have confidence—can look after your property and investments, pay bills, and distribute trust funds to you or your family if you're ever disabled. An RLT isn't required for disability planning: a will can be paired with a power of attorney to address disability concerns. (See Chapter 11.) The RLT just offers the ability to do disability planning in one document.

The document that creates an RLT looks similar to a will, with the three basic parts discussed above. But instead of authorizing an executor to shepherd your will through probate and then distribute your property, the trust authorizes your successor trustee to transfer trust assets, after your death, to the beneficiaries named in the trust document. No probate will be necessary.

Many RLTs feature a fourth section causing the RLT to spring into action before your death should you become disabled. It will include a definition of disability, how disability is determined (usually by your primary physician and a second opinion), and name a successor trustee to act as long as the disability lasts.

Although fully revocable during your lifetime, the RLT becomes irrevocable at death. It also may become irrevocable during periods of disability. Irrevocable means that the trust's terms harden like concrete and can no longer be changed. So at your death or disability, the assets you've put in the trust become locked up. Only your successor trustee can access them, and then only for the purposes you specified in the RLT.

What's So Bad About Probate?

Aside from disability planning, the main reason to create an RLT instead of a will is to spare your family the hassle, delay, and expense of probate. But is probate really so bad?

Probate is a court process designed to ensure the genuineness of a deceased person's will and grant the executor of the will the power to pay the debts of the estate and distribute the remaining probate assets to the intended beneficiaries. Probate courts hear challenges to wills—for example, when a child or beneficiary seeks to invalidate a will on the grounds that the deceased person wasn't mentally capable of signing a will at the time he or she signed it, or that the deceased person was under the controlling influence of another person.

Most executors hire lawyers to guide them through the court process, file the forms, and make sure all of the paperwork is completed and notices are given appropriately. The lawyer's fees are normally based on the amount of time the lawyer spends on the estate and can run from under a thousand dollars for small, uncontested matters to several thousand dollars for larger estates. Some lawyers may quote a flat fee. In some states, however, lawyers can charge a fee that's a percentage of the deceased person's gross estate. California, for example, is notorious for its probate costs. No matter what state you're in, if there's a challenge to the will, it likely won't get resolved without lawyers on all sides, each of whom may have fees in the thousands, if not tens of thousands, of dollars.

The court will charge fees as well, which are usually several hundred dollars. There may also be costs of filing notices in the newspaper, which are usually small in comparison to the other fees. The lawyer's fees and court and other costs are paid out of the deceased person's estate.

Some promoters of RLTs overestimate the costs and burdens of probate, as if probate were an incurable, life-threatening, rapidly spreading toe fungus. Critics argue that the process takes too long, is too expensive, and makes your will and all of your financial information public. In some states, probate may indeed be costly, time-consuming, and unnecessarily burdensome on the executor charged with administering the estate, and should be avoided.

In other states, the costs and hassles of establishing and maintaining an RLT may greatly outweigh the inconvenience of the probate procedure. In these states, probate is neither painful nor expensive. Depending on the state and the will, the executor may not have to post a bond (a kind of insurance policy to protect the estate from loss due to the misconduct of the executor) in order to serve or have to file an inventory (of estate property) or an accounting, so sensitive financial information never becomes public.

It really depends on the state (and sometimes the county) you live in. Your attorney should be able to advise you what the risks and costs of probate are in your area. Some attorneys are adamant about protecting their clients from probate; others may see it as less of an issue. Some (although not many, I hope) might just as soon have the estate go through probate because they see it as an opportunity for another fee.

Be wary of promoters who attribute extraordinary powers to RLTs in language more appropriate for chain letters. As a practitioner in a state where the will is the primary estate planning device, I'm always somewhat dubious over the need in my state for an RLT for the average 50-year-old in good health, just because it can be an irritant to transfer your property to the RLT and then maintain the RLT properly. If the RLT doesn't provide a clear benefit, I'd rather my clients not have to go through the trouble. You can always start out with a will and consider an RLT as you get older.

That said, it's a good technique in the right circumstances, even in my state. For example, let's say you're in your 60s and in good health, but you're concerned about what might happen to your investments and property if you became unable to manage them yourself. You don't want your spouse and your children at odds over where the money's going if something happens to you, and you don't want to give anyone in your family a blank check over your assets. In that case, an RLT may be right for you. With the population aging and the potential for abuse of elderly and incapacitated people increasing, I think more and more seniors are going to be better served by an RLT than a traditional will, and I see the popularity of RLTs increasing, even in historically will-centric states.

To sum up, an RLT is an appropriate estate planning device for many people, especially those who:

- live in states where probate is time-consuming, expensive, and an all-around hassle
- wish to have a mechanism in place to pay their bills and manage their assets should they become disabled through accident, stroke, or illness, or
- wish to keep their estate plan private following their death.

CAUTION

There's no such thing as a free lunch (or dinner). Watch out for promoters who send out flyers or advertise in the local newspaper and offer you a free steak dinner to hear the RLT testimony. Often, their expensive "custom" plan is nothing more than a kit that might or might not work in your state. My personal feeling is that if someone is willing to buy you dinner, then they're trying to sell you something, whether it's a trust, an insurance plan, an annuity, a water softener, or a multilevel marketing program. Take the pitch with a grain of salt and have a disinterested professional review the claims. If they won't tell you what their solution or product is unless you commit, then walk the other way. Some of these companies are adept at preying on the hopes and fears of seniors. Reputable companies should tell you what they're pitching and let you have someone else review it.

Providing for Your Spouse but Making Sure Your Children Ultimately Get Your Stuff

The most common goal in estate planning for blended families is to provide for a surviving spouse, then benefit your children once your spouse passes. Here we'll look at several potential ways to accomplish this. You'll see that perhaps the most commonly used technique—making an outright gift to surviving spouse—actually provides the least certainty that your children will ultimately end up with anything. You'll also see that two tools historically used to save on estate tax, the credit shelter trust and the QTIP trust, can be very useful for blended families even if you're not worried about estate tax.

The techniques are:

- making an outright gift to your spouse
- making a separate agreement with your spouse over how property will be passed down
- leaving your spouse a life estate, with what's left (the remainder) passing to your children at your spouse's death
- creating a credit shelter trust, and
- creating a QTIP trust.

Leaving Everything Outright to Your Spouse: Probably Not a Good Idea

One very simple option is to leave your assets outright to your loved ones, no strings attached. This leaves the recipients free to do whatever they wish with the assets: use and enjoy them or give them away, and eventually leave them to a third person.

> **EXAMPLE:** Carlo leaves his prized Corvette outright to his wife, Cordelia, at his death. Cordelia can drive the car, sell it, or give it to a new boyfriend. At her death, she can leave it to Carlo's children or to anyone else she chooses.

Leaving assets outright is the simplest way to leave them to a spouse, but in blended families it's rarely the best way. If your goal is to make sure your children end up with something at your spouse's death, an outright transfer to your spouse doesn't ensure that you'll accomplish that goal. Instead, it gives your spouse total control over what you've left. This creates the possibility that your estate plan will fail if you're the first to die and your spouse changes his or her mind after your death.

You and your spouse may decide to leave everything outright to each other with the "understanding" that the second spouse to die will split everything up equally. Even if you sign wills that do this, either of you is going to be able to change your mind unless you have a separate binding agreement. You and your spouse are always free to change your wills as long as you are mentally capable of doing so. That means you or your spouse can also—without the consent of the other—amend your will to deviate from the original plan.

> **EXAMPLE:** Theo and Emily execute mirror-image wills in which the first-to-die spouse leaves everything to the survivor, no strings attached. Each will divides what remains at the second person's death equally among their children (his two daughters, her son). Theo dies, leaves everything to Emily and nothing to his daughters. A few months after Theo's death, Emily revises her will to leave everything to her son, Orlando, and specifically disinherits Theo's daughters. The daughters can't do anything about it.

You may well say, "I trust my spouse to do the right thing, so I'm not concerned about him or her misusing an outright gift." But this is not about trust—it's about making sure both your spouse and your children benefit from your years of work and sacrifice. After your death, your spouse is going to be subject to competing demands on his or her resources. Your spouse's children may have a need your spouse will feel obligated to fill, even if it's at the expense of your children.

> **EXAMPLE:** Carlo leaves an investment account outright to his wife, Cordelia, at his death, with the intention that Cordelia use what she needs during her life and then leave the rest to his children from a prior marriage. But after Carlo's death, Cordelia's son divorces, gets laid off, hurts his back, and loses his house. Cordelia spends the bulk of what she's received from Carlo helping her son get back on his feet and leaves nothing from the account to Carlo's children at her death.

That's one reason why putting assets in trusts (discussed below) is so important in blended family estate planning. If you leave an asset to an irrevocable trust, your spouse can't later leave it to someone else.

> **EXAMPLE:** Michael leaves an investment account in trust for his wife, Cathryn, at his death. The terms of the trust will dictate when, how much, and for what purposes Cathryn may receive money from the trust. The trust also directs that any assets remaining in the trust at Cathryn's death pass to Michael's children from a former marriage. Cathryn can use and enjoy only as much of the trust assets and income as the trustee gives her. The trustee, not Cathryn, decides when to make distributions in accordance with the trust agreement. Michael's children end up with what's left even if Cathryn signs a will leaving all her property to her children.

Because of the possibility that a surviving spouse could take what's left to him or her and leave it to your spouse's children or someone other than the deceased spouse's children, I don't usually recommend that people leave everything outright to a spouse. In fact, I think that one of the keys to successful estate planning in blended families is to attach some strings to what you leave to a surviving spouse. Life estates, credit shelter trusts, QTIP trusts, and contracts among spouses provide the strings you need to get the assets where you want them to go. We'll look at these tools next.

Some Gifts Are Just Fine

This isn't to say that you shouldn't leave anything to your spouse outright. Some unrestricted gifts make perfect sense. For example, couples commonly leave one another household furnishings, cars, mementos they've collected, and other items they've purchased together. What I'm advising against is giving to your spouse the things that you really, really want to pass to your children (such as family heirlooms and other family property), unless your spouse has a critical need for them during his or her life. If your spouse has that need and getting the item to your children is equally important to you, then I'd suggest using one of the techniques discussed here and attaching some strings to the item so your children get to enjoy them someday.

Prenups and Postnups, Contracts to Make a Will, and Joint Wills

Many people who've been married before sign a prenuptial agreement ("prenup") before they remarry. A prenup sets out each spouse's obligations to the other upon death or divorce. Because both parties have agreed to the prenup, they can't later freely change their minds without amending the prenup.

> EXAMPLE: Before their marriage, Theo and Emily sign a prenup in which they agree to sign mirror-image wills in which the first-to-die spouse leaves everything outright to the other spouse. The prenup also requires that each will divide what remains at the second person's death equally among their children (his two daughters, her son). But a few months after Theo's death, Emily revises her will to leave everything to her son, and specifically disinherits Theo's daughters. When Emily dies, Theo's daughters could sue Emily's estate for failing to honor the prenup, and insist that they inherit in accordance with its terms.

Comparing Some Estate Planning Tools

	Outright Gift to Spouse	Life Estate to Spouse, Remainder to Heirs	Credit Shelter Trust	QTIP Trust
Provides for surviving spouse during lifetime	Yes	Yes	Yes	Yes
Provides for other heirs during surviving spouse's lifetime	No	No	Yes	No
Ensures that what remains upon surviving spouse's death passes to your children (or other desired beneficiaries)	No	Yes	Yes	Yes
Saves on estate tax at surviving spouse's death	No	Some—partially uses first-to-die spouse's applicable exclusion amount based on what the remainder is considered to be worth at first spouse's death	Yes	No—amounts remaining in QTIP trust are includable in surviving spouse's estate
Third party manages assets at death of first spouse	No	No	Yes—requires use of trustee, which can be expensive	Yes—requires use of trustee, which can be expensive
Principal disadvantages	No assurance that your children will ultimately receive anything	May create tension between surviving spouse and children over maintenance and taxes; limits ability to borrow against the property unless surviving spouse and all beneficiaries agree		All income must be paid to surviving spouse, even if he or she remarries or doesn't need money

So if you're contemplating marriage and preserving your assets for your children is critical, I'd suggest considering a prenup to clarify what assets are whose and how assets will be divided on death or divorce. There are a few things to factor in as you're deciding whether to ask for a prenup:

- Each of you will need to hire a lawyer to make the prenup binding on both of you.
- Prenups can cost thousands of dollars.
- Most prenups require you to disclose fully your financial position to your spouse and attach financial statements and tax returns to the document.
- Prenups require you to be very specific about the rights of each spouse on death or divorce, including how assets will be divided, bills will be paid, and whether either spouse is responsible for supporting the other spouse and for how long.
- Prenups generally can't fix child support for children born during the marriage—that's determined by state law.
- Many people (often the less-wealthy spouses) do not like to be asked to sign a prenup. It hurts their feelings and can create lingering tension in the relationship.

If you and your spouse didn't sign a prenup before your marriage, it's not too late. A postnuptial agreement ("postnup") is an agreement you enter into with your spouse after your marriage. Like a prenup, a postnup can set out each spouse's obligations to the other upon death or divorce. With a postnup, you don't have to have a trust to remove your spouse's ability to leave your assets to someone else at your spouse's death. The postnup could obligate each spouse to leave whatever remains of an inheritance from the first-to-die spouse to the first-to-die spouse's children.

> **EXAMPLE:** Carla and Kevin have a comfortable, not lavish, net worth. Carla wants to provide for Kevin should he survive her, yet make sure that what remains of what she left him passes to her children, Candy and Carol. Carla is concerned that the costs of having a trustee manage the funds during Kevin's lifetime will only further drain away her estate, but is also uncomfortable

with Kevin's having the uncontrolled ability to leave the funds to whomever he wants should he remarry following Carla's death. Carla and Kevin enter into a postnup. Each agrees to sign a will providing for the balance of what's left at the second spouse's death to be divided appropriately among both spouses' children to ensure that the children of the first-to-die spouse get their fair share.

Similar to a prenup, a community property agreement is used in those states (Arizona, California, Idaho, Louisiana, Nevada, New Mexico, Texas, Washington, Wisconsin, and sometimes Alaska) that grant spouses equal rights in assets and earnings arising during the marriage. A community property agreement can specify what's jointly owned and what remains separate.

One disadvantage to a postnup is that it doesn't ensure that there will be anything left when the surviving spouse dies—a big difference in the level of protection for your children, when compared to a trust. With a postnup, the surviving spouse may be able to use up what was left, or sell it to an innocent third party. Getting the asset or the funds back may be impossible for your children.

Two similar techniques are joint wills and a contract to make a will. Using these, one or both spouses make particular provision in their wills and cannot change or amend them, even after the death of the first spouse. With the rise in prenups and postnups and the specific case law interpreting them, these are probably not as common as they once were. Some lawyers advise them in blended family planning, so you may hear more about them from your lawyer. The principal drawback to these is their lack of flexibility.

> **EXAMPLE:** Lacey and Cliff sign a joint will in which they agree that their house will pass to Cliff's children after the second spouse dies. Cliff dies in 2009. Lacey won't be able to sell or transfer the house without the consent of all of Cliff's children, even if the house is in a declining neighborhood, she needs the money, or she needs to move to a different climate for health reasons.

Realize that protecting assets with any of these techniques will bind the affected property and limit the surviving spouse's rights to sell or dispose of the property, even if selling the property is in everyone's best interests.

RESOURCE

More information on prenups. *Prenuptial Agreements,* by Katherine Stoner and Shae Irving (Nolo), goes through all the issues, explains the process, and shows you how to draft an agreement to take to lawyers for each person.

Life Estates: An Oldie But a Goodie

A life estate is what it sounds like: a right to use property for life. You can give someone a life estate in your will or revocable living trust or in a real estate deed. A life estate can be for real estate or personal property. For example, you could give your spouse the right to use your house and its contents (furniture and so forth) during your spouse's life, and say that your children get it when your spouse dies. You can also give away property that you own while reserving a life estate for yourself to use the property for the rest of your life.

Life estates were very popular in the early to mid 20th century. In rural areas, farms were often left to a surviving spouse, then to the children at the surviving spouse's death. Nowadays, they have been largely replaced by trusts, which can be tailored more closely to a family's individual needs.

In blended families, a life estate can be a useful technique because it's a simple way to provide for yourself or your spouse while still ensuring that something ultimately passes to your kids. There are drawbacks, though. Your spouse may not be able to borrow money against the property unless your children agree to be on the loan

It's also very common for disputes to arise over who is responsible for maintaining the property and paying for repairs or taxes. If you're leaving a life estate, you want to make sure there's money earmarked toward upkeep, taxes, and maintenance. You may want to have your attorney draw up an agreement so that your spouse agrees to pay taxes, insurance, and maintenance from funds you're leaving your spouse for that purpose.

> **EXAMPLE:** Britt leaves Debbie a life estate in his large Victorian house. At Debbie's death, the house will pass to Britt's children. The interior walls of the house are horsehair plaster and have cracked extensively over the years. Britt's children want Debbie to pay for new sheetrock; Debbie settles for inexpensive paneling. Britt's children want Debbie to pay for repainting and repairing the exterior of the home; Debbie chooses vinyl siding.

It's a good idea to run through some "what-if" scenarios in your mind. For example, what if your spouse remarried, needed to move into assisted living, or just decided to move out? Would you want the house still in your spouse's name and unavailable to your children? If a grown stepchild were living in the house with your spouse, would he or she have to pay rent?

Life estates don't work well if the person who gets the property for life (the life tenant) and the people who eventually inherit it (the remainder beneficiaries) don't get along. They don't work well when there's a mortgage on the property, because the person who gets only a lifetime right to the house may resent making monthly mortgage payments so that the ultimate beneficiaries will get the house free and clear. There may be tax consequences to the person with the lifetime right as well when making payments.

If the spouses are relatively young and the house is subject to a mortgage and is expected to appreciate, it may be to the advantage of the surviving spouse (and that spouse's children) to sell the house, reinvest his or her half in a new residence, and put the other in an account for the first-to-die spouse's beneficiaries. Under this approach, when the surviving spouse is making payments on the new home she would be making them solely for the benefit of her children. Otherwise, a surviving spouse who makes a lot of mortgage payments on the new home, would be doing so half for his or her children and half for her late spouse's children.

The principal benefits of a life estate are its simplicity and low cost: You don't need a 50-page trust agreement or even a trustee to ensure your children end up with the property at your spouse's death. Life estates work best when they're for a reasonably short period of time (better suited for a 65-year-old surviving spouse than a 40-year-old one), when the property is expected to remain in the family, and when family ties are strong.

> **EXAMPLE:** Donna and Sanjaya enjoy living in Donna's spacious mansion in Chicago's Hyde Park. Donna is willing to let Sanjaya use the house should he survive her, but wants to keep it in her family. Donna leaves Sanjaya a life estate in the house and specifies that it will pass, at his death, to her children. Donna also leaves a checking account to her children designated for home maintenance, to relieve Sanjaya of the burden of having to pay for house repairs.

As we've seen, one disadvantage to a life estate is that the person who gets the house for life (the life tenant) generally can't sell the house without the consent of the ultimate beneficiaries. You can remove this drawback by providing that the life tenant may sell the house, as long as the proceeds pass to your children at your spouse's death or are reinvested in a different house that will pass to your children at your spouse's death (The latter option works best if you think your children would agree with your spouse's tastes in the choice of a substitute residence.)

> **EXAMPLE:** Deborah and Karl enjoy living in Deborah's trendy Upper East Side co-op. She is willing to let Karl use the co-op should he survive her, but wants to make sure her investment in the co-op ultimately passes to her family. Deborah can leave Karl a life estate in the co-op, yet permit him to sell it and reinvest the proceeds in another home. At Karl's death, the new home would pass to Deborah's children.

A life estate is a simple, although imperfect, tool best suited when the conditions are right (older life tenant, debt-free home, money to maintain, and good relationship between the life tenant and ultimate beneficiaries). Another option is to put the home in one of the trusts discussed next or in a trust set up just for the house.

QTIP and Credit Shelter Trusts: Estate Planning Workhorses

Historically used a means of minimizing estate tax, credit shelter and QTIP trusts are both good planning vehicles for blended families even if estate tax isn't a concern. Either trust can help achieve your goal of providing for a surviving spouse, yet ultimately benefiting whom you wish, rather than leaving that decision to your spouse.

The two trusts basically work like this. You create the trust in your will or revocable living trust (RLT). Assets don't go into the trust until your death. At that time, the property that you've designated to be held in trust is transferred to a trustee you've chosen. The trustee manages the property, invests it, and makes distributions, all as you specified in your will or trust document. Most trusts provide for the support of a surviving spouse and the support and education of children. (Your spouse and children, who *benefit* from the trust, are called *beneficiaries*.) At some point, at your spouse's death or when your children reach certain ages, the trust terminates, and what's left goes to your children.

So what are the differences between the two trusts? There are some significant ones. In a QTIP trust:

- The trustee *must* regularly distribute any income the trust property earns to the surviving spouse.
- The surviving spouse *is the only one* who can get distributions from the trust while the surviving spouse is alive.

By contrast, in a credit shelter trust:

- Distributions are *discretionary*—there is no requirement that income be distributed to either your spouse or children.
- The trust can benefit *both your spouse and your children* during your spouse's life.

Key Features of QTIP and Credit Shelter Trusts		
	While Surviving Spouse Is Alive	**After Surviving Spouse's Death**
QTIP	Money may be used only for benefit of surviving spouse; income must go to surviving spouse	Trust assets go to children outright or at ages specified in trust
Credit shelter	Money may be used for benefit of surviving spouse and/or children; no requirement that income be distributed to either	Trust assets go to children outright or at ages specified in trust

If you're not concerned about estate tax, you'll probably choose between the trusts based on whether or not you want money available for your children during your spouse's life (a credit shelter trust) or only after the surviving spouse's death (QTIP).

If estate tax is a concern (you have a net worth of $3.5 million or more), then you might use both trusts. Typically, the entire applicable exclusion amount (the federal estate tax threshold, $3.5 million for deaths in 2009) would go in the credit shelter trust, with the rest going to the QTIP trust. But now that the exclusion amount has gone up so much, to $3.5 million, you might choose to have less go into the credit shelter trust just so there will be something available to leave outright to your spouse or to put in a QTIP trust.

Blended families for whom estate tax isn't a concern may still be better off putting assets in both trusts because of the different way they provide for the surviving spouse and the first-to-die spouse's intended beneficiaries.

> EXAMPLE: Beth wants to provide for her spouse, Manny, and her children. She has a net worth of $2 million. Beth decides to create two trusts, each with $1 million in assets. One trust will be a QTIP trust for the primary benefit of Manny during his life; the other trust will be primarily for the benefit of her children during Manny's life. Manny will receive all income the QTIP trust earns

during his life. If he needs more money, he can ask the trustee for funds from the QTIP trust. If that isn't enough, Manny can request distributions from the credit shelter trust.

The biggest advantage of a QTIP or a credit shelter trust is also its biggest disadvantage: you have to have a trustee. Trustees can be friends, relatives, or paid professionals, such as corporate trustees affiliated with a bank or brokerage company, lawyers, and accountants. (I talk about selecting trustees in Chapter 10.) Trustees can provide much-needed management of your assets and impartiality when dealing with your loved ones. Non-family-member trustees also cost money. Trustees control the purse strings, which can be a source of irritation to a child or a surviving spouse. People don't like to have to go to other people to ask for money. Be aware of that natural reaction as you look at determining which option is right for you and your family.

Where Are You on the Control Continuum?

Some people are comfortable with distributing their wealth with no strings attached. Others want to exert some control from beyond the grave. A charter member of this extreme end of the control spectrum, media mogul Sumner Redstone, once said: "I'm in control now and I'll be in control when I die." (Quoted in "Family Feud," by Robert Lenzner with Devon Pendleton, *Forbes*, November 12, 2007.)

QTIP Trusts

"QTIP" trusts, shorthand for the cumbersome "qualified terminable interest property" trusts, are also called marital deduction trusts. That's because they take advantage of the federal tax law that says you can leave everything to your spouse at your death estate-tax free if your spouse is a U.S. citizen. In tax jargon, there's an unlimited marital deduction from estate tax for amounts going to your spouse.

If established as part of your will or RLT (as is typical), a QTIP trust becomes irrevocable at your death. Your executor normally decides which of your assets to put in the QTIP trust. Typically, the surviving spouse gets a specific amount or what remains in your estate after making your other bequests and establishing the credit shelter trusts if you're using two trusts. But the trust also ensures that what remains at your spouse's death passes to your children or others you've chosen.

The QTIP trust makes it clear that at your spouse's death the only people who may receive your assets are your blood descendants. You can give your surviving spouse a "power of appointment," which allows your spouse to adjust and vary the percentages that each of your descendants receives at your spouse's death, or you can set the percentages. Setting percentages might be appropriate if you're concerned that a spouse may favor a particular child—say, the child the two of you have from your current marriage—over your children from a previous relationship.

> EXAMPLE: In her will, Danielle establishes a QTIP trust for her husband, Desmond. When Danielle dies, Desmond will get to stay in his and Danielle's house. He'll also receive income from the trust assets for the rest of his life. If Desmond needs money, he can request an additional distribution from the trustee. The trustee will look at the terms of the trust to determine whether Desmond qualifies for an additional distribution. The trustee has the power to say yes or no (based on the directions in the trust document) to Desmond's request. When Desmond dies, none of the trust assets will go to his children from a previous relationship, but will pass in equal shares to Danielle's children from her previous marriage and the child she has with Desmond.

QTIP trusts have a number of requirements, including that income earned on the trust assets (for example, dividends from stock) be frequently distributed to the surviving spouse during his or her lifetime. The income can be paid only to your surviving spouse. Also, only your spouse may request and receive additional distributions (called encroachments) from the principal of your trust. Plus, you can't turn off the spigot in the event your surviving spouse remarries or has a problem with creditors—he or she will still be entitled to regular income distributions.

The amount set aside in a QTIP trust is not subject to estate tax at the first spouse's death. What remains at the surviving spouse's death, however, will be included in his or her estate for estate tax purposes.

> **EXAMPLE:** You die leaving $2 million in a QTIP trust to your spouse. At the time of your spouse's death, the QTIP trust has $1.5 million in assets left. Your spouse also has $3 million in separate assets. Your spouse's total estate will be $4.5 million:
>
> | | |
> |---|---|
> | Assets in QTIP | $ 1.5 million |
> | Assets owned outright | + 3.0 million |
> | Total estate for tax purposes | $ 4.5 million |

Credit Shelter Trusts

The second workhorse in most plans is the credit shelter trust. A credit shelter trust is a way to provide for your surviving spouse during the surviving spouse's lifetime, with the remainder passing to your descendants. And it can reduce estate tax, if you think you'll leave enough money or property to make that a concern. (Fewer and fewer estates are now subject to the estate tax, as the applicable exclusion amount has risen.)

A credit shelter trust is typically designed to hold the maximum amount that can pass to children free of estate tax ($3.5 million in 2009). Because so much can now be held in a credit shelter trust, it may be larger than the QTIP trust if you use both trusts in your planning and fund the credit shelter trust with the maximum amount it can shelter from estate tax.

> **EXAMPLE:** Phil dies with an $8 million estate. He set up both a QTIP and a credit shelter trust. If the applicable exclusion amount in the year of Phil's death is $3.5 million, then the credit shelter trust will hold $3.5 million; $4.5 million will be in the QTIP trust.

Most times, if you're using both trusts, your credit shelter trust gets set up first and equals the applicable exclusion amount. Your QTIP trust gets what's left. If you don't have enough money in your estate to set up both, the credit shelter trust will be established with what you do have. You don't have to put the full $3.5 million in the credit shelter trust— you can put a set amount or percentage in the QTIP trust, or leave your spouse a specific amount of cash or property.

> EXAMPLE 1: Susan dies with a $3 million estate. She sets up both a credit shelter trust and a QTIP trust in her will. If the applicable exclusion amount in the year of Susan's death is $3.5 million, then $3 million will go into the credit shelter trust and nothing will go into the QTIP trust unless she makes a specific provision for her QTIP trust.

> EXAMPLE 2: Same facts, but Susan directs that the amount going into the QTIP trust should be equal to one-half of her estate. So $1.5 million will go into the credit shelter trust, and $1.5 million will go into the QTIP trust.

Unlike a QTIP trust, a credit shelter trust can pay a portion of trust income to your descendants during your spouse's lifetime. Both your spouse and your descendants may ask the trustee for payments (encroachments) on the principal. The trust document will specify the general approach you want taken for distributions, whether you want to encourage distributions and not worry about what's in the trust or whether you want to discourage distributions to preserve the trust principal. Frequently, the trust will provide for the support of your spouse and the support and education of your children.

Your trustee will look at the language of the trust in deciding whether to make distributions.

> EXAMPLE: Ren creates a credit shelter trust for Connie and his three children. The trust allows the trustee to make distributions for Connie's support and to keep her in her accustomed manner

of living. Connie makes a request of the trustee to liquidate the modest trust so she can go on a year-long cruise around the world. The trustee will deny the request if it's inconsistent with the terms of the trust and Ren's intention.

The assets in a credit shelter trust may be divided at the surviving spouse's death into shares for each child or kept in one trust for the benefit of all. The one-for-all trust is often called a "pot" trust because everything goes into one pot. A pot trust normally keeps all the assets together until the youngest child should have finished with education (age 25 is common). Along the way, the trustee can use the property in the trust to pay for the children's education and whatever else is allowed by the terms of the trust. Then, the remaining assets are distributed outright or divided into new trusts for the children.

> **EXAMPLE:** Clyde and Betty are married. Clyde has two boys from his first marriage, Clyde, Jr. and Dylan. To preserve his $3.5 million applicable exclusion amount, Clyde sets up a credit shelter trust in his will. That means the executor puts $3.5 million in assets into the credit shelter trust. The rest, depending on the will, is distributed outright to the beneficiaries or placed in another trust, such as a QTIP trust. Should Betty survive Clyde, the credit shelter trust will help to provide for Betty. At Betty's death, Clyde, Jr. and Dylan will get anything that's left in the trust—Betty can't leave it to her children or to a new beau. The credit shelter trust can spread out when distributions are made so that Clyde, Jr. and Dylan won't receive everything at once.

If a beneficiary has a problem with creditors, the credit shelter trust can suspend distributions to the beneficiary to avoid having creditor claims exhaust the trust assets.

> **EXAMPLE:** Romeo creates a credit shelter trust for his son Romeo, Jr. Romeo, Jr. has a car accident that badly injures Nelly. Nelly tries to sue the trustee of the credit shelter trust so that she can get

the distributions that Romeo, Jr. would get from the trust. Rather than make the payments to the creditor, the trustee can suspend payments to Romeo, Jr. and keep the principal and income safe from Nelly.

If you include both a credit shelter trust and a QTIP trust in your revocable living trust, the trustee will funnel assets into the QTIP and credit shelter trusts at your death, as shown in the diagram below.

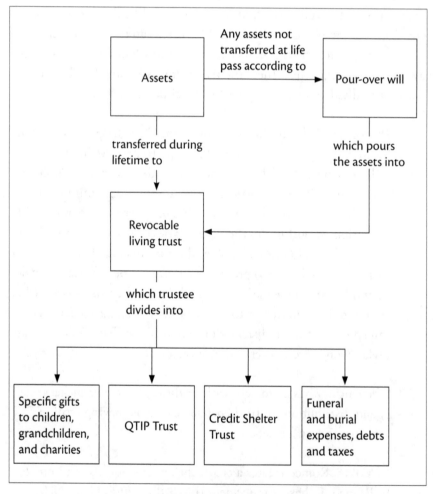

Living Trust With QTIP and Credit Shelter Trust

Nonprobate assets (insurance, accounts with beneficiary designations, property which passes automatically to a survivor) won't go into your revocable living trust unless you specifically direct them to the trust.

If you used a will to create this kind of arrangement, your executor would parcel out your assets to the trusts, as in the diagram below.

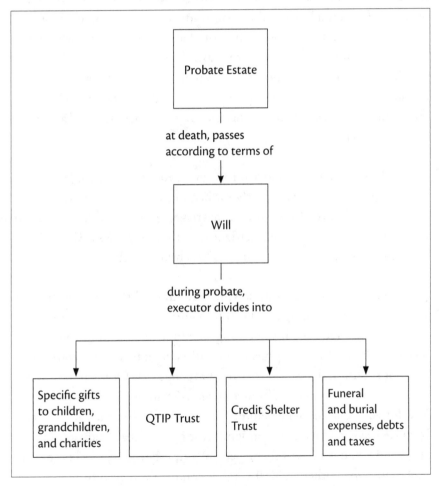

Will With QTIP and Credit Shelter Trusts

Providing Cash for Loved Ones With Life Insurance

After a death, family members will probably need money to pay living expenses, and they may face large additional expenses such as estate tax. You don't want them to be forced to quickly sell assets—real estate or stocks, for example—to raise cash. And if you're leaving much of your estate in trust, you need to be sure that family members who don't inherit right away have access to the cash they need.

Buying life insurance now is one way to provide necessary cash, quickly. If the life insurance is properly set up, the benefit won't add to your estate tax or cost your beneficiaries any tax. (See "Other Tax-Saving Tools," below.)

> **EXAMPLE:** Barry is married to a much younger woman, Jade. He wants to provide generously for her, but doesn't want to make his grown children from his first marriage, Jennifer and Jason, wait to inherit anything until after Jade's death. Barry buys a $2 million life insurance policy and names his children as beneficiaries.

Life insurance (or annuities, which are similar but pay a benefit over years instead of in a lump sum) can be a great tool to provide needed cash for your loved ones if something should happen to you, your spouse, or both of you. For blended families, it's a nice way to provide for your spouse and any children you have together. Or it can be a way to make sure your children from a previous relationship won't have to wait for your spouse to die before receiving the bulk of their inheritance. If you're leaving a business or a significant piece of real estate to one child and you don't have other assets in your estate to leave a comparable inheritance to another child, insurance can help you even things out among your children.

Buying Life Insurance

Life insurance comes in two basic types: term and permanent.

Term life is issued for a set period of years (ten, 20, or 30), throughout which the premiums remain the same. At the end of the term, the premiums increase substantially, so most term life isn't kept after the term expires. Term life is a good way to replace the income that would be lost if you die young. You generally don't build any value in a term policy, and if you stop paying the premium, the policy lapses. The initial premiums on term life are typically much lower than on other policies. But as you age, you may not be able to replace term life insurance with another policy if you want to keep life insurance as part of your portfolio.

Permanent insurance policies (whole life, variable life, universal life, and variable universal life) are designed to stay in effect throughout your life. They aren't expected to lapse at the end of a set term like a term policy is. They're more expensive initially than a term policy. Their premiums may adjust based on the performance of the policy. In some cases, the policy can become fully paid up, meaning you won't have to pay any further premiums. You're essentially investing funds with the insurance company in return for the death benefit. If the insurance company does well with its investments, your policy's performance improves as well.

Second-to-die policies pay at the second spouse's death. They can be term or another kind of policy. They can be cheaper than an individual policy, because the insurance company has to pay only when the second of you goes. A second-to-die policy can be helpful for paying taxes.

For me, term life is the easiest product to get my mind around—you know what the benefit is, and you know what the premiums are going to be. You know the insurance isn't going to be there forever, so you make other investments to provide for your loved ones if you outlast the term of the policy.

Insurance advisers may recommend term or other types of policies. Be sure to check the policies out carefully and ask what happens to the policy if the market doesn't go up as fast as predicted, or decreases.

How much insurance should you get? I've seen various ways of calculating the amount of coverage you need, from completing extensive worksheets that look at your lost income and ongoing expenses to rules of thumb that say five to seven times the primary breadwinner's income.

Your insurance adviser should be able to help you out. Just keep in mind that your adviser is a salesperson, so shop around and do your research to back up what your adviser recommends.

RESOURCE

More information on buying life insurance.

- www.kiplinger.com offers information on group and individual coverage
- www.smartmoney.com describes differences between policies and links to major providers
- Life and Health Foundation for Education, www.lifehappens.org, is an industry group sponsored by insurers; its website includes guides to various kinds of insurance and provides a printable consumer brochure under disability insurance
- A.M. Best www.ambest.com/consumer: A.M. Best is a rating organization for insurance carriers. Its website allows you to search by state for carriers who provide insurance in your state and contains helpful consumer information.

Special Life Insurance Considerations in Community Property States

Whether life insurance is treated as separate or community property can affect who has a right to at least some of the eventual proceeds. The answer may depend on the state.

Some states look at whether premiums were paid with separate or community property. If the premiums came from community property, then the surviving spouse may be a part owner of the policy, as well as have a right to a portion of the death benefits.

EXAMPLE: Tim and Sally live in a community property state that looks at the source of premiums for determining who owns a life insurance policy. If Tim pays premiums on a life insurance policy out of his and Sally's community property, then Sally may be entitled to part of the death benefit, even if Tim named his daughters as beneficiaries.

Other states look at when the policy was issued to determine whether it's community or separate property.

EXAMPLE: Leonard buys a life insurance policy before he gets married. His state's rules look at when a policy is purchased, so the policy is Leonard's, and he can designate his children as beneficiaries. Leonard's wife Leona isn't an owner of the policy or entitled to its death benefit under state law. She might, however, be entitled to reimbursement of half of premiums paid if Leonard used their community property to pay premiums as they came due.

In any event, you'll want to check with your adviser if you intend to name someone other than your spouse as the beneficiary of a life insurance policy. For example, your spouse may need to consent to treating the policy as separate property in order for you to leave the policy proceeds to your children, or you may have to pay all of the premiums out of your separate property.

Sharing the Wealth Now: Making Gifts During Your Life

You don't have make loved ones wait until after your death to share some of your good fortune. Three tools are particularly good at helping you provide for your loved ones through lifetime giving. They are:
- making tax-free "annual exclusion" gifts
- contributing to Section 529 plans to help pay for college, and
- paying education and medical expenses directly.

Giving to children while you can see them enjoy the benefits can be very gratifying. In addition to being good things to do, these techniques help you save taxes—a bonus!

Making Tax-Free "Annual Exclusion" Gifts

Annual exclusion gifts are simply "no strings attached" gifts to children, stepchildren, or anyone else you choose. In 2009, you can give $13,000 per year to anyone (and any number of anyones) other than your spouse without owing federal gift tax. (There's no limit on how much you can give your spouse free of gift tax, unless your spouse isn't a U.S. citizen—in that case, the tax-free limit is $133,000 per year.)

If you and your spouse elect to split gifts, you can give $26,000 a year per recipient. Why is splitting gifts a good technique? It reduces your taxable estate. Plus, it can be a relationship-smoother as well. By using both spouse's credits, you can make larger, tax-free gifts to children and stepchildren than you could if you weren't married (alone you can give $13,000 per year; with spouse $26,000). If your children think your new spouse is going to get all your money, you can start sharing with them now to show them otherwise. A little money may go a long way in helping everyone get along.

> EXAMPLE: Kristin and Jorge have enough money to burn a wet mule. To reduce their potentially taxable estates, they make annual exclusion gifts of $26,000 to each of their children. Kristin can give the full amount to each of her kids; Jorge can do the same with his. Or Jorge can fund all of the gifts. Just because they've agreed to split gifts for tax purposes, it doesn't mean that both spouses have to contribute. The money can come from just one spouse.

Giving to Meet a Need: Section 529 Plans

Section 529 plans are an excellent tool to help pay for college. Named after Internal Revenue Code Section 529, these state-sponsored investment plans offer participants the ability to accumulate benefits tax-free to pay college education expenses. Amounts given within the annual exclusion amount avoid gift tax, and are not included in the giver's estate (and so avoid estate tax). You also get a tax deduction for your contributions in many states. Any income the account earns isn't subject to income or capital gains tax. Proceeds from a Section 529 plan can be used for room and board (not just tuition) while the recipient is enrolled in an educational institution. You can even front-load the plans by putting in five years' worth of your annual exclusion gifts ($65,000) into an account to get it going.

You can establish a Section 529 account directly with the provider or through your financial adviser. Most states offer several investment options, from very conservative to aggressive.

EXAMPLE: Winona wishes to help her young stepchildren pay for college. As long as she and her husband elect to split gifts, she can contribute up to $26,000 per year per stepchild to Section 529 plans set up for them.

RESOURCE
More information on Section 529 plans. Check out what each state offers at www.savingforcollege.com or search online under your state's name and "Section 529 plan."

Paying Tuition or Medical Expenses

You can pay any amount for someone's tuition or medical expenses without worrying about a gift tax, as long as you pay the provider directly. These gifts are unlimited; you can make them even if you've already used your annual exclusion gift amounts. This can be a goodwill booster for a stepparent if you are willing to fund a portion of a stepchild's or stepgrandchild's education. Note the limitation to tuition—payments for room and board are generally not exempted from gift tax. Unlike a Section 529 plan, though, you can pay for private elementary or high school, not just college. These payments are good for estate tax planning, because they get these gifts out of your estate. Plus, you don't have to pay a gift tax. They're even better for the benefits you're giving a child or stepchild: education and medical care.

> **EXAMPLE:** Winona wishes to help her young stepchildren pay for education, but she's already made annual exclusion gifts to each of them. She can pay the tuition directly to Wellington Prep School for the stepchildren, while continuing to make annual exclusion gifts.

There are some limits. Generally, these payments must be made directly to the provider—not the child or stepchild—to qualify. In addition, to qualify for the educational exclusion, the payment must be for tuition, not room and board.

> **EXAMPLE:** Steve's stepson Seth blows out his knee while snowboarding in Snowmass. Seth's surgery costs $13,000. Steve can pay Seth's orthopedic bills without the stipend siphoning his annual gift exclusion amount. Provided Steve sends the payments straight to the surgeon, there's not a gift tax issue. Steve can't write the check to Seth; it has to be made out to the provider.

Other Tax-Saving Tools

If you're one of the decreasing number of Americans concerned about federal estate tax, you might want to explore some other tax-saving tools, in addition to the trusts discussed above.

Joint Revocable Trusts

A joint revocable trust is one you and your spouse both sign. Joint revocable trusts started in community property states, because so much property in those states is held jointly, rather than in one spouse's name or another. A joint revocable trust would be your primary estate planning device. With a joint revocable trust, you and your spouse would contribute virtually all of your property to the trust. During your lifetimes, you'd be the trustees for the trust. After one death, the trust becomes irrevocable, and the surviving spouse can't change it. Up until that time, you can change the trust. Although you pool your property in the trust, it doesn't get divided equally among your beneficiaries (unless that's your intent), but gets divided according to the trust terms. Each of you can ultimately leave your assets to your children unless you want to do otherwise.

These benefits can make a joint trust worthwhile whether or not you're concerned about the estate tax. But there are tax benefits as well. A joint revocable trust uses each spouse's applicable exclusion amount without the wealthier spouse having to transfer assets outright to the less wealthy spouse. Joint revocable trusts work well when you're trying to provide for the spouse, yet ensure that your children end up with more and the government less, particularly if one spouse is much wealthier than the other and doesn't want to make a no-strings-attached gift of millions of dollars to the other spouse. They allow you to put assets in your spouse's estate for tax purposes without losing control over them.

> **EXAMPLE:** Raul and Sylvia have been married for two years. Sylvia's net worth dipped precipitously when she and her previous husband, Justin, divorced. But she still has $7 million, much more than Raul (who has few assets to his name) and twice the 2009 applicable exclusion amount. Sylvia wouldn't feel comfortable transferring $3.5 million to Raul, but she doesn't want to lose the use of his applicable exclusion amount should he pass away first. Sylvia establishes a joint revocable trust with Raul, which allows her to keep her assets under her control, but use his applicable exclusion amount should he pass away first.

Lifetime QTIP Trusts

Unlike the effective-on-death QTIP trusts discussed above, which are usually created by a will or an RLT, a lifetime QTIP is a separate, irrevocable trust. It's another way to provide for your spouse but ensure that what remains passes to your children, and it can provide estate tax savings when one spouse has much more money than the other.

Unlike a will or revocable trust, a lifetime QTIP is irrevocable as soon as you sign it. Once you set it up, there's no going back. It's like tattooing your new spouse's name and number on your bank account. So why use one? Typically, a wealthier spouse who's concerned about estate tax establishes a lifetime QTIP for the less wealthy spouse's benefit. It is better than giving the spouse a large sum of money, only to hear a week later that "things just aren't working out" and the money is gone. An estranged spouse wouldn't be able to clean out a QTIP trust like a bank account.

A lifetime QTIP works as if you passed away the day you signed a will with a QTIP provision in it, with one big exception. The lifetime QTIP can fund your spouse's applicable exclusion amount even if your spouse dies before you. A QTIP in your will would help fund your spouse's applicable exclusion amount only if you died first.

A lifetime QTIP has a number of requirements, including that income the trust earns be frequently distributed to your spouse during his or her life. Plus, you can't turn off the spigot if you divorce and your spouse remarries—he or she will still be entitled to the funds. This is the principal drawback to a lifetime QTIP. If your relationship doesn't last, the trust can't be terminated. The amount set aside in a QTIP trust is not subject to estate tax at the death of the spouse who created the trust, but will be included in the other spouse's estate for estate tax purposes.

> EXAMPLE: Wealthy Paula wishes to provide for poor Pete, her husband, yet ensure that her children end up with the balance of her assets. Paula wants to use Pete's applicable exclusion amount, but doesn't want to transfer $3.5 million into his name. Paula can set up a lifetime QTIP for Pete. Once the lifetime QTIP is established, Pete will receive quarterly distributions of income for the rest of his life. At his death, the trust assets pass to Paula's children tax free. By using Pete's applicable exclusion amount, Paula can pass to her children—tax free—twice the amount she could have passed on her own.

Without lifetime QTIP:

Estate	$ 7,000,000
Federal estate tax	− 1,575,000
Paula's children receive	$ 5,425,000

With lifetime QTIP:

Estate	$ 7,000,000
Federal estate tax	− 0
Paula's children receive	$ 7,000,000

Life Insurance Owned by Children

If you've bought life insurance for your children (often a good idea, as discussed above), the value of the policy proceeds will be part of your estate, for estate tax purposes, unless you take steps now. One way to get those proceeds out of your estate is for your children to own the policy on your life.

To make this happen, you assist your children in the paperwork and medical exams that the company needs to issue the insurance. The children own the policy and are its beneficiaries. You make annual exclusion gifts to your children to pay the premiums on the policy. (Remember, gifts of up to $13,000 per recipient per year aren't subject to gift tax.) The death benefit will not be subject to income tax in the hands of your children, and will not be included in your estate.

> EXAMPLE: Timothy's sons Dimitri and Pasqual apply for and hold an insurance policy on their father's life. Timothy can pay for the insurance by making gifts of the premium amount to the children through annual exclusion gifts. The children pay the premium on the policy from the money Timothy gives to them. Provided they keep the insurance in place, Dimitri and Pasqual will inherit the full amount of the life insurance, but the proceeds won't be included in Timothy's estate, because he doesn't own the policy.

Irrevocable Life Insurance Trusts

There's another way to get life insurance proceeds out of your taxable estate, if you are concerned about your children maintaining a life insurance policy with the money you've given them or if your children are minors. You can create an irrevocable life insurance trust (ILIT) to hold the policy. Like life insurance owned by your children, life insurance in an ILIT won't be part of your estate.

With an ILIT, the life insurance proceeds don't have to be paid outright to your children, but can be held in trust. Another benefit is that the trust can be used to help provide funds so your estate can pay any estate tax owed. For tax reasons, the ILIT can't just write a check to the IRS for estate tax owed by your estate, but the insurance proceeds can be used to buy assets out of your estate or lend money to your estate so there will be funds available for your estate to write the check.

Without an ILIT, if you owned the insurance, the death benefit would be included in your estate for estate tax purposes. Not only is the death benefit excluded from your taxable estate, but because it's life insurance, the recipients of the death benefit won't have to pay income tax on the death benefit. Your beneficiaries don't even have to pay for the insurance.

You start by creating a trust. You name a trustee, who should be someone other than you, your spouse, or your child (an accountant, for example). You either contribute money to the trust to enable the trustee to purchase a life insurance policy or you put an existing life insurance policy in the trust. Ideally, the trust applies for and purchases the life insurance, because if you transfer an existing policy to a trust it takes three years before the life insurance is out of your estate. If the trust applies for the policy, the three-year waiting period doesn't apply. The death benefit is not part of your estate.

Before premiums become due, you make a gift of the premiums into the ILIT. Now, here's where it gets a little tricky. Before the trustee can pay the premiums, the trustee has to notify the trust's beneficiaries (your children) that a gift has been made into the trust. To make the gift qualify for tax reasons, the children have to have a right to withdraw a portion of the premiums for a time period specified in the notice (often 30 days). Once the beneficiaries' right to withdraw a part of the gift lapses, then the trustee pays the premium keeping the policy in force.

> EXAMPLE: Timothy, a successful businessman in his early 50s, is married to Rachel, a designer of children's clothes. She is approximately the same age as Timothy's younger son, Pasqual. Timothy wishes to provide generously for her, but is concerned that Pasqual and his brother Dimitri will grow weary of waiting on Rachel to pass away before receiving their inheritance. Timothy puts a life insurance policy with a $3 million death benefit into a trust for the benefit of his sons. If Timothy lives at least three years after the transfer, Dimitri and Pasqual will inherit the full amount of the life insurance without its being included in Timothy's otherwise taxable estate. The ILIT has allowed $3 million to pass to the two children free of estate tax. And like any inheritance, the children don't have to pay income tax on it, either.

In community property states, ILITs are better used to provide for children, rather than spouses—because of the joint property ownership rules of community property states, naming a spouse as one of the trust beneficiaries may pull the proceeds of the policy into your spouse's estate for tax purposes, which you're generally trying to avoid.

Qualified Personal Residence Trusts

Qualified personal residence trusts (QPRTs, pronounced "kew-perts") can be a great way to get a major asset, such as your house or a vacation home, out of your estate and into the hands of your beneficiaries at a relatively low tax cost. Here's how a QPRT works. You put your house in trust for a fixed number of years (say, ten or 15). While the trust lasts, you keep the use of your home. Once it ends, your house passes to the people you've chosen, typically your children.

Who would want to do this? Someone who wants to make sure their children end up with their home or vacation home at a low tax cost. Because here's the good news:

- the house passes to your children
- you don't have to pay a lot of tax to get the house to your children, and
- all of the increase in value of your house (appreciation) after you've set up the trust gets taken out of your estate.

Of course there's a big wrinkle in all that good news. If you want to stay in or use the home after the trust ends, you have to pay rent to the beneficiaries of the trust—your children—at fair market value. Or your beneficiaries have to set up a QPRT of their own (a reverse QPRT—seriously, that's what it's called) and give YOU the right to use the house for a period of time (say, one or two years) before it comes back to them, and keep setting these up as long as you want to live in the house.

As we're all aware, house prices across the country have dipped recently. If you think the value of your home or vacation home is going to go back up, a QPRT is a good technique to get it out of your estate while prices are low. A QPRT can also be a blended family relationship-smoother if your children are concerned about ultimately ending up with a treasured family home or vacation place. You can go to your children and say, "I'm giving you the beach house by putting it in a trust. No matter what, it's coming to you when the trust is over."

Transferring your home into the trust is a taxable gift for gift tax purposes because its value will surely be over the annual exclusion amount ($13,000 in 2009). The value of the gift is reduced, however, because you're not parting with the home immediately, but only at the end of the trust. So, if you give away a $400,000 home, the value of the gift will be much less than $400,000 because you've kept the right to stay in it for ten years. This will be true even if the house is worth more than $400,000 once your children get it.

Most people use their lifetime gift tax credit to avoid paying a gift tax when setting up a QPRT, so they don't actually have to write a check to the IRS for any gift tax.

EXAMPLE: Celia and Tomas live in Tomas's mountaintop home outside of Telluride, Colorado. Tomas has two daughters, Pilar and Rosalita, from a previous marriage. By establishing a QPRT, Tomas can ensure that Pilar and Rosalita end up owning the house. Tomas can take a large asset out of his otherwise taxable estate and get it in his daughters' names.

The principal advantages of a QPRT are:

- **Estate tax savings.** The house, any appreciation on the house, and any rent you pay your children once the trust ends aren't included in your estate. If you waited to put the house in a trust at your death, all of this would be part of your estate.
- **Peace of mind.** You know your children will end up with the home.

The main disadvantages of a QPRT are:

- **Possibility of more taxable gifts.** They don't work well if you have a mortgage on the house during the trust, because if you pay the mortgage it could be deemed an additional gift to your children.
- **Your kids are your landlord.** If you or your spouse does stay in the house after the trust ends, you have to pay rent to your children or ask your children to do a QPRT for you.
- **Loss of control.** Your children get the house outright when the trust terminates, and they can do with it what they wish. They don't have to rent it to you (or give you the right to use it) or to your spouse if you're the first to die. They might disagree among themselves if one wants to sell and others don't—and any one of them could force a sale. The house could be subject to claims from the children's creditors, even if you're still living there and paying rent.
- **To get the benefits, you have to outlive the term.** If you die before the end of the trust term, the trust terminates, and the house gets pulled back into your estate. You haven't lost anything (other than the legal fees from setting it up), but you don't get the tax benefits.

7

Spouses of Unequal Wealth

Talk, Talk, and Keep on Talking 154
Should You Help Out the Stepchildren? 156
Good Tools for Spouses of Unequal Means 157
Good Tools for Both Spouses 157
Good Tools for the Wealthier Spouse 162
Tools for the Less-Wealthy Spouse 163

Her pot has a lot and his does not.
Do you combine the pots and use what you got
To spend your days upon the yacht
Or squirrel them away in a shanty hot?
Would answers have come to questions thought
Before you ever tied the knot?
To chart your course, to plot your lot,
Or not?

Back when you and your spouse were dating, every week brought something new:

- shared experiences ("next stop: Graceland!")
- awestruck discoveries of similar experiences in the past ("you hated high school, too?")
- growing intimacy ("I like the way you smell") and, of course,
- late-night confessions about previous relationships, hopes, and fears.

One thing you may not have talked about much was money. Sure, you may have had some clues about what the other one had or didn't have, but you probably weren't exchanging financial statements over brunch. Although counselors preach the importance of making sure your financial views are compatible before marriage, most of us don't talk about finances much. Most couples enter a blended relationship without an exact financial picture.

And that's appropriate for the premarital (aka constant cuddling), stage in the relationship. You've just met this wonderful person; you don't want to screw it up (or have it progress for the wrong reasons) by saying, "Oh, by the way, I'm broke," or, for that matter, "Oh, by the way, I'm rich Rich RICH!!!" But at some point, whether it's in a prenuptial agreement or a postnuptial confession, you may find that one of you has a lot more money than the other.

When planning for people of different means, I've found that the different means matter. While it can certainly be a blessing to have those resources available, money has the ability to draw out deep feelings in us all. Not all of these feelings are positive. If one partner has much more than the other, it can become a point of resentment, a source of tension (for both spouses), and a power-shifter in the relationship. Even if you and your spouse are at ease over the disparity, if you both have children, there can be resentment between the ones raised without a lot of money and those with trust fund checks left forgotten and uncashed in their dresser drawers.

Financial status likely will affect how each of you looks at finances, career choices, how money should be managed and spent, debt, and expectations and involvement in your children's upbringing. The source of the money (earned vs. inherited) may weigh heavily on your perceptions. Each of you will have emotions about money, whether it's guilt (which seems to be common with inherited wealth), viewing it with satisfaction as a reward for a job well done, viewing it as inadequate (near-universal), or, for a few, contentment.

You and your spouse have probably already noticed some differences in your views on money, support, and child-raising. For example, virtually everyone wants their children to be well educated. But well educated means different things to different people: Is it graduating from a local college or university, or will only the Ivy League do? Are you looking at two years, four years, or all the way through graduate school?

What you wish to be responsible for affects your estate planning. A wealthier spouse may be concerned about avoiding estate tax, providing for the less-wealthy spouse, and making sure the wealthier spouse's children are the ultimate recipients of the wealthier spouse's assets. Planning to achieve these goals can get quite complex, frequently involving trusts to provide for the spouse while preserving the wealth for the next generation.

Planning for the less-wealthy spouse's estate is simpler, though no less important. The less-wealthy spouse is usually most interested in passing on limited resources to his or her children as quickly as possible at death. Because the wealthier spouse is typically not relying on the assets of the other spouse, the focus is on the children.

How you handle day-to-day finances also affects your planning. What will you spend your money on? You might feel more than a little guilt if your spouse wants to whisk you away for a nice vacation when your child's having trouble making ends meet. But your spouse may not want to skimp on luxuries for the two of you in order to support your children.

Talk, Talk, and Keep on Talking

It's hard to come to terms with your differences if you haven't thought them through before you're sitting in the lawyer's office. From my perspective, the couples who get the best results when doing their estate planning are the ones who have talked about things up front and have invested time in their relationships with children and stepchildren. Before setting foot in the lawyer's office, you and your spouse should take some time in a relaxed, nonthreatening location (poolside at the Ritz-Carlton seems to work well) and talk about your expectations and values. You may find that you're not that far apart when it comes to what you want to accomplish; you may just have different ideas of how to get there. At least, you'll know what the other is thinking so there shouldn't be any surprises by the time you do visit your lawyer.

As with so many emotional issues, sometimes we aren't conscious of our feelings on money, and these feelings may be difficult to tease out. As you talk, it may be helpful for each of you to consider:

- how money was talked about during your childhood (if it was talked about at all)
- what your family's resources were like while you were growing up, whether there were any times of particular hardship, and how that affects your perception of abundance and scarcity
- how your family spent its money on you and your brothers and sisters when you were growing up, how you spend money on your children, and how you determine what's appropriate to give your children, and
- your experiences with money since leaving home.

These questions may help bring to light your and your spouse's attitudes, emotions, and fears regarding money. Age and generation may play a role as well: People who grew up poor during the Great Depression famously have very distinct and conservative views on money. It may be that each generation has its own perspective.

If She Is the One With the Money

Because of societal and gender issues, tensions likely will increase where the man is the less wealthy of the two. Two articles, one in *Worth* magazine, the other in *The New York Times*, highlight feelings (and sometime frustrations) that result when a man marries a much wealthier woman.

Both mention the importance of being able to talk about money, using outside facilitators or counselors as necessary, honoring the contributions of the less-wealthy mate, and avoiding feelings of dependence on the wealthier spouse.

The lessons seem to be that, if you're the wealthier wife, remember we males are very sensitive about this stuff. Encourage your husband in his career, delight in his successes, and involve him as best you can in money issues.

And if you're the guy, rather than resent the wealth of your spouse, look at it as your good fortune and as part of who she is. You want to establish boundaries, but don't insist on going it alone or surviving on your salary alone just to prove a point. Sure, there'll be some tensions, but learn to accept and enjoy the money for what it is—a tool—not a verdict on your adequacy as a breadwinner.

Dwight Cass, "For Richer, For Poorer—Marriages of Fiscal Unequals," *Worth Magazine* (July 2004). www.worth.com/Editorial/Money-Meaning/Family-Matters/Features-For-Richer-For-Poorer.asp

Tamar Lewin, "A Marriage of Unequals," *The New York Times* (May 17, 2005). www.nytimes.com/2005/05/19/national/class/MARRIAGE-FINAL.html.

Should You Help Out the Stepchildren?

Most folks, wealthy or not, wish to provide for both their spouse and their children as their resources permit. (In Chapters 2 and 3 I talk about fairness and providing for your spouse, kids, and stepkids.)

But what if you have more than enough to live on, and your spouse and children are already going to be well provided for? At what point do you decide to benefit your stepchildren?

There is no monetary formula, nor is there an objective way to determine what is right. It all depends on your wishes and your relationship with the stepchildren. Obviously, if you've helped rear your beautiful stepdaughter from age two, you may inclined to leave her a generous bequest. Not so for a belligerent, belching stepson you welcomed into the blended family on his 39th birthday, which also happened to be the 19th anniversary of his last holding down a regular job.

Fairness involves taking into account your needs and resources, the needs of your spouse and children, your relationship with your stepchildren, the needs of your stepchildren and any inheritances they might receive, and the likelihood that a bequest or gift will be used constructively or squandered.

> EXAMPLE: Rena is well off because of a substantial inheritance from her grandmother. Rena's husband, Gary, has a son, Jason, age 27. Jason was laid off from his job recently and is struggling to pay the rent on his apartment. Rena offers to pay up to six months' rent for Jason to help him get back on his feet.

Bottom line: If there's a real need, and you can contribute without doing damage to the stepchild (such as enabling an addiction or removing an incentive to be gainfully employed), and you have the means, then go ahead. A gift or bequest can help you (think of how happy your spouse will be), plus help the stepchildren in their time of need. It's a win-win.

Helping stepchildren struggling with the cost of higher education can be a particularly good way to benefit the whole family. You may find it cheaper in the long run to underwrite some educational expenses than to support them once they're out in the real world and can't support themselves (or, perhaps more drastically, wanting to move in with YOU because they can't support themselves).

Do this because it's the right thing to do, not because you're expecting to get a lot of thanks, because thanks may not be coming (in the short term, anyway). And don't expect the recipient to become some miniature version of yourself. Work ethics, values, and interests all are shaped at an early age. Finally, make sure you, your spouse, and your stepchild are very clear about the terms of the arrangement, how long any assistance will last, and what happens if the stepchild doesn't live up to her end of the bargain.

> **EXAMPLE:** Susan's less wealthy husband, Nick, has a daughter, Brittany, from a previous marriage. Brittany, age 22, attended two semesters at the local college before dropping out and has held a series of low-paying jobs since then, barely getting by. She comes to Nick and announces a heartfelt intention to return to school and complete her education. Susan and Nick make a deal with Brittany that if she will maintain a B average, Susan will pay the college tuition. Because Susan will pay the tuition directly to the college, there are no gift tax issues (see Chapter 5) and also no opportunity for Brittany to take her college money and spend it on something else.

Good Tools for Spouses of Unequal Means

Here are some good estate planning tools to consider if you and your spouse have very different financial resources.

Good Tools for Both Spouses

A number of tools work best when both spouses participate, even though the bulk of the money may be coming from the wealthier spouse.

Give When It Works

You and your spouse can give each child and stepchild up to $26,000 in any calendar year without raising a federal gift tax issue. Even if the money comes from just one spouse, you can give the full $26,000 if your spouse agrees. (Such "split gifts" are discussed in Chapter 6.) You can give this outright or contribute it to a Section 529 college savings plan. You can further fund education and medical expenses by making the payments of any size directly to the provider. These direct "ed/med" payments don't count against the $26,000 limit. (See Chapter 6 for more on gifts.)

Honor the Prenuptial Agreement

If you and your spouse have a prenuptial agreement, you'll need to make sure your estate plan is consistent with its terms. If your will or trust doesn't follow what's required by the prenup, there can be problems later. You don't want there to be a discussion or dispute over whether the will or the prenuptial agreement should control.

> EXAMPLE: Wealthy Coolidge and penniless Betty sign a prenuptial agreement before their marriage. In the prenup, Coolidge agrees to leave to Betty at his death a dollar amount based on the number of years they've been married at the time of his death. A few months before his death, Coolidge signs a will leaving Betty more property than she's entitled to under the prenup. After Coolidge's death, Coolidge's children attempt to challenge the will and argue that the prenup should control.

Bottom line: If your prenuptial agreement no longer reflects your current wishes, then amend it as part of your estate planning.

Reduce Overall Estate Tax

The applicable exclusion amount is the amount each of us can leave estate-tax-free at our death to someone other than our surviving spouse or a charity. In 2009, that amount is $3.5 million. Under current law, if a spouse dies without fully using the spouse's applicable exclusion amount, then the ability to shield that money from estate tax is lost. (There's been some talk about changing this so that the second spouse to die can use any unused portion from the first spouse; check with your attorney to get the latest information.)

If you're the less-wealthy spouse, it probably doesn't matter to you much. You can leave what you have to your children and not worry that the estate tax will take a bite out of it. But if you're the wealthier spouse, it may matter a great deal. That's because if you were able to use your spouse's applicable exclusion amount, you could potentially save your estate up to $1,575,000 in taxes ($3.5 million x 45% tax rate), all of which could go to your heirs instead of the IRS.

> **EXAMPLE:** Bob has a net worth of $7 million; his wife, Brenda, has a net worth of $0. If Brenda passes away first, she won't have used any of her applicable exclusion amount. If Bob can use Brenda's applicable exclusion amount as part of his planning, he can pass up to $3,500,000, estate tax free, to his heirs. If Bob doesn't use Brenda's applicable exclusion amount and leaves his entire $7 million estate to his children, then his estate will pay $1,925,000 in tax that could have been completely avoided.

Without Brenda's applicable exclusion amount:

Bob's estate	$7,000,000
Exclusion	− 3,500,000
Taxable estate	$3,500,000
Estate tax rate	x 0.45
Estate tax	1,925,000
Amount to heirs	$5,075,000 (estate less estate taxes)

With Brenda's applicable exclusion amount:

Bob's estate	$7,000,000
Estate taxes	$0
Amount to heirs	$7,000,000

So if you have a taxable estate and your spouse doesn't, you likely are looking at your spouse's applicable exclusion amount the way Wile E. Coyote used to look at the Road Runner (you know, when the Road Runner's body is replaced with a cooked chicken dinner). Why? Because as we've seen, if you can use your spouse's applicable exclusion amount, you can pass more down to your children tax free.

If one of you has more than $3.5 million, and the other far less, you may want to take a close look at using one of the following techniques. They let you use the less-wealthy spouse's applicable exclusion amount should that spouse pass away first. All of these are discussed in detail in Chapter 6.

Outright gift of assets to spouse during life. The easiest (but perhaps least desirable) way to make sure your spouse's applicable exclusion amount gets used is to give enough money or property to your spouse so that your spouse ends up with assets approximately equal to the applicable exclusion amount. Even in first marriages, it's a gift the wealthier spouse frequently doesn't want to make. If you're divorced and saw a large portion of your net worth go to a former spouse in the divorce, you may be even more reluctant to leave large sums outright, or transfer assets to your new, less wealthy spouse, even if it may achieve some tax savings.

> EXAMPLE: Ellen, a successful executive in the software industry, divorced Frank four years ago. As part of the divorce settlement, she transferred her interest in their Silicon Valley home (worth over $1 million) and other cash and assets to Frank. Ellen's current net worth is $5 million. Newly remarried, she is reluctant to transfer $1.5 million outright to her less-wealthy husband to take advantage of his applicable exclusion amount, even if it would save estate taxes. She doesn't want to take the risk that comes from losing control over the assets.

To qualify for the unlimited marital deduction (and be gift tax free), gifts to the less wealthy spouse must have no strings attached. Once you've made the gift, your spouse will be free to do whatever your spouse wants with the gift. The obvious problem is that you have to trust your spouse to dispose of the assets at your spouse's death as you would wish. If your spouse creates a will leaving everything to your children, all is well. But what if your spouse creates a will leaving everything to your stepchildren or to a new spouse? Perhaps not so good.

Lifetime QTIP trust. Basically, the wealthier spouse creates an irrevocable trust to benefit the less-wealthy spouse during the less-wealthy spouse's lifetime. At the death of the less-wealthy spouse, the assets in the trust pass according to the way the wealthier spouse set it up in the trust. This way, the less-wealthy spouse can't take the trust assets and leave them to his or her children or a new spouse. The disadvantage to this approach? *For the rest of his or her life,* the less-wealthy spouse is entitled to all of the income off of the trust assets, even if the spouses divorce; the spigot cannot be turned off.

Joint revocable trust. The joint revocable trust is a way to use the less-wealthy spouse's applicable exclusion amount without giving the assets outright or placing them in a trust that can't be undone. Both spouses sign one trust agreement, put their assets into the trust, and manage them during their lives. The joint revocable trust can provide for the surviving spouse, yet make sure that each spouse's wealth ultimately passes to his or her children.

Insure Each Spouse

Here I'm primarily talking about two kinds of insurance: health insurance and life insurance. Disability insurance is also a good idea, though. (See Chapter 11.) You'll want to make sure each spouse has adequate health insurance to protect against catastrophic medical bills and to avoid claims by health care providers against joint assets or assets of the wealthier spouse.

As hospitals struggle, and as Medicare and Medicaid constantly seem to be getting cut, having good health insurance for both spouses is a necessity. Hospitals are becoming more aggressive in pursuing those with the perceived means to pay now that hospitals are losing so much money on indigent care. We all want the best health care possible for our loved ones, which is rarely what the government safety net provides.

Paying for the less-wealthy spouse's health insurance coverage may be cheaper for the wealthier spouse in the long run. (After all, you don't want unpleasant discussions like "I know you need that open heart surgery, honey, but I promised the kids a new ski boat.") Having insurance in place also may make the wealthier spouse's children less likely to worry about a catastrophic claim wiping out their inheritance.

Life insurance may also be a good tool for two reasons. First, insuring the life of the less-wealthy spouse can provide a cash source for that spouse's children, so they will get something at their parent's death. Second, if estate tax is a concern, life insurance on the wealthier spouse's life can provide a source of liquid assets to pay taxes or meet other needs at that spouse's death. Holding the insurance in an irrevocable life insurance trust or having the children own the insurance boosts the amount that can pass free of estate tax, as discussed in Chapter 6.

Good Tools for the Wealthier Spouse

The wealthier spouse may require sophisticated planning to accomplish the common goals of providing for the surviving spouse and preserving the balance of the wealth for the next generation.

Use Credit Shelter and QTIP Trusts

A wealthier spouse who doesn't use a lifetime QTIP or joint revocable trust discussed above typically uses a will or revocable living trust to establish credit shelter and QTIP trusts to take effect at death. (These are discussed in Chapter 6.) Assets left in these trusts will benefit the surviving spouse during life while also benefiting the wealthier spouse's children. Credit shelter and QTIP trusts also save on estate tax for the wealthier spouse.

> EXAMPLE: Bernie has assets of approximately $300,000. His wife, Harriet, has millions. Her will creates credit shelter and QTIP trusts. If Harriet passes first, the credit shelter and QTIP trusts will provide for Bernie during his life. The credit shelter trust will also be a resource for Harriet's children during Bernie's life. At

Bernie's death, the amounts in the credit shelter and QTIP trusts will pass to Harriet's children. If Bernie dies first, at Harriet's death her estate will pass to her children.

Buy Insurance

The wealthier spouse also should work carefully with a trusted insurance adviser to make sure that property, casualty, automobile, and umbrella coverages are in place with appropriate limits (which, in the case of automobile insurance, should be well in excess of statutory minimums). This will shield assets from third-party claims. Be sure to check your policies. You may have less coverage than you think. The time to act is today, before you've had a car accident or someone is injured while working on your property.

Tools for the Less-Wealthy Spouse

Just because one spouse has less money, the planning isn't any less important. The less-wealthy spouse will need a will or revocable living trust (RLT) to make sure assets go where he or she wishes.

Estate tax may not be a concern for the less-wealthy spouse. Again, the key number we're looking for is whether the less-wealthy spouse has $3.5 million in assets. If not, and the wealthier spouse doesn't need any support, the less-wealthy one will provide mainly for his or her own children at death.

If you're the less-wealthy spouse, you may still leave your interest in the marital home, furniture, and furnishings to your spouse, but your primary focus will be on providing for your children. Depending on the amount left and ages of the recipient, a less-wealthy spouse may or may not need to use trusts.

EXAMPLE 1: Jack has assets of approximately $300,000. His wife, Sophia, has millions. Jack's children are 29 and 32. His will leaves his assets outright to his two children. Jack also coordinates his beneficiary designations on his retirement plan and other accounts to make his children the primary beneficiaries, and gets Sophia's consent to the changes where required. Regardless of whether Jack or Sophia dies first, Jack's children will receive his estate.

EXAMPLE 2: Lucy has children who are 9 and 12. She has assets of approximately $300,000. Lucy uses a will to leave her assets in trusts for the children, to be distributed to them outright when they turn 25. She also coordinates her beneficiary designations on her retirement plan and other accounts to make her children's trusts the primary beneficiaries and gets her husband's consent to the changes where required.

The May-December Romance

Providing for the Younger Spouse 167

Providing for the Older Spouse's Children 171

Providing for Children From the Current Relationship 173

Her face is ever passing fair
His skin, a few more wrinkles there
Her eyes bereft of worry lines
His brow, it sags from pull of time
But tho' he's lost his youthful wiles
The years fade when at her he smiles

You and your spouse may be close in love, but not in age. Blended families often unite people with more than a few years separating them. And while you may enjoy a wonderful relationship with your spouse, things can get a little strained with the children of the older spouse, particularly if the younger spouse is closer in age to them than to the older spouse.

It's that tension—between the younger spouse and the children of the older spouse—that you'll want to address in your planning. Like any blended family, individuals in May-December relationships often must reconcile supporting a surviving spouse with providing for children. But striking the right balance may be tougher because the younger spouse likely will outlive the older one by many years.

If your estate planning doesn't address the difference in life expectancy, it can affect the older spouse's children in two ways:

- **They likely will inherit *less*.** If the surviving spouse is depending on the older spouse's estate for support, more years of support mean less money will ultimately be available for children.
- **They will likely inherit *later*.** In most estate plans, the children receive the bulk of their inheritance at the death of the surviving spouse. If the surviving spouse isn't too much older than the children, then the children may be waiting to receive their inheritance for a very long time—well past the age when they could have used it most.

Without planning, money struggles can sour the relationship between the surviving spouse and the children. But with planning, you can provide for both the surviving spouse and the children in a way that doesn't pit their interests against one another. There may be mistrust, but by acknowledging the displacement that a new, younger spouse brings, you may be able to avoid lasting divisions if you'll proceed cautiously before making drastic changes.

Because typically the younger spouse outlives the older one and has fewer assets, most of this chapter talks about what the older spouse can do to plan for distribution of his or her wealth. But of course, illness or accident could mean that the younger spouse passes away first, so the younger spouse will want his or her own plan. It's really up to the younger spouse's wishes. A younger spouse who wishes to provide for the older spouse can do so. If it's children that the younger spouse wishes to benefit, then outright gifts or trusts may be used as appropriate. (See Chapter 6.)

Celebrity May-December Romances

You're not alone. Here's a sampling of celebrity relationships, with the older spouse listed first:

- Demi Moore and Ashton Kutcher (15 years' difference)
- Jerry and Jessica Seinfeld (18 years)
- Geena Davis and Dr. Reza Jarrahy (15 years)
- Mary Tyler Moore and Dr. Robert Levine (18 years)
- Francesa Annis and Ralph Fiennes (19 years)
- Clint and Dina Eastwood (35 years)
- Michael Douglas and Catherine Zeta-Jones (25 years)
- Donald Trump and Melanie Knauss (28 years)
- John and Cindy McCain (18 years)
- Woody Allen and Soon-Yi Previn (35 years).

Providing for the Younger Spouse

The threshold issue in planning for blended families is how to divide your resources among your spouse and children. I talk about this more fully in Chapter 3, which covers determining how much there is to go around, taking into account prenuptial agreements, and addressing the needs and resources of each spouse and child.

May-December relationships present additional considerations. You need to look out over a longer period of time to take into account the extended life expectancy of the surviving spouse. You'll want to factor in the surviving spouse's needs for support over that longer time period. As part of the calculation, the plan needs to contemplate whether the younger spouse has been encouraged to leave the work force and the impact that will have on the younger spouse's future needs and resources.

> EXAMPLE: Andrew, 50, and Maryanne, 30, meet and marry. Andrew encourages Maryanne to leave her job at a publishing company so she'll have time to travel, be at home with the children they plan to have, and support him in his busy career as an advertising executive. If Andrew dies at age 70, Maryanne, now 50, will have given up her most productive working years in support of the family. She'll require more financial assistance today and throughout the rest of her life than if she had continued working and saving for retirement. Andrew's estate plan should respect Maryanne's requirements for support.

You'll also want to look carefully at your financial resources and requirements and at what you're trying to accomplish. If the goal is to make sure that whatever remains at the surviving spouse's death goes to the children of the older spouse, then a good way to accomplish that is to put the surviving spouse's share in a trust.

> EXAMPLE: Sam, age 45, and Shelly, age 30, are setting up their estate plan. Sam has two young children from a previous relationship. He wants to ensure that his children receive what's left of Shelly's share at her death, but also make sure they are cared for before her death. Sam divides his estate into two equal trusts. One-half of his estate goes into a trust that supports Shelly during her lifetime. At her death, that trust will distribute what's left to

his children. Sam puts the other half of his estate in a trust for his minor children.

If you're the older spouse and you're not concerned about what happens to the surviving spouse's share, you may be comfortable with giving the surviving spouse control over a portion of your estate. In that situation, an outright gift to the surviving spouse is appropriate.

> EXAMPLE: Sam, from the previous example, isn't concerned about his children receiving what's left of Shelly's share at her death. So he leaves Shelly half of his estate outright, which means she can use it, spend it, and leave what's left however she wishes. Sam puts the other half of his estate in a trust for his children.

In both of these examples, the key is the division of the estate at the first spouse's death. With a division at death, the children aren't competing with the surviving spouse for funds in a common trust or being forced to wait until the second spouse's death to receive all of their inheritance.

You may be tempted to put everything into one trust for the surviving spouse and the children to make things simpler. But one trust doesn't address the key tension in May-December relationships. Simpler probably isn't better here.

> EXAMPLE: Let's go back to Sam and Shelly. If Sam puts his estate into one trust for Shelly and his children, then throughout Shelly's life, the trustee will decide when and how much to distribute to Shelly and the children. Both Shelly and the children will receive distributions from the trust during Shelly's life. At Shelly's death, what's left goes to the children.

In this example, Sam has provided for his wife and children, but at a cost. By putting all of his estate into one trust, he has put Shelly and the children at odds with one another. If Shelly doesn't feel that the distributions from the trust are adequate to support her lifestyle, she may

Don't Forget to Plan for the House

The marital home is probably the biggest single asset you and your spouse own. Because of its financial and emotional importance, you'll want to consider the house separately from other assets. You and your spouse need to decide what you want to have happen after the death of one spouse.

- Do you want the surviving spouse to live in the house as long as the surviving spouse wishes? If so, what funds need to be set aside to pay for the mortgage, taxes, and insurance?
- Do you want the house to be sold at your death and the proceeds divided among the spouse and your children?
- Do you want your children to inherit the house?

You can specify in your estate plan what you want to have happen. Keep in mind the need for flexibility. You may picture the family home being passed down through the generations, but the needs and wishes of your spouse and children may warrant a different result.

Options for houses include:

- Leaving the house and funds to maintain it in a trust for your spouse. The trustee can be a family member (other than your spouse), a friend, an accountant, a lawyer, or a bank or trust company. The trust can be part of your will or revocable living trust and can be used for a number of your assets or be limited to the house and its upkeep. At your death, the house can be sold and proceeds divided or distributed outright to your children. (See Chapter 6.)
- Leaving a life estate to your spouse, with your children getting the house at your spouse's death. This usually works best if the house does not have any debt on it, the spouse is able and willing to keep up the house, and the spouse and children have a good relationship. (Chapter 6 has more information on life estates.)

Not recommended:

- Leaving the house outright to the surviving spouse (unless your children don't care if they get the house)
- Leaving the house jointly to your spouse and children. There are too many competing interests in this situation—conflict is almost inevitable, and any co-owner could go to court and force a sale.

ask the trustee for more. If the children find out, they may protest or be resentful. Similarly, one or both of the children can request more money from the trustee, which Shelly may resist. It's not an arrangement that promotes family harmony.

Similarly, you don't want to name your spouse and children cotrustees of trusts for their benefit, because their competing interests can lead to disagreements over how the trust should be managed and over who gets what money out of the trust. Disagreements can lead to deadlock and litigation.

Providing for the Older Spouse's Children

As we've seen, a key consideration in May-December romances is getting the inheritance to the older spouse's children from the previous relationship soon enough for them to make productive use of it. I recommend a division at the older spouse's death to lessen the tensions between the children and the surviving spouse.

Here are some ways to get a portion of the inheritance in the hands of the older, wealthier spouse's children sooner rather than later:

Establish a trust for children who are not yet ready to handle an inheritance. Putting property in a trust can make the money available for the children while they need assistance, and later pay the money out in stages when they're ready to handle it. The trustee can be a family member (other than your spouse), a friend, an accountant, a lawyer, or a professional trustee, such as a bank or trust company.

Make an outright gift to adult children at death. Consider making an outright gift to the children at the older spouse's death, rather than keeping everything in trust until the younger spouse dies.

> EXAMPLE: Angelo, 53, and Holly, 32, are recently married. Angelo has three children in their 20s from a previous relationship. Angelo leaves each child $100,000 at his death, and places the rest in trust for Holly, with whatever is left at her death going to the children. (Angelo will be wise to keep an eye on the size of his

total estate—if it shrinks significantly due to a market downturn, there might not be enough left over for Holly after the cash gifts to his children.)

Buy life insurance. If the older spouse has or can get life insurance, then a life insurance policy naming the older spouse's children as beneficiaries can provide funds for them. This not only divides the pie, it makes the pie larger so there's more to go around. If estate taxes are a concern, life insurance can be a way to get money out of your estate tax-free. Also, life insurance can be put into a trust, which lets you arrange for money to be distributed to your children over time when they're at an age to handle the funds.

Don't wait: give today. The older spouse can make gifts during life to the children to place needed funds and prized possessions in their hands, see their enjoyment, and receive their thanks.

The Wrong Stuff: A Cautionary Tale

In 2003, famed test pilot General Chuck Yeager married Victoria Scott D'Angelo—a woman 36 years his junior. The marriage triggered a dispute with his four adult children that estranged Yeager and his children.

After his first wife's death and before his remarriage, General Yeager's adult daughter lived next door to him and managed his money. When he remarried, he sought to regain management of his finances, which his children resisted strongly. In 2006, a judge ordered Yeager's adult daughter to repay almost $1 million in funds after she sold some assets belonging to Yeager. He later sued his children in federal court over other disagreements.

Whether the dispute could have been lessened had Yeager elected to put the management of his funds into the hands of a third party—rather than wresting them from the control of his daughter in order to give his new wife a greater say—is hard to tell. The lesson to learn is to tread slowly, carefully, and after a good deal of discussion. Clearly, once positions hardened and the lawsuits started flying, prospects for reconciliation were dim.

Providing for Children From the Current Relationship

I've been talking about "the children" here as the adult children of the older spouse. But of course, many couples in May-December romances have children of their own. If that's possible in your relationship, then your planning needs to take that into account. When planning for children, you can make outright gifts or buy life insurance and name them as beneficiaries. You also can set up a trust that provides for the surviving spouse and those children, since the biological connection between parent and child may avoid some of the tension that exists in stepparent/stepchild relations.

EXAMPLE: Tom is 20 years older than Tammy, who is close in age to Tom's two children from his previous marriage, Brandon and Emily. Brandon and Emily have finished their college education, which Tom paid for. Tom and Tammy also have a child, Jordan. Tom has assets worth approximately $2 million. Tom decides to leave his estate as follows:
- house (valued at $500,000): outright to Tammy
- $200,000 each to Brandon and Emily
- $100,000 in a college fund for Jordan, and
- $1 million in a trust designed to support Tammy and Jordan. At Tammy's death, the remainder of the trust assets will be divided among each of Tom's three children.

Dos and Don'ts in Planning for May-December Marriages

DO take into account the younger spouse's life expectancy in the estate plan and the potential for friction between the younger spouse and the children of the older spouse.

DO keep in mind that if the younger spouse and the children of the older spouse have similar life expectancies, you don't want the children waiting until the younger spouse's death to receive their inheritance.

DO look at ways to provide both for the surviving spouse and the children, rather than making an outright gift to the surviving spouse or setting up a trust that provides only for the surviving spouse without making separate provision for children.

DON'T leave everything to the younger spouse and force the older spouse's children to wait for the younger spouse to die before receiving their inheritance.

DON'T put assets in joint ownership between the surviving spouse and the children of the older spouse.

DON'T combine assets into one trust for your children and their stepparent, or name them as cotrustees of any trusts.

Family Property

Heirlooms.. 176

    Making Gifts Now 177

    Leaving an Heirloom to Your Spouse and Then Your Children 178

    Divvying Up the Treasure 179

    Making Your Intentions Known.. 180

Real Estate.. 181

    Your House and Your Spouse 182

    Several Pieces of Property... 183

The Family Farm 185

A Family Business 188

    What Do Your Children Want? 188

    Your Spouse's Role 189

    Your Main Alternatives... 191

    Working Now to Make Things Smoother Later 192

Trust Assets 193

    Trusts With a Power of Appointment.. 193

    Trusts That Don't Give You a Power of Appointment................................ 195

Each of us strives to make our mark
To carry on the eternal spark,
But legacies we choose to leave
Of what we have ourselves received
From loved ones who have passed before
Preserves our memory, if not more.

My mother has a little cast iron bank named "Fido Buckingham" that she received as a child. For as long as I can remember, Fido has sat on a shelf in my parents' house, filled with old pennies. I can remember when I was very little disassembling Fido, poring over the pennies, and then watching my mother carefully put him back together. Market value? Probably not $50. Value to my brother, whose name is written in my mother's handwriting and taped to the bottom? As the commercial says, "priceless."

This chapter discusses this kind of heirloom and other family property and suggests how to make sure they pass as you wish. By "family property," I mean those possessions you treasure and want to keep in your family. Family property doesn't have to have been in your family since the arrival of the Pilgrims; it's just something that's important to you that you want to pass on to your family.

I'll talk about four types of family property:

- heirlooms
- real estate and farms
- businesses, and
- trusts you control.

Heirlooms

Each of us has personal items, some grand, some not so, that we'd like to give our children or other favored relatives some day. Naming a loved one to receive a cherished heirloom is a wonderful way to leave a happy legacy. Your children, grandchildren, and other relatives will have a fond, tangible remembrance of you to treasure.

My advice in blended families is to go on and give the items away during your life or specifically leave them at your death. Don't leave them to your spouse, expecting that they'll go to the right people once your spouse dies. Your spouse may have no way of knowing the meaning behind Aunt Martha's treasured shell necklace, and how your favorite niece would love to have it.

My wife and I tend to be packrats—we keep everything. Other people may gravitate to the opposite extreme and wish to "clean house" on behalf of a parent, whether the parent wishes it or not. Without clear instructions, your beloved possessions can end up online, in the garbage, in a garage sale, or in your stepchildren's house.

I've seen situations in blended families in which people didn't specifically leave items at their death, and then sometime between their death and the death of the surviving spouse, items went missing. This creates unnecessary tension and suspicion between the children of one spouse and children of the other.

Making Gifts Now

Disputes over personal possessions can be some of the most contentious, so be clear about what you want to have happen. If you think there might be a fuss over gifts you have already made, then leave a list with your personal papers showing your significant gifts and who received them. You don't want someone to whom you've given a gift to be pressured into returning it just because they can't show that you intended for them to have it permanently. Which of the following scenarios would you prefer?

> EXAMPLE 1: Brenda regularly visits her mother and stepfather. Her siblings do not. One day, Brenda's mother hands her the family silver chest and says she wants Brenda to have it. After the mother dies, Brenda's brothers and sisters want to know what happened to the family silver. Brenda says, "Mom gave it to me," but doesn't have anything in writing from her mother. After some heated bickering among the siblings (including some mutterings about

Brenda having "made off with the silver"), Brenda agrees to divide the silver chest and its contents with her brothers and sisters.

EXAMPLE 2: When Brenda's mother dies and her will is read, there's a provision that reads, "In recognition of the care and attention Brenda gave to me, I have previously given Brenda the family silver." Brenda keeps the silver chest and its contents.

Leaving an Heirloom to Your Spouse and Then Your Children

You might want your spouse to enjoy a family item during his or her lifetime, but make sure your children receive it eventually. Leaving it to your spouse might work out fine, but remember that any option other than putting the beloved item in your children's hands carries with it a risk that they ultimately won't get it—it might be lost, stolen, sold, or given away without your children ever knowing it's gone until it's too late.

EXAMPLE: Myra has a painting that's been in her family for many years. It hangs prominently in her and her husband Carl's home. Myra would like for Carl to keep the painting if she should die first, but she ultimately would like for her son Ted to have it.
Myra has three options:
1. She could leave the painting to Ted, and express her wish that he allow Carl to enjoy it during his life. This makes sure Ted owns the painting and lets him decide whether to keep it in the house. It doesn't make sure that Carl will get to enjoy the painting. It also doesn't make sure that Ted will get the painting in the end if he does leave it at Carl's—it could be damaged or stolen while it's there. This option works best if Myra expects her son to honor her wishes or if Ted and Carl have a good relationship.

2. She could leave the painting to Carl and express her wish that he leave it to Ted. This makes sure Carl gets to enjoy the painting, but offers no protection for Ted.

3. In her will, she could leave a life estate in the painting to Carl, with the painting passing to Ted at Carl's death. This achieves both goals. (Chapter 6 discusses life estates.)

Divvying Up the Treasure

If you know a group of people (children, grandchildren, stepchildren, some combination of the above) whom you would like to inherit your treasured possessions, but don't have a strong preference as to who receives what, you can allow them to pick during your life. A common way is simply to have people tag the items they wish to receive.

EXAMPLE: One Saturday during the holidays, Renee gathers the family and allows each person to select a family memento they would like to have. Renee writes the name of each person on a piece of tape on the bottom of the item, and makes a master list that she keeps with her important papers and refers to in her will.

Or, you can establish a procedure in your will so that at your death the recipients can pick according to a predetermined procedure, such as using an order pulled out of a hat. Whoever draws number one gets to pick first, and the rest go in order according to the number drawn.

RESOURCE

Help with the heart stuff. The University of Minnesota Extension Service maintains a website called "Who Gets Grandma's Yellow Pie Plate?" that's devoted to assisting people divide up family mementos. It offers resources and suggestions at www.yellowpieplate.umn.edu.

Making Your Intentions Known

Once you've decided who gets what, you have a couple of ways of making your intentions known and legally binding. You can list everything and where it's going in your will or trust, or make a list apart from your will or trust.

Putting the list of items and recipients in your will or trust gives your wishes the strongest legal protection. It's hard to challenge where the collection of lawn gnomes goes when it's laid out in the will or trust.

The problem is that people's wishes change over time. Once it's in your will, it's there to stay. If granddaughter Stephanie decides she doesn't want your wedding dress, you have to redo your will to leave it to someone who does. If you have more than a few items or beneficiaries or change your mind frequently, this can get costly and inconvenient.

Another option is to maintain a separate list of who gets what, and refer to that list in your will or trust. This allows you to change your list from time to time without going back to the lawyer's office. Depending on your state, a separate list may not be as strong as putting it in your will or trust; in other states referring to a list gives it legal protection. So a list may not be well-suited for big-ticket items over which there likely will be a fuss. But for most items and most families, the list works just fine.

If you decide to go with the separate list route, make sure you mention it in your will or trust, keep your list up-to-date, keep it with your important papers, and sign and date each list you make. You may want to tear up your old lists or draw a line through them on the first page to confirm that the list is out of date.

If the person you would like to receive the item is too young to appreciate it or care for it, you may want to designate that it be left to a parent or guardian to be held until a birthday or wedding date. Every state except South Carolina and Vermont has adopted a uniform law regarding transfers to minors that allows you to designate a custodian for an item until the person turns 18 or 21 (or even 25, in some states). The person you choose to be custodian controls the property until the ultimate recipient is old enough to receive it.

And while you're at it, go on and attach a little note to the item so that future generations will have an idea of where it came from. This is what the antiques folks call establishing the provenance of the piece. Who knows? Maybe in some version of "Antiques Roadshow" 50 years from now, your lucky great-grandniece will be showing off your porcelain owl collection to the astonishment and delight of the expert appraisers!

At the end of the day, although five-carat, flawless yellow diamonds can be both a comfort and a treasure, what you're really passing down is part of your family's history, part of the story that is your family. And that's what you preserve by making sure the family heirlooms stay in the family.

Tips for Heirlooms

- Leave them sooner rather than later.
- Specify whom you'd like to receive what in your will or trust or in a separate list that's mentioned in your will or trust.
- Take time to write down the history of what you're leaving.

Real Estate

If you've been fortunate enough to amass real estate or receive it from your family, it's important enough to take the time to ensure you pass it on wisely. In Chapter 6 I talk about tools for dividing property you and your spouse purchased together, and making sure your children ultimately get their share. Here, I'm talking about real estate you or your family had that you want to stay in the family, not be divided between you and your spouse.

Leaving real estate can be tricky. Unlike shares of stock of a publicly traded company, in which each share is exactly like the other, real estate doesn't divide neatly. This makes it more difficult to treat your children equally if real estate is a significant part of your estate. You might not have enough property to give a separate piece to each child. (And even if you did have four beach homes and four children, odds are that the values of the different properties would vary widely, either today or in the future.)

If real estate or a farm is a large part of your estate, planning now to diversify your investments may allow you to hold your wealth in assets that will be more easily divisible among your loved ones. But if you really want that property to pass to your children, you probably don't want to sell it just to make it easier to divide down the road.

As you build and manage your real estate, in the back of your mind think about how you might want to divide it for the benefit of your family. The earlier you start planning, the better the result is likely to be. Here are some common real estate issues:

- letting a spouse use the property for life while ensuring that it eventually passes to your children, rather than the spouse's children or another person
- balancing inheritances equally among your children while providing for your spouse
- listening to what your children want, and
- leaving property in joint ownership to your children in a way that brings them together as opposed to driving them apart.

Your House and Your Spouse

If just one of you owns the house in which you and your spouse live, take a minute and think about what might happen if the owner died. Would the surviving spouse suddenly be living in a house owned by his or her stepchildren? Not always a good idea, as you can imagine.

So if you would want your spouse to be able to go on living in the house, then consider giving your spouse a life estate in the property or putting it in a trust for the surviving spouse's lifetime. Either of these methods gives your spouse the right to use the house until death. That way, you can still ensure the property passes to your children while continuing to meet your spouse's needs. (I talk about life estates and trusts in Chapter 6.)

EXAMPLE: Betty owns the home in which she and Frank live. Should Betty die first, she wants Frank to live in the house as long as he wishes, and then have the house go to her two children. Betty grants Frank a life estate in the house; at his death, the house passes to her children.

Several Pieces of Property

If you have several pieces of real estate and want to leave them to your children (either at your death or at the death of your surviving spouse), you have many options.

One for Each

If each piece of property has a roughly equal value in today's market, you might be tempted to give or leave each child his or her own piece. Be careful. Changing property values, zoning, or road access between the time you make your will and the time your children inherit the property could vary the values widely. Rather than make a strict division, you might wish to state your preference in your will or trust as to which child receives which piece of property. You can allow your executor or trustee to even things out by making adjustments based on the appraised market values at your death.

Alternatively, you could put the real estate in a trust to be managed by a professional trustee on behalf of all your children for a set period of time (ten years, 15 years) after your death or until your youngest child reaches a certain age.

EXAMPLE: Reginald has three children and four pieces of income-producing property he inherited from his mother. He decides to put all of the property in a trust at his death. In his will, he creates a separate trust to hold the property and appoints a local trust company to hold the property, manage and maintain it, and make distributions of income to the children until his youngest child turns 25.

> **TIP**
>
> **Find out what the kids want.** If your children are old enough, talk to them about what they might inherit. One child might want to take on the job of managing real estate; another might want to sell and get out.

Everything to Everybody

You might think that combining your real estate and leaving everything to your children in equal shares is the easiest way to make sure that everyone receives equal treatment. But for most families, joint ownership by the children is not the best option. Rarely will all of the children agree on the best use of the real estate, nor will each child use or enjoy it equally. Think of the family house: Would one child want to live there and the others sell? Could one afford to buy the others out? What about a vacation home?

Even if you think your children won't disagree, remember they might have spouses who could stir the pot. Divorce or debt problems can also cause friction. You might be the glue holding everything together for now, but disagreements often fly once the parents are gone.

If you're determined to insist on joint ownership, then I would recommend two things. First, discuss your plans and your reasoning with your children. Explain that you want them to enjoy the benefits of ownership with one another and don't wish it to be a burden. Recommend that they talk regularly to avoid disputes. Second, put in place a mechanism to manage the property. This may be part of your will or trust. It could also involve putting the property in a limited liability company or other entity. Limited liability companies also work well for vacation homes to specify how the home will be used and enjoyed and how maintenance and other costs will be paid.

> **EXAMPLE:** Rebecca has three children and a vacation home on a lake in upstate New York. The home has been in the family for generations, and each of Rebecca's children have spent a number of summers at the lake. Rebecca puts the lake home in a limited liability company and gives each of her children a small share

in the company. In the operating agreement for the company, Rebecca addresses how weekends and holidays are to be allocated during peak times, how off-season use will be permitted, and how and who will be responsible for the upkeep. Rebecca makes annual gifts of interests in the lake home to her children. At her death, she'll leave her remaining interests in the cabin to her children.

RESOURCE

Saving the Family Cottage: A Guide to Succession Planning for Your Cottage, Cabin, Camp or Vacation Home, by Stuart Hollander, David Fry, and Rose Hollander (Nolo), gives an excellent explanation of the almost inevitable problems that come up when siblings inherit a vacation home as tenants in common. It also explains how to avoid strife and keep a cottage in the family by creating a limited liability company with an operating agreement tailored to your family's needs.

Don't Forget the Costs

When leaving your properties, don't forget the annual costs of maintenance, taxes, and insurance that come with real estate. If your favored inheritor of the property can't pay to keep it up, then you'd better address that in your will as well. Even if you're able to leave the house to a son or daughter without a mortgage, the annual expenses can run in the tens of thousands of dollars. If your beneficiary can't afford that, then you'll need to leave more money to help them keep the property, or make different plans.

The Family Farm

In my area of the country, farming is still a big part of the economy. In the current environment, though, fewer and fewer people are able or willing to farm full time. Often a family will come to me with a farm that has been in the family for many, many years that they want to pass down to the next generation. One child might still work on the farm and depend on it for a livelihood, but the other children live and work in the city.

Leaving the farm to the children jointly is typically unwise, because the interests of the children are so divergent. The farmer is going to want to continue to work the farm; the others would like to see some cash coming in from their ownership. Even if the farming child were to be successful, it likely won't be enough to satisfy the remaining children, who may prefer to sell the property and spend or invest the money elsewhere, and any child will probably be able to go to court and force a sale, even if the others object. The farming child may not be able to buy out the others. Another potential problem is losing the farm to creditors (or a divorcing spouse) of a co-owner.

What to do? If you have enough other assets, you could leave the farm to the farming child and leave other assets to the other children.

If there aren't other significant assets, but the tract is large enough to divide, you may wish to have a survey prepared that would parcel out the tract based on the number of children you have. Because some of the land (with a home, road frontage, or a pond) can be more valuable than the other portions, each share doesn't have to have the same number of acres. With a well thought out survey, you may be able to leave the farming child the working portion of the farm, and leave the other children the farmhouse or scenic areas of the farm. You'll want to check your state or local law, because you may be limited in how you divide your property (in some areas, lots must be a minimum number of acres). If your property receives a break on property taxes because it's agricultural, that break can be lost depending on how and when the property is divided and for what purpose.

If the farm can't be easily divided and you don't have a lot of other assets, think about buying life insurance. The insurance proceeds might give your estate extra cash to balance your children's inheritances.

EXAMPLE: Howard wishes to leave his family farm to his three children, Howard, Jr., Evelyn, and Stanley. Howard, Jr. farms with his father; Evelyn and Stanley live and work in the city. Stanley has little emotional attachment to the farm. Howard divides his farm to give the working part of the farm to Howard, Jr., the homestead to Evelyn, and a small tract with road frontage to Stanley. Stanley's piece is the smallest by far, so Howard purchases an insurance policy and names Stanley a beneficiary to bring the value of Stanley's inheritance in line with that of his brother and sister.

If you don't have a full-time farmer in the family, planning so the arable land can be rented (this often means paying for adequate irrigation systems) or that the farm can be devoted to a less labor-intensive use such as forestry can be a big help. Plant those pine trees now, and your children may well be the ones to benefit.

How About a Conservation Easement?

If the property has distinctive features that might make it attractive for research or simply being preserved in its current state and not developed, one solution might be to preserve those features forever with a conservation easement. This involves dedicating a portion of your property for preservation or research. You still own the land and you can still use it, but you agree with a third party (called a land trust) to prevent further wide-scale development of the property. The land trust monitors use of the land to make sure there isn't any development that violates the terms of the easement. Properly structured, conservation easements can offer attractive income, estate, and property tax benefits. And you can ensure that even once the property changes hands, your beloved swimming hole won't become the site of a new strip shopping center.

You know your children better than anyone else. If you live in South Texas and your daughter lives in Nova Scotia and has no desire to return, perhaps leaving her the family farm isn't the best idea. You may have to look beyond your children if you want to keep it in the family.

Again, talk with your children to get an idea of their preferences. Once you've made a decision, speak with them to let them know why you're doing what you propose to do. This can go a long way toward preventing hurt feelings in the future and avoiding nasty surprises.

A Family Business

You might have spent a lifetime nurturing a successful business that you created or received from a family member. Family businesses can be a source of great pride, as well as valuable for the wealth they produce. On the negative side, family businesses present many of the same issues as real estate. They are hard to split up and can create deep division within a family if not dealt with appropriately.

Many people want to pass down their businesses to their children, but fail to do the planning along the way that is crucial to a successful transition. The sad reality is that, without a clear succession plan, most family businesses suffer dramatically at the owner's death. Great value in the business can be lost if untrained survivors are forced to sell or liquidate the once-successful business now reeling from the owner's death.

It doesn't seem to matter whether the business is worth thousands or millions, most people don't plan. Don't let your business be one of those that struggles or fails because you didn't plan when you had the chance. Most clients who come to me for planning a business transition get it done and are so glad they did. The peace of mind can't be beat.

What Do Your Children Want?

You might have dreams of your children taking over the family business once you are gone. Your children might have other ideas. With help, you can assess carefully whether passing the business down to the children is in their best interests or the family as a whole, and make a well-informed decision.

Again, communication with your spouse and children is the key. You may want to bring in an outside adviser. One of the benefits of an outside adviser is the adviser's ability to discuss options with your spouse and children and get a sense of what they truly want, as well as their abilities.

Your Spouse's Role

A key issue in blended families is to sort out what role, if any, your spouse will play in the business if you should pass away first and what income your spouse will need from the business during your spouse's life. If your spouse will be depending on income from the business to make ends meet, then you'll want to try to make that income available without creating tension between your spouse and your children.

Most of the time, it will be best if your children are prepared and able to take over at your death, and if you don't make your spouse a co-owner of the business with your children or have an employment or consulting agreement that compels the business to hire your spouse. Your children likely will want the freedom to run the business as they see fit, which will be hard enough to do without your spouse looking over their shoulder.

> EXAMPLE: Claire builds a successful printing business. Her second husband, Don, is a part-time employee in the business. Claire wants the business to pass to her son at her death. Don will still need some income from the business. Claire doesn't want to put Don and her son at odds, so she doesn't want to make them co-owners or require the business to employ Don. Some options for Claire:
> - Buy life insurance to provide cash for Don.
> - Leave a majority of the business to her son and require that he purchase the remainder from her using a promissory note. She then leaves the note to Don, who gets the income from the note.

- Leave Don a life estate in the building the business occupies, and leave the business to her son, together with a long-term lease that pays a favorable rent to Don. (The lease would require the business to pay taxes, maintenance, and insurance on the building, so there won't be a potential for disagreements between Don and her son over those issues.) Don will receive rent from the business for the rest of his life.

Keys to Planning for Businesses

- Plan! Most family businesses fail to survive the founder's death because of inadequate or outdated succession planning.
- Carefully consider what your spouse's needs are and find a way to meet them without making your spouse a co-owner or employee of the business.
- Don't leave a business jointly to children employed by the business and children who work outside the business. Consider other ways to compensate the children who work outside the business so that the business won't become a source of discord among your children.
- As you plan, get help from outside advisers experienced in family business transition planning.

If you have a family business interest that is a large part of your estate, then you need to hire an adviser who specializes in succession planning. Often that can be your estate planning lawyer. For businesses of a significant size, you may need to bring in a business counselor or financial adviser who can value your business, help you assess the potential options and successors, and facilitate family meetings to discuss your and the family's vision for the future. Talk with other business owners you know and look for specialists who can help you bring your vision to reality.

Your Main Alternatives

You have a number of alternatives when it comes to planning.

Do Nothing

You don't have to do anything. You can hope your spouse and children are able to sort it out. This is usually the worst alternative—the business can get tied up in disagreements among your spouse and children, and its value can plummet while everything's being sorted out.

Leave the Business in Equal Shares to Your Children

You can hope that they'll sort it out. Again, this is rarely the best option because your children will have different objectives and different visions for the business. One child might wish to expand the business; another might want to sell it. The potential for conflict is too great to leave it to chance.

Leave the Business Only to Your Children Who Will Work in It

If your goal is to leave the business to your children, this is often the best alternative. If one child works in the business and another doesn't, it's common for them to clash over salaries and distributions, perks, and purchases.

If you're leaving the family business for one child to run, make separate arrangements for the other children's inheritances rather than making all of the children shareholders in a business that only one runs. This is a tough issue, because a lot of times the business is the most valuable asset in the estate. Absent extraordinary circumstances (and I mean truly extraordinary), it is a bad idea to leave the business to two or more children when only one child is expected to work in the business.

Some years ago, author and business transition counselor Gerald Le Van identified the "parasite vs. plunderer" syndrome to describe this situation. The child not involved in running the business (the outsider) views the child running the business (the insider) as a plunderer. The outsider looks at the salary and perks enjoyed by the insider and thinks the insider is bleeding the business dry and diverting what otherwise would be a nice, fat dividend coming to the outsider.

The insider, however, sees the outsider as free of all of the stresses, challenges, and ulcers of running the business and views the outsider as a parasite whose constant complaints and demands for dividends drag the business down.

You don't want your children viewing one another as plunderers OR parasites. So do something about it. Find assets to give to the outsider, purchase life insurance, designate retirement funds—just don't leave the business to the both of them.

Sell the Business and Distribute the Proceeds

If you analyze your options and decide that selling the business is the best alternative, consider selling before your death. After all, you have the skills, you have the experience and the knowledge of the industry. Aren't you a better choice to find a potential buyer and maximize what can be obtained than a child who's not involved in the business, who might simply conduct a fire sale once you're gone?

Working Now to Make Things Smoother Later

It may be that your children are capable of managing a portion, but not all, of your various investments and enterprises. Liquidating some of these investments (that is, turning them into cash) may make it easier and more manageable for your children to tackle what remains.

As part of the succession plan, family members who will be called upon to run the business when they inherit it should be cross-trained in each area of the business to obtain the necessary expertise. If your children are interested and able, bring them in the business and let them learn from the master—that is, *you*. Let them see the operation of the business from a number of levels, including sales, marketing, production, administration, and customer relations. This will increase their skills and let you assess their interests and abilities.

If your business relies on the presence and commitment of a senior employee, use an employment agreement, with incentive compensation as appropriate, to ensure the person will be around to assist your child when help is needed most.

> **EXAMPLE:** Tonya has a successful dry-cleaning business. Her head account representative, Jose, has worked with her for many years. Tonya recognizes that losing him would cripple the business if she were to have passed away. Tonya enters into a multiyear employment agreement with Jose that gives him additional performance-based incentives for each year he stays with the company.

Trust Assets

You may be the beneficiary of a credit shelter or generation-skipping trust set up by family members, or a credit shelter or marital trust set up by a late spouse. (These kinds of trusts are discussed in Chapter 6.) If you're the beneficiary of a trust, you'll want to look carefully at its terms as part of your planning. You might have a say in what happens to trust property at your death.

Trusts With a Power of Appointment

Back when the trust was set up, the maker may have put in provisions that allow you to specify what happens to the trust assets at your death. These provisions are called powers of appointment. You might have the right to say to whom, in what percentages, and how the trust assets will pass. To exercise a power of appointment, you must specifically mention it in your will.

Usually, a power of appointment is not unlimited; for example, it may allow you only to leave trust assets to your descendants or the trust maker's descendants. Powers of appointment normally prevent you from using what's in the trust for your spouse's benefit at your death. For example, you probably can't designate "your estate" as a beneficiary and then leave everything to your new spouse, unless the trust specifically grants you that power. So you shouldn't rely on the trust to provide for your spouse after your death in most circumstances.

You'll need to review the trust provisions very carefully to see:
- what you can do
- what you can't do, and
- what happens if you do nothing.

Powers of appointment are generally buried deep in lengthy and dense trust documents. How and when you exercise them can affect the amount of tax your estate owes or even trigger taxes that wouldn't have been owed. This is why it's so important to share copies of trust agreements and wills containing active trusts with your estate planning attorney so you can discuss alternatives and consequences.

Often, when you read a trust, you'll find that if you do nothing, the trust decides where the assets go, which may not be what you want to happen. You may have the ability to alter the percentages your children would receive or have assets pass outright or put into a new trust with the provisions that you desire. That way, you can incorporate these assets into your estate plan so that they'll be disposed of in a way that's consistent with your overall desires.

> EXAMPLE 1: Helen holds a power of appointment allowing her to divide what's left in her grandmother's trust among her three children:
> - Gay, who is independently wealthy
> - Tammy, who has had debt problems and is in a troubled marriage, and
> - Martha, who works in a rewarding but low-paying position as an advocate for the homeless.
>
> Helen decides not to appoint the trust assets in equal thirds, but decides to leave more to Tammy and Martha based on their needs. Gay gets a small fraction outright. To protect Tammy's inheritance, Helen appoints Tammy's share to a new trust that will insulate what's in the trust from Tammy's creditors and her husband. Helen leaves Martha's share to her outright.

EXAMPLE 2: Stacy is the holder of a power of appointment over assets in a trust established by her late grandfather, Colonel Biggs. The trust provides that if Stacy doesn't exercise her power of appointment, the assets will pass outright and free of trust in equal shares to Stacy's four children. Stacy wishes to disinherit one of her children, Renaldo, who tried to set a fire at the family reunion. In her will, Stacy exercises her power of appointment to eliminate Renaldo from the beneficiaries of the trust.

EXAMPLE 3: One of Stacy's children, Hank, has a substance abuse issue, and she does not want him to receive money outright, knowing it would be swiftly squandered. With the help of her attorney, Stacy decides to appoint Hank's portion to a trust for Hank's benefit, with clearly defined guidelines for the trustee to avoid enabling Hank's addiction. Stacy decides that the rest of her children will be able to handle the money at her passing, so she exercises her power of appointment to confirm that they'll receive their share of the assets outright as the trust intended.

Keys to Powers of Appointment

Share trust documents with an estate planning attorney. If the trust's terms would create a bad result and don't grant you powers of appointment, don't despair. There still may be ways to achieve the estate planning result you desire. The trustee may be able to help or your state's laws may provide a solution.

Trusts That Don't Give You a Power of Appointment

Some trusts don't have a power of appointment to allow you to make the adjustments you wish to make. Using Example 2 above, what happens if the trust says that at your death, trust assets go to your children, but you have a drug-abusing child?

Don't despair, because there are often solutions. First, look to the trustee. The trustee may be able to help you achieve a good result using authority granted by the trust. Professional trustees are familiar with reading trust agreements and crafting solutions within the language of the trust and applicable law. For example, the trustee might be able to divide the trust into shares now and include precautions in the trust for the substance abusing child.

Several states have adopted what are known as "decanting" statutes, which may allow your trustee to take an existing trust and decant it, like a fine red wine, into a new trust. This new trust may contain the protections that the old one lacked. So, if there's $500,000 in a trust that would be divided equally at your death, the trustee may be able to use a decanting provision to put the $500,000 into a new trust that divides the money into shares at your death and contains protections for the substance abusing child.

Even if the trust is irrevocable and its terms say it can't be amended, and the trustee can't find a way to work around it, a court may allow you to amend the trust if you can show that implementation in the way it's set up now would not be consistent with what the maker would have wanted or the purposes for establishing the trust. The laws of your state or the state in which the trust was set up will provide the standards under which an otherwise unchangeable trust may be changed. Using this procedure is reserved for situations where there's enough money in the trust—and the result under the existing trust would be so bad— that litigation is worth the expense.

Choosing Executors and Trustees

What Do Executors and Trustees Do? 200

    The Many Hats of an Executor 200

    Duties of a Trustee 201

Potential Candidates for Executor or Trustee 203

    Family Members or Friends 205

    Accountants 210

    Attorneys 211

    Banks and Trust Companies 211

    Family Member Plus Professional: The Best of Both Worlds? 215

Helping Your Executor and Trustee 215

There's nothing very lusty
About serving as a trustee.
There's nothing too particular
About being an executor.
Better make the right selection
To give your plan expression.
Care will see your choice rewarded,
Keep your plan from being thwarted.

One of the best parts about estate planning is that you get to pick who is responsible for handling your estate once you're gone. Having well-designed wills and trusts is only part of the job. Getting the right people to serve as executor and trustee—the people charged with carrying out the terms of your will and trust—is a key component of an effective estate plan.

Good executors and trustees do things the way you would have them done. They:

- keep close track of your money
- carefully follow the terms of your will and trust
- pay attention to deadlines
- act quickly to keep things moving
- communicate with your beneficiaries
- treat your beneficiaries fairly, and
- work well with attorneys, accountants, and other advisers.

It's an important job, and a time-consuming one. That's why you want to pick the best executor or trustee you can. We all have different strengths and weaknesses, and not everyone you know will be well-suited to the task or have the time to serve.

Even though it is frequently a thankless job and the pay (especially for family members) is low, you might have a number of family members who would like to serve. Choosing among them can be hard because you don't want to disappoint someone. But you have to choose the best to get the results you want. In any family, feelings can get hurt and relationships strained because of who has been chosen to represent an estate, how the executor administers the estate, or how the trustee makes distributions under a trust.

For blended families, executor and trustee choices become even more critical because there are more cooks stirring the pot. Often the ties among stepbrothers and stepsisters are not strong, nor are the ties between children and stepparents. In slicing limited resources into more pieces, there is more potential for hurt feelings.

Once the parent is out of the picture, hurt feelings are a common source of bitterness in blended families. In extreme situations, the surviving spouse or one or more of the children may seek to avenge these hurt feelings by going to court. That kind of rupture to relationships is what you're trying to avoid.

Think back to your goals in your estate planning. If you're like many people, keeping family members close, or even bringing them closer than they were before your death, is an important goal. For some families, that may include continuing important traditions, like gathering for the holidays or spending time with one another on vacation.

Contrast that with what you DON'T want: your family feuding with or even suing one another following your death, as distant as two sides at war. Choosing the right executors and trustees can help keep the family together.

What's a "Fiduciary"?

Executors and trustees have similar responsibilities to beneficiaries. Lawyers call these responsibilities fiduciary duties (think fidelity, faithfulness), which is a way of saying that executors and trustees must act at the highest levels of honor and integrity. They're supposed to act the way politicians promise to act during campaigns. Both executors and trustees are referred to as fiduciaries.

What Do Executors and Trustees Do?

Put simply, your executor is the person who gathers up the assets of your estate, pays debts and taxes, and distributes what's left to beneficiaries. The trustee administers the funds in any trusts you have set up. An executor's job has a term limit: managing an estate from start to finish usually takes from 12 to 24 months. A trustee's job may go on for many years, depending on the terms of the trust.

The Many Hats of an Executor

Like a cat juggler, an executor simultaneously performs—or hires a professional to perform—a number of tricky roles.

Part of the executor's job is paperwork:

- reading the will and following its instructions
- preparing probate court documents, if necessary
- communicating with beneficiaries throughout the administration of the estate—following up to get signatures on important documents, letting them know of important dates, and arranging for them to pick up or select personal items
- applying for life insurance proceeds and other death benefits
- notifying banks and other institutions where the deceased person had accounts
- notifying creditors of the estate
- keeping good records of bills paid and monies in the estate, and
- making any required periodic reports to the probate court and beneficiaries.

Part of the executor's job is working with others, including:

- accountants, to make the right tax decisions for the estate and making sure that tax returns get filed on time
- appraisers, if necessary to value assets
- attorneys, throughout the probate process
- financial advisers, to oversee, transfer, divide, and distribute investments, and
- banks and other financial institutions.

Part of the executor's job is handling stuff:

- keeping property safe
- making sure items go where they're supposed to under the will and arranging to get assets in the hands of beneficiaries
- selling assets if necessary to raise cash for expenses, and
- if the will calls for creating trusts, deciding which assets go into which trust and transferring the assets to the trustee.

But the most vital job of the executor is to fulfill your wishes and demonstrate openness, fairness, impartiality, tact, and empathy to the beneficiaries. So essentially, you need someone who has:

- an accountant's brain
- the heart of a saint, and
- a lawyer's love of the mundane.

Duties of a Trustee

A trustee's role is in many ways similar to that of an executor. A trustee's primary functions are to manage the trust assets, invest them wisely, and make distributions to beneficiaries, all the while following the trust document's instructions.

Part of the trustee's job is paperwork:

- reading the trust agreement and following its instructions
- keeping good records of bills paid and amounts in the trust, and
- making any required periodic reports to the beneficiaries.

Part of the trustee's job is working with others:

- accountants, to make the right tax decisions for the trust and make sure tax returns get filed on time
- attorneys, to interpret the trust and comply with applicable law
- investment advisers, for assistance with the financial part of the job discussed below, and
- banks and financial institutions.

Part of the trustee's job is financial, which the trustee may do or outsource to an investment manager:

- investing assets to meet the requirements of the trust agreement (or state law, if the trust doesn't give instructions) and the needs of the beneficiaries
- diversifying the assets in the trust to avoid becoming too dependent on the performance of one asset, and
- distributing income and principal as required under the trust agreement.

The Importance of Diversification

State law and prudent investment practices usually require keeping a portfolio from being too heavily dependent on one asset—say, a single stock or industry. If trust investments are concentrated in a single area, your trustee may diversity the portfolio. Diversification is the opposite of putting all your eggs in one basket. It's finding the right mix of stocks, bonds, cash, and other investments that helps the trust portfolio do well in good times and lessens the blow in bad times.

A large part of the trustee's job is judgment. Beneficiaries may repeatedly pressure the trustee for more money, now. The trustee is going to need to assess the interests of the trust and all of the beneficiaries in light of what you intended. The trustee is going to need to be able to say no, if the circumstances warrant.

A good trustee will be able to:
- decide whether to grant beneficiaries' requests for money or other assets from the trust
- resolve differences if beneficiaries make competing requests, and
- choose whether to honor a request for money today if that would adversely affect the trust tomorrow and frustrate your wishes in setting up the trust.

But your trustee's most important job is to fulfill your wishes and be open, fair, impartial, tactful, and empathetic to the beneficiaries.

Potential Candidates for Executor or Trustee

The complexity of your estate is a big consideration when you're thinking about who should be your executor or trustee. It also may help you to decide whether to select an individual, a trust company, or a law or accounting firm. Among the factors going into the choice of a fiduciary:

- **The size of the estate.** How much do you expect there will be?
- **The potential for conflict.** Is there tension among your beneficiaries today, or do they all get along? Even if they get along now, do you see a chance that they won't when it comes time to divide everything up?
- **How long the job will last.** An executor shouldn't be on the hook for more than a year, but it's open-ended for a trustee. A couple of years until a teenager becomes an adult? Ten or 20 years? Generations?

When selecting an executor or trustee, most people choose a family member or close friend, a corporate trustee, or an accountant or attorney.

Larger estates and longer-lasting trusts are more likely to need expert help than smaller estates or shorter trusts. The bigger the estate or trust is, and the longer it lasts, the better you'll be served by going outside your family and heading to the pros. On the other hand, if it's a smaller estate or trust, or if it won't last very long, you may want to look at a family member or friend, accountant or attorney.

Good Choices for Trustee		
	How long will the trust last?	
How big is the trust?	**Short time**	**Many years**
Large ($1 million plus)	Bank or trust company; accounting or law firm	Bank or trust company
Middle ($250,000 to $1 million)	Accounting or law firm; family member or friend	Bank or trust company; accounting or law firm
Modest (up to $250,000)	Family member or friend	Accounting or law firm; younger family member or friend

Remember, the job of an executor is generally less complicated and stressful than that of a trustee. Even in relatively complex estates, someone who is fair and good at working with people may be well-suited to be an executor. Even someone who doesn't have any experience in this area can still do a fine job with assistance. A trustee, however, may be serving for years and is likely to need more financial sophistication.

EXAMPLE 1: Dale has two sons, Ron and Edward. Edward has a six-month-old daughter, Darlene. Dale plans to leave her modest estate outright to her two sons, but in case Edward should pass away before her, she provides that Darlene's share will be held by a trustee until Darlene turns 21. Because of the size of her estate and the strong likelihood that Edward will survive her, Dale provides that her sister, Edwina, will serve as trustee should Edward pass first and Darlene's trust be needed. This is a perfectly reasonable choice. In the unlikely event that Edwina must take on the job of trustee, she can hire expert help (paid for from trust assets), and the trust assets will probably be used up in Darlene's childhood (or college, at least), anyway.

EXAMPLE 2: Ellen is married to Roger and has two children, Vince and Vickie, from a previous marriage. Ellen plans to leave her multimillion-dollar estate in a "dynasty trust" (one that could last a very long time) to benefit Roger and her children for the remainder of Roger's life, and then her children during their lives. After her children's death, the trust assets will go to any grandchildren when they reach ages 30, 35, and 40. Because of the size of her estate and the great likelihood that the trust will be in place for many years, Ellen selects a professional trustee to manage the trust.

What Should We Do With Auntie Enid's Place Mats?

Deciding who gets personal items, mementos, and keepsakes is often one of the most contentious issues in the administration of an estate. If the will doesn't tell the executor what to do, the executor may set up a procedure that allows the beneficiaries to see the items and choose based on their preferences using an order drawn out of a hat. Or the executor may decide for the beneficiaries and throw everything in a box for them.

Picking an impartial executor and leaving detailed instructions on how you wish your items divided (as opposed to trusting a family member to "do the right thing") can help defuse a potentially explosive situation. For more tips on handling heirlooms, see Chapter 9.

Family Members or Friends

Most peoples' first choice for a fiduciary is a family member. They reason that the family member has the most knowledge of what they would have wanted. Plus, the family member is not as likely to charge large fees as would a third party. And for most estates, even relatively complex ones, a well-qualified family member may have the capacity to serve as an executor quite well with help from a lawyer and an accountant.

Particularly in blended families, however, a family member will be the best choice only if he or she has a sparkling relationship with the rest of the family. That's because beneficiaries will likely view a fellow beneficiary who is also a fiduciary as having a conflict of interest. They may fear that the fiduciary will benefit the fiduciary or the fiduciary's side of the family to the detriment of the others. If it's a good relationship and the person is otherwise qualified, a family member can be a good choice; if the relationship tends to the sour rather than the sweet, another option may be advisable.

EXAMPLE: Rick has two grown children from a previous relationship; his wife Bobbie has one. Rick's older child is a hard-charging stockbroker used to giving orders; the other is an artist using recycled materials. Rick is tempted to choose his stockbroker son as executor of his estate because he's older and has expertise with finances. On reflection, Rick decides that his artist daughter may be the better choice because she gets along well with his wife and her son, and would be able to carry out Rick's wishes without alienating the rest of the family.

Executors and trustees exercise a lot of discretion in fulfilling their roles. The beneficiaries are going to be looking closely at the choices your appointed one makes for signs of self-dealing or favoritism. If their relationship with the fiduciary isn't the best, they'll be looking all the more closely.

Family relationships tend to become more strained rather than less following a death, and people often underestimate just how emotional and unpleasant this process can become. Rather than place a loved one in the position of being second-guessed (and challenged), you might do well to select a neutral third party.

Lawsuits over estates are becoming more and more common. I have witnessed some of these battles. Frequently, estate litigation stems from hurt feelings, becomes very emotional very quickly, and sparks a "win at all costs" attitude rather than an objective analysis. No one wins. Once a dispute becomes all about the principle of the matter, it's very hard to resolve early, even when resolution is in everyone's best interest. My colleagues who now make a living handling such cases confirm my observations.

Another reason to think long and hard before selecting a family member is that you want your fiduciary choice to line up with your estate plan. So, for example, if your estate plan calls for providing for your spouse, but puts the money you leave him or her in trust so that your children ultimately receive a healthy portion of it, then you might not wish to name your spouse as trustee. Why? Because a surviving spouse who has control over the assets might frustrate your intentions (where your assets end up) or your tax planning (keeping those assets out of your spouse's estate for tax purposes). Naming your spouse as trustee is inconsistent with putting the money in trust in the first place. I'm not saying that your spouse would do anything untoward, I'm just saying that in this area appearances often matter more than the reality if someone comes along later and wants to challenge something a trustee has done.

Picking Your Executor or Trustee	
Good Choice	**Bad Choice**
Has good relationship with family	Is frequently at odds with one or more family members
Is fair	Looks out only for himself or herself
Lives in your home state	Lives three states away
Keeps good records	Is disorganized
Has a good financial history	Has problems dealing with money
Is legally qualified to serve	Is a minor or a convicted felon (even if it's something from many years ago)
Has a life expectancy greater than yours	Is aging, with competency issues, or is no longer up to the task

Popular Reasons for Making Bad Choices

People frequently make the wrong choice of executor or trustee for one of the following reasons:

- "He's the oldest." Many people have a vague, nagging feeling that they should name their oldest child. But if all your children are of age to serve, then just being the oldest isn't a qualification. As we've seen, being an executor or trustee is a tough job. If your oldest child isn't the best for the task, don't let birth order sway you. (I am assuming there are no religious or cultural imperatives mandating that you name the oldest child. If your culture is such that it would be a disgrace to the oldest child, then do take that into account.)

- "Her feelings will get hurt if she doesn't get picked." Parents don't like to disappoint their children. I've seen parents respond to a child's likely overreaction by naming a child who isn't the best choice, but would complain the loudest. Again, being a good fiduciary requires that the person look beyond their own needs and concerns. If they're likely to throw a fit if they're not chosen, would they be a good fit for a role that requires maturity and conscientiousness?

- "He's putting pressure on me to choose him." A child who gets a whiff of your planning might begin lobbying for the job. You want to pick the person who will do the best job, not the one who is trying to muscle into your decision.

- "I owe it to her." Again, look at the variety of hats the fiduciary wears—administrative, financial, and record-keeping. You don't need to choose someone out of a feeling of obligation. If you want to do something special for someone, you can do that in your will or trust rather than naming them to a role for which they're ill-suited. And remember that the job isn't an honorary position—it requires a lot of work. The greater favor might be to let someone else do it.

How About Naming Them All?

Many parents come up with the idea of naming multiple family members as fiduciaries to avoid controversy. In most cases, this is a bad idea. For example, if you have three children, you might be tempted to appoint all three and let the majority decide. But that can lead to deadlock, or alliances between two to the detriment of the third.

In my experience, it's better to go on and make the hard decision. If you name everyone and hope for the best, it can lead to the worst. To lessen any hurt feelings, you may want to discuss with your child the choice you have made and why. And remember that just because only one child is the executor or trustee, it doesn't mean that siblings can't be involved in discussions, decision making, and just plain helping out. There will be enough work for everyone.

Estate Tax Considerations

When your goals include reducing the impact of estate tax, then the tax laws may make it less advantageous for you to pick a close family member as trustee.

Let's say you don't want your spouse to be taxed on any money you leave to your spouse in trust, because your goal is to get the money down to your children free of estate tax. If you're trying to keep assets out your spouse's estate for tax purposes, then you normally don't want your spouse to be the sole trustee over the assets. Your spouse might not be able to serve as a trustee at all over funds you don't want being included in her estate unless your spouse's power is tightly restricted.

So, avoid naming as trustee:

- a beneficiary (Ben establishes a trust for his children Glenn and Jen, and names Jen the trustee), or
- someone whose estate is not supposed to include the trust assets for tax purposes (Ben establishes a trust for his grandchildren, Finn and Win, and names his children Glenn and Jen as the trustees).

If beneficiaries are named as trustees over their own funds (or parents named as trustees over funds that benefit their children), typically the trust agreement must limit the trustee's ability to make distributions. These limits are typically called using an "ascertainable standard" which proposed distributions must meet. Ascertainable standard means the trustee can't make distributions on a whim, but usually only to meet the demonstrable needs of the beneficiary for health, education, support, or maintenance.

> EXAMPLE: Lorraine has two children and two grandchildren. She sets up trusts to benefit the grandchildren and names her children as trustee. To keep the money in the trust from being included in Lorraine's children's estates, Lorraine prohibits the parents' ability to distribute money out of the trusts for reasons other than health, education, support, or maintenance.

Naming one of these individuals is not always a bad idea, but you'll want to work closely with your attorney before you make a decision.

Accountants

Accounting firms frequently serve as fiduciaries. An experienced firm offers certain advantages:

- Accountants are good with figures.
- They have professional liability insurance, so if they lose money through carelessness your relatives should be able to recover.
- You aren't dependent on any one person; the whole firm should be responsive.
- They charge by the hour, rather than by a percentage of what you have, which may be cheaper than a bank or trust company.
- Accountants normally won't handle the investments themselves, they'll farm that out; with a bank, you're going to get the investing department down the hall.

Accountants also may have certain disadvantages:

- Your grieving relatives will be asking an accountant for money, and your accountant may not be as liberal with distributions as you might wish. (These are the same people who won't let you deduct that hamburger in Honduras because you don't have the right receipt.)
- Some accountants may not have their antennae set to the soft issues and think of things solely in financial terms.
- Because they likely will farm out the investment work, you don't have the leverage to get reduced fees as you might with a bank that's performing both the administrative and the investment work.

As with any professional relationship, you need to ask whether you're there for the firm or only one individual. If your accountant retired or died, are there other people at the firm you would trust?

Attorneys

In many places, attorneys offer fiduciary services and employ extra staff to assist with estate and trust management and accounting. Those firms have the advantages of accounting firms, plus they're experienced with reading and interpreting law to make sure your trust is being managed appropriately. And of course there are potential problems. If someone challenges the will or trust your attorney drafted, the attorney may have a conflict of interest.

At a minimum, the person that you select should have experience with similar estates or trusts and appropriate professional insurance. And be sure you know who would serve as fiduciary if the person you choose wasn't able to.

Banks and Trust Companies

Normally, you won't name a bank or trust company to be your *executor* if there's a suitable family member available—that's something an individual can do and it will cost a whole lot less. If there's not a good family choice and your estate is large, you might appoint an attorney or a bank or trust company to do the job.

But you might well want to consider a bank or trust company to serve as your *trustee*, if the trust is large enough.

A "small" trust for many corporate trustees is one under $250,000; $1 million is the threshold for others. Some corporate trustees have even higher minimums, which they justify by offering higher levels of service and extras. At some companies out there, if you don't have $10 million, you don't get in.

So, obviously, when you're shopping around for a corporate fiduciary, ask about the average size of trusts that the corporate trustee has under its management. You will also want to see whether your trustee is experienced in dealing with any special items in your estate such as an ongoing business, large tracts of land, or developable property. If your trust falls neatly in the range that the fiduciary manages, and your fiduciary has experience with the kind of assets you have, then you may have some comfort that you'll receive the attention you're promised.

A company must be licensed in your state to serve as your fiduciary. Most banks and brokerage companies offer these services through their related companies, often called trust companies—you'll see the word "trust" somewhere in their name. A good place to start may be in asking your bank or broker for information on what its trust company provides.

For their services, they typically charge a percentage of the value of the assets they're managing, with a minimum fee. If you don't negotiate a fee arrangement, they have a standard fee schedule. Fee schedules differ dramatically from state to state, so I can't tell you what to expect or what's a fair fee in your state. You will see a higher percentage for the first $1 million the trustee manages; the percentage decreases from there. The best way to figure out what's customary in your state is to get fee schedules from a number of different corporate fiduciaries there and discuss them with your attorney or accountant.

Some trust companies won't invest your assets themselves; instead, they hire a related company to do the work, which will generate an additional charge to your account. You'll want to ask in advance whether investments and buying and selling stocks are included in the management fee, or whether they are extra.

The Beauty of Competition?

If you use a corporate trustee, you may want to allow for some competition to enable your trust to get a better deal on fees. If the executor, the beneficiaries, or an independent third party has the power to remove the trustee, there may be more leverage in negotiating fees.

EXAMPLE: Betty appoints Big Trust Co. to serve as her trustee, but gives her accountant the right to negotiate the fees to be paid with Big Trust Co. and to select another trustee if a satisfactory arrangement can't be reached. If the estate is large enough, Big Trust Co. may be willing to reduce its standard fee to keep the account.

There are quite a few advantages of using a corporate trustee when you have a blended family.

Experience. Individuals may serve as an executor or trustee only once or twice in a lifetime. Corporate trustees do it all day, every day. It's not something extra they agreed to do, it's their business.

Independence. Corporate trustees aren't tied to one side or the other in a blended family. Frequently, decisions that individual trustees make affect them or their family. For example, a family member serving as trustee could find herself in situations where one decision means more money to her or to her children, and another means the other side of the family benefits and her side gets less. Corporate trustees don't face this choice. They won't be as likely to prefer one side over the other because of emotional ties, relationship history, or likes or dislikes.

Good reporting capabilities. Corporate trustees have reporting systems in place, so your beneficiaries won't be kept in the dark.

Access to expertise. They can call on good accounting and other resources, such as tax planning, which can affect the amount of tax the trust and the beneficiaries are required to pay.

Recourse if something goes wrong. Unlike individual fiduciaries, corporate trustees carry insurance and have substantial other assets that can be tapped in the event of theft or misconduct. Your beneficiaries won't have to worry about tracking down or suing a relative if the money is mishandled.

Continuity. They're here today, here tomorrow. Under most circumstances, you, your estate, or your trust won't outlive the fiduciary. And even if a bank fails, it's generally taken over seamlessly by another one.

Access to investment professionals. You may be able to negotiate a lower commission for investments that the trust makes if you're using the trust company for trust services.

There are also disadvantages to using a corporate trustee.

Cost. This is the number one reason people are fearful of choosing a corporate trustee—they think the trust's value will be eroded by all of the fees. That's why it's important you know in advance what the fees are for your situation.

Potential for a conflict of interest. Some trust companies use a related company to make trades in your account and charge extra for the service. The investment arm may be paid on commission, so there's a chance they could push commission-generating trades.

Lack of continuity. There's always a chance that the local trust officer with whom you have a relationship today will be across town at another bank tomorrow or part of Mega Mega Bank after a merger. Many years ago, trust officers stayed with banks for a long time, they developed relationships, and there was a reasonable expectation that the person you saw today was going to be the same person your loved ones would be dealing with long after you were gone. Now it is no longer the case. Trust departments expand and contract with the economy and how the department fits in with the overall vision of the bank. Trust officers move around much more than they once did. So you have to go into the relationship thinking, "if Alan were gone tomorrow, would I still want my assets at this bank?"

In the end, you need to weigh the advantages of the corporate trustee and be realistic about your alternatives. Will a family member be able to devote the time to the job? Do they have the capabilities? Is the cost of the corporate trustee justified when you look at the alternatives?

Boutiques: Good for Shoes—How About Trust Services?

Some quick-thinking businesses have responded to the fact that people want experience, but don't want to pay the corporate trustee rate; people want to deal with a person, but they're afraid that the person they see today may be gone tomorrow. These fiduciary "boutiques" say they offer the best of both worlds. They're small, approachable, and local; they're experienced, but not as pricey as bank trust companies. The people running these boutiques may be accountants, attorneys, or financial professionals. Ask your accountant or attorney whether your town offers a reputable boutique fiduciary. As with any small business, make sure the firm is licensed and carries sufficient insurance so beneficiaries will have recourse should something go wrong. You'll also want to verify that the firm has a succession plan so you're not relying on just one individual.

Family Member Plus Professional: The Best of Both Worlds?

One way to get the benefits that a family member offers, while buffering against claims of favoritism, is to pair the family member with a professional fiduciary to serve as cofiduciaries. I've heard of this called pairing the "head" (professional) with the "heart" (family member).

I'm not sure this works as well with blended families because you still have the potential that the family member will act (or be perceived to act) unfairly when it comes to one side of the family or the other. The potential for hurt feelings and suspicion remains when you elevate one family member over the others by your selection. You'll also want to review carefully the compensation schedule of the proposed trustee—some charge *more* when they're serving as a cotrustee than when they're serving by themselves. If you're already concerned about fees, this may not be the best choice.

Helping Your Executor and Trustee

You can help your executor and trustee and make their job go much more smoothly if you:

- Keep good records. This includes a list of all of your bank, stock, and retirement accounts, with account number and institution name, kept in a safe place (safe deposit box, fireproof home safe), with a copy at your attorney's or accountant's office.
- Keep a list of significant property you own, particularly if it's something your fiduciary might not be aware of.
- Don't forget to write down computer passwords, safe combinations, and where to find safe deposit box keys.
- Leave notes for your executor in a couple of places as to where your estate planning documents are. Give your attorney and accountant a note as well.
- Make your intentions clear about whether your executor or trustee is to get paid for the job (and remember that it's a lot of work).

In any family, but especially in a blended one, pay particular attention to relationships that could be strained after your death. Cultivate good relationships with your children and stepchildren. Consider putting a statement in your will as to your love for all of your children and your desire that they work cooperatively with your fiduciaries in settling your estate.

If you think there might be hurt feelings over your choice for executor or trustee (or how you've left your property), take steps now. Communicate your intentions and try to soothe the feelings of those who might have wanted to be the fiduciary by talking to them about your reasons for making your selection. For example, if your executor lives in your town and your other children do not, let the out-of-towners know what you're doing and why you're doing it. It will lessen the likelihood that they'll blame your plan on your executor and think it was your executor's doing, rather than your own. This also saves your executor from being the bearer of bad news (or at least unpleasant surprises) later.

Remember that a family member appointed as executor or trustee likely will need help. They may not know where to go. If you could suggest an accountant, a lawyer or other adviser for your executor to hire, that might help them get the expertise they need. Because these people have your blessing and may already be familiar with your situation, that can be a great relief.

Meet with your future executor or trustee, discuss your expectations, and make it clear how you want people to be treated. Don't, however, involve your future executor or trustee in your planning. For example, when you meet with your lawyer, don't have the child you plan to name executor come with you. Even if it's all your idea, this may make your plan more open to challenge down the road, because another child might claiming that the one who attended meetings with you improperly influenced you.

If you think there's a potential for some ill will, let your attorney know. That way, you can plan to minimize disputes. For example, if you know that your youngest son is likely to challenge to the plan, then tell your attorney why you think he may want to raise a fuss. Your attorney will be able to offer suggestions to lessen the likelihood of a challenge.

Calling All Packrats, Collectors, and Acquirers of Memorabilia

If you have a valuable collection, keep good records about what everything is. For example, make a file with a short description of your major memorabilia, where you got it, how much it cost, and why it's valuable. Received a ruby ring from your aunt on your tenth birthday? A pocketknife from your grandfather? Write it down somewhere so your children and stepchildren will know where it came from.

Quite valuable things can look like candidates for the trash to the unknowing. Keep on hand any books you may have that could tell your executor about your collection and mention the books in a letter to your executor, noting any items in them that you have in your collection. If you favor antique Chinese porcelains, but your executor knows nothing about them, you don't want her using the Ming vase as a planter or turning your treasures into someone else's amazing bargain at an estate sale.

Take the story of Evan Lattimer, called on to sort through the piles of Lincoln memorabilia, oddities, and unlabeled relics left behind by her father, a prodigious collector. As reported in *The New York Times*, "She learned one important lesson early on: just because an article looks like junk doesn't mean it is. Bothered by the sight of three connected chairs with a broken leg, she took action. 'I put them out on the street and went back into the house,' she said. Twenty minutes later, once they were gone, it struck her that they might have been seats from the Ford's Theater in Washington." (Kassie Bracken and Erik Olsen, "In a Father's Clutter, Historic Oddities," *The New York Times* (August 20, 2008).)

Yes, that would be the Ford's Theater where President Lincoln was assassinated. Most of us don't have items quite that valuable, but if you know the story behind something, better to make sure you're not the only one who knows it.

You might also wish to consider selling or donating special assets while you're alive and can convey the full value of your treasures. If you want to hang onto things, think about having them appraised by an expert. This will give your executor both an idea of their worth and a name to contact if an updated appraisal is someday needed.

Preparing for Disability and End-of-Life Decisions

Premature Disability: How Would You Pay the Bills? 222

    Do You Need Disability Insurance? 222

    Shopping for a Policy 223

    Paying the Premiums 225

Age-Related Disability 227

    Long-Term Care Insurance 227

    Managing Assets 231

    Health Care Issues—Who Makes Decisions If You
       Can't Speak for Yourself? 236

Throughout your life, there comes a time
To make your choices known,
To spare the tears, the fears and cares
Of loved ones left alone.

For most of this book, I've focused on helping you plan today so that your wishes will be respected after your death. But estate planning is more than that. A comprehensive estate plan will also ensure that you and your assets are protected if you are disabled before death. Planning allows you to appoint someone to make health care decisions on your behalf and to say how you wish to be treated if you're unable to speak for yourself.

This chapter shows how you can plan for these possibilities.

When I meet with couples in my practice, I always try to discuss these topics. Some of them are difficult to think about, but working through them is a necessary part of your planning. Let your family know what your wishes are should something happen to you.

As part of a blended family, you want to minimize disagreements between your spouse and your children. Conflicts are more likely to happen if you haven't specified your wishes in advance. Planning is a way to eliminate many of the conflicts your blended family could face over you and your care.

When considering what you want to have happen, it's helpful to separate how you want your money managed from your health issues, because different tools are used for each. Unfortunately, the tools have similar names, which can be confusing. For a quick reference, see "Disability Planning Tools," below.

Disability can come in many forms. I find it useful to divide it into two types:

- **Premature disability,** from accident or illness before age 65, and
- **Age-related disability,** from normal aging, dementia, or illness later in life.

With a premature disability, the concerns are primarily income-related. If you can't work, how are you going to pay the bills? There are certainly financial issues with care when you're older, but age-related disability issues often have more to do with getting assistance. If you need help, who is going to assist you? How can you make sure your helper doesn't take advantage of you?

Disability Planning Tools		
Tool	**What It Does**	**When It's Effective**
Financial Power of Attorney	Gives another person the authority to manage your finances and pay your bills	You choose—either when you sign it or if you become disabled
Health Care Power of Attorney	Gives another person the ability to make health care decisions for you	If you cannot make or communicate decisions for yourself
Living Will	Specifies what you wish to have happen regarding life support, food, and water if you're in a coma or have a terminal condition and are not expected to improve	If you cannot speak for yourself
Advance Directive (also called Advance Medical Directive or Medical Directive)	Like a living will, specifies your end-of-life wishes; may also include health care power of attorney	If you are unable to make or communicate decisions for yourself
Last Will and Testament	Specifies who inherits your property after your death	At your death

Premature Disability: How Would You Pay the Bills?

Here's a quick question with an obvious answer that you may not have thought about: If you're under 50 and in reasonably good health, why is disability insurance more expensive than life insurance? The answer is that the odds are greater that you'll become disabled, rather than die, before you're 65. That's why term life insurance can offer a high death benefit for a low premium, while a disability policy provides for a much smaller benefit and a higher premium.

Do You Need Disability Insurance?

If you're 45, the likelihood of premature disability (a lingering, prolonged, or permanent condition that prevents you from working for months or years at a time) for either sex is about twice as great as the risk of death before 65. (This figure is from a 2004 study by the Actuarial Foundation, *Disability Insurance: A Missing Piece in the Financial Security Puzzle*.)

If disability poses the greater threat, then why do most people plan for a premature death but not for disability? I think it has to do with common misconceptions regarding premature disability.

I used to assume that only surgeons or people with hazardous jobs needed disability insurance. Picture linemen with the electric company: they're up in the bucket truck swaying back and forth trying to repair a snapped power line in the middle of a hurricane. Of course, I thought, they need disability insurance. Not me—I'm a lawyer. The biggest job hazard I face is a paper cut.

The statistics tell a different story. According to the Actuarial Foundation study, most disability claims don't stem from on-the-job accidents, but from illnesses. Disabling illnesses include cancer, heart disease, mental illness, severe arthritis, or musculoskeletal disease. These affect the sedentary office worker as much as (if not more than) active workers in hazardous jobs.

A premature disability can be so devastating because it packs a double whammy. Not only have you lost your primary source of income, you're also not putting away money for your retirement.

What to do?

It's in your best interest to get long-term disability insurance. It covers disabilities that last longer than 90 or 180 days, depending on the policy.

If you don't have coverage, you may be forced to rely on government benefits, which are pretty small and don't pay for much. The primary provider is the federal government through its Supplemental Security Income, Social Security Disability Insurance, and veterans and vocational rehabilitation programs. To qualify, you have to produce medical evidence of the disability, plus you must generally have exhausted your other assets and be at a poverty level to receive full financial benefits. Most people don't qualify on the first attempt. For those who do, benefits are often less than what private insurance provides. Federal benefits can be an important safety net if you don't have disability insurance or if your benefits have run out, but with the hassles and low benefit amounts, you don't want to rely on them if you can pay for private insurance.

Shopping for a Policy

Disability policies fall into one of two types: group and individual. Group coverage is usually much cheaper than individual coverage. Check and see if your employer offers disability insurance coverage; many companies do. Some employers provide it for free. You may be able to supplement group coverage or pay for any portion your employer doesn't cover through payroll deductions.

If you're a member of any professional associations, see if they offer disability insurance as a benefit. You may be able to purchase insurance through an association and get a group rate even if your employer doesn't offer the insurance.

If you choose employer-provided insurance, remember that your coverage may last only as long as you're with that company. If you switch jobs, you'll need to get coverage through your new employer or on your own. As you get older, individual coverage will get harder and more expensive to get, so factor that in when you're deciding whether to buy individual coverage or elect your employer's coverage. If there's a job change on your horizon, you may want to look at individual coverage while you can purchase it more cheaply, so you'll have it while you're between jobs or if your new employer doesn't provide it.

How much should you get? An easy answer is to say as much as the insurance company will sell you. Disability insurance is usually available up to a certain percentage of your current salary. Typical group plans cover up to 60% of your salary up to certain caps, say a maximum benefit of $60,000 annually. Individual plans may go higher, as much as 80% or 90% of your salary. If you're highly compensated, the caps on coverage in a group plan will limit you to much less than 60% of your salary, so you'll want to look at individual coverage to supplement your group coverage to make up more of your lost income.

So, if you're a $75,000-per-year salaried worker, you can't buy disability insurance that would pay you $500,000 a year. You won't even find coverage or be able to combine policies to pay you $75,000 a year. Insurance companies try hard to make sure you don't have an incentive to qualify as disabled.

The definition of what constitutes a disability varies among policies. Some policies protect you if you can no longer perform your current job; for others, the coverage kicks in only if you can't do any job. Some policies pay benefits for a maximum number of years; others pay through age 65.

Because you won't be able to purchase insurance coverage that would totally replace your current salary, you need to get with your adviser to see what your true, basic financial needs are and work from there. Also, the benefits won't start until after a 90- or 180-day period, so your disability plan will need to include your saving enough money or purchasing a short-term disability insurance policy to get you to where the benefits start with your permanent policy. Your insurance adviser can help you navigate through the different policy types and levels of coverage.

What to Look for in Disability Policies

- Strength of the company (several companies, listed below, rate insurance carriers)
- Benefit amount
- Benefit increases based on inflation or cost-of-living adjustments
- Waiting period to qualify (90 days? 180 days?)
- How disability is defined. Must you be totally unable to work or just unable to work in your current field?
- How long benefits will be paid. Two years? Until you reach age 65?

RESOURCE

Rating disability carriers. The following companies rate insurance carriers. Review one or more ratings companies to gauge the health of your proposed insurer.

- A.M. Best (www.ambest.com)
- Moody's Investors Services (www.moodys.com)
- Standard & Poor's Insurance Ratings Service (www.standardandpoor.com).

Paying the Premiums

You may have different options on how you can pay for your insurance. If your employer pays for your insurance, or if you pay for it using before-tax dollars (out of a cafeteria plan, for example), then if you ever start drawing benefits, you may have to pay income tax on them. If you pay for disability insurance out of your pocket using after-tax dollars, the benefits may be income-tax free if you ever need them.

Paying with after-tax dollars is better if you ever need to use the insurance, because insurance benefits won't be subject to tax. Paying with before-tax dollars works best if you never need the insurance.

EXAMPLE: Anita's employer offers two options for disability insurance. She can pay for the insurance using either before-tax dollars or after-tax dollars. Anita elects to use after-tax dollars. Her net paycheck after taxes is reduced by the cost of the disability insurance. Should Anita become disabled and qualify for benefits, she won't have to have pay federal income tax on the benefits—a good thing, because her check already will be less than her previous salary. If Anita had opted to use before-tax dollars (that is, from her gross pay before taxes), the benefits would be subject to income tax, and Anita would receive less in her time of need.

If your employer offers a choice of using before- or after-tax dollars, look closely at costs to you of the insurance both ways, and compare those with your need for disability insurance amid other resources. For most people, it makes sense to use after-tax dollars if you can swing it. Why? Because you're already only getting a percentage of your salary. If you take tax out of that, there will be less to live on, certainly much less than what you have now. If you would be relying solely on the disability insurance, you may want to pay with after-tax dollars. If you have substantial other resources, you may consider paying with before-tax dollars. Women may want to pay for disability insurance with after-tax dollars because of their higher rates of disability.

Like most insurance, the older you get, the more expensive disability insurance gets and the harder it is to qualify. Group coverage is easier to obtain than individual.

RESOURCE

Online help with disability insurance.

- www.kiplinger.com offers information on group and individual coverage
- www.smartmoney.com describes differences between policies and links to major providers
- The Consumer Federation of American and the American Council of Life Insurers offer a guide at www.consumerfed.org/pdfs/ltdbrochure.pdf.
- Life and Health Foundation for Education, www.lifehappens.org. An industry group sponsored by insurers, the Foundation website includes guides to various kinds of insurance and provides a printable consumer brochure under disability insurance.

- The Council for Disability Awareness, www.disabilitycanhappen.org, is a nonprofit organization that raises awareness about disability and the need for insurance. It is sponsored by a number of national insurance carriers. The website offers statistics and consumer guides.
- A.M. Best, www.ambest.com/consumer, is a rating organization for insurance carriers. Its website allows you to search by state for carriers who provide insurance in your state and also contains helpful consumer information.

Age-Related Disability

As you age, you may need a little help managing your day-to-day affairs from time to time. Most people do. Disability planning for later in life is designed to make sure you get the help and care you need, and that your assets are protected once you're no longer making the bank deposits and paying the bills.

Long-Term Care Insurance

The price of nursing home care continues to rise rapidly—in 2008, a private room cost $74,560 a year on average, according to Genworth Financial Services' annual survey. These costs can take a huge bite out of anyone's estate. (Medicare does not pay a penny for most long-term care.)

For most people, it used to be that you paid for nursing home care out of your own pocket and then, once you spent and sold most everything you had, Medicaid would step in and pay. Medicaid is a federal program administered by the states. Each state has its own rules as to who qualifies, how much they can keep in assets, and what assets aren't counted in what they're allowed to keep (like a modest home or certain annuities). Medicaid pays only once you have exhausted your other resources.

Now there's another option: long-term care insurance.

Long-term care insurance pays for in-home and nursing home care. Like any insurance, you pay premiums now to get a benefit later if you need it. The amount of the benefit depends on the policy you buy. After you pass the medical exams and get through the waiting period (the length of which depends on the policy), long-term care insurance will pay or reimburse you for in-home and nursing home costs. The policies have a lifetime maximum benefit—if you exceed it, then you or Medicaid will have to pay after that.

Don't Jeopardize Your Medicaid Eligibility

For Medicaid to pay for long-term care, you basically have to be at a poverty level of income and resources. Many people would like Medicaid to pay for their care, but don't want to exhaust a lifetime of savings before qualifying—and so are susceptible to pitches for programs or techniques that purport to help them keep assets but still qualify for Medicaid.

My advice is to tread carefully. In recent years Congress plugged many of the loopholes that once existed. If someone encourages you to make large gifts to your children or transfer property out of your name now to qualify for Medicaid, you might actually end up disqualifying yourself from Medicaid at a time when you really need it.

To find an attorney who can describe sound alternatives, check out www.nolo.com or the National Association of Elder Law Attorneys at www.naela.org.

Who Benefits?

Buying long-term care insurance while you're still relatively young can be a good hedge against having your life savings depleted by nursing home costs. The downside? The older you get, the harder it is to qualify and the more it costs. Most long-term care insurance buyers are in their 50s, with some in their late 40s or early 60s. Also, you need to check the insurer's record of rate increases. A recent study showed a major national insurer averaged 18% in annual premium increases from 1998 through 2005. ("The Good and the Very Bad," by Michael Gilfix and Bernard A. Krooks, *Trusts and Estates* (January 2009).)

Long-term care insurance is probably not appropriate for families at either end of the economic spectrum: wealthy families can afford the cost of care and poorer families can't afford the insurance. For those of us in the middle, it may be a good safety net.

Your employer or a professional association might provide a long-term care insurance group policy, so don't forget to check those if you're interested in long-term care insurance. The premiums may be much lower than individual policies.

Do your homework to ensure that the proposed carrier has an excellent rating so it will be around when you need it. As with any sales proposal, you'll want to ask specific questions as to the types of coverage that are recommended, the benefit provided (whether strictly nursing home care or in-home care as well), how the benefit is paid (does it pay the provider, or do you have to pay the provider up front and get reimbursed), and how long the benefit will last once you start drawing on it. Be warned: Some of the sales literature may use assumptions of an extended, decades-long nursing home stay, when the actual typical occupancy period for people in nursing homes is much shorter. Most nursing home stays are less than three months, according to the Centers for Disease Control's *National Nursing Home Study* (June 2002).

Long-term care insurance can be a good relationship-smoother for you and your spouse so that your children and stepchildren don't worry that the cost of your care will deplete their inheritances.

> EXAMPLE: Elaine and George are in their early 50s and in good health. After the death of his mother, George became concerned that the costs of their final care might eat away at their children's inheritances. In addition, George's children are nagging him to "do something" so that caring for him and Elaine won't consume their inheritance. Elaine and George buy long-term care insurance, tell the kids not to worry, and pledge to take more expensive vacations.

States With Special Long-Term Care Insurance Programs

Some states offer what's called a "Long-Term Care Partnership Program," intended to encourage people who might otherwise depend on Medicaid to buy their own long-term care policies. These partnership programs are authorized by federal law.

Private companies offer the insurance policies, which must meet certain criteria under federal law. What's really special about these policies is that if you eventually use up all the policy benefits and apply for Medicaid, you can keep a specific amount of assets and still qualify for Medicaid (if you are otherwise eligible for Medicaid).

Commonly, you can protect assets up to the amount of the insurance benefits you've received. But in some states (including New York), you can buy a policy that lets you protect all of your assets. Because the asset limit for qualifying for Medicaid is so low—just a few thousand dollars—this feature could make the difference when it comes to qualifying for Medicaid.

> **EXAMPLE:** Phyllis buys a long-term care insurance policy that has a lifetime benefit of $100,000. If she exhausts her insurance benefits and applies for Medicaid, then $100,000 or more (depending on the state) of her assets won't be counted when determining her eligibility for Medicaid.

Currently, more than half the states either have active partnership programs or are in the process of setting them up. Check with your state's insurance department to see whether or not your state has an active program yet.

RESOURCE

Long-term care insurance information.

- www.kiplinger.com offers information on group and individual coverage
- www.smartmoney.com describes differences between policies and links to major providers
- The Life and Health Foundation for Education, www.lifehappens.org, an industry group sponsored by insurers, maintains a website that includes guides to various kinds of insurance and provides a printable consumer brochure about long-term care insurance.

Managing Assets

A huge issue for many older people is the day-to-day management of their financial matters. There are several good ways to deal with this issue, giving someone you trust authority over (not ownership of) your assets.

Powers of Attorney

Durable financial powers of attorney are a popular technique for dealing with disability. Here's how they work: You (the principal) appoint someone (your agent) to have the authority to deal with your financial affairs. That person can typically do just about anything you can do with your money, checking accounts, brokerage accounts, retirement accounts, and real estate.

Durable? Sounds Like a Truck Commercial

These documents are called "durable" financial powers of attorney because they stay in effect if you become incapacitated. Traditional powers of attorney end if the principal becomes incapacitated. Traditional powers are used mostly for limited, short-term events—for example, you're out of the country on a trip, or you've moved and want to authorize someone to sign the closing papers on your old house in your old state.

You can give your agent the power immediately, or you can make your agent's power conditioned on your disability. Powers of attorney that wait to kick in until disability are called springing powers of attorney. Who decides whether you're disabled? Normally, it takes one or two physicians to certify that you're no longer capable of managing your affairs in order for the power of attorney to be effective.

Deciding whether a power of attorney should be effective immediately or spring into effect at disability is a matter of preference. In my practice, blended families choose springing powers of attorney more often than nonblended families do. If you and your spouse maintain separate checking accounts and try hard to keep separate assets separate, then you may want to think about using a springing power of attorney. That way, you'll have it, but it's only there if you need it. If you and your spouse put everything into one big pot, you may be more comfortable with a power of attorney that's effective immediately, but have an understanding with your spouse that it's to be used only if you're incapacitated. It's up to you.

Powers of attorney can be very helpful. Your agent will be able to pay bills, sell real estate, and buy and sell investments. Certainly, if you have a family history of dementia, you should sign a power of attorney so that your loved ones are able to manage your affairs. But really, financial durable powers of attorney are always a good idea, regardless of age or family history. Anyone, at any age, can be in an accident.

> **EXAMPLE 1:** Bertie and Max have been married a number of years. Bertie wants Max to be able to pay her bills and manage her investments should she become incapacitated. She signs a power of attorney that has a springing feature so it's there if needed.

> **EXAMPLE 2:** Belinda owns a business in which her son Samuel works. Belinda wants Samuel to be able to run the business should something happen to her. Belinda gives Samuel a power of attorney with respect to the business so he'll be able to sign payroll checks, pay vendors, and sign contracts if she becomes disabled.

Powers of attorney can also be very dangerous. Think of the word *power* in the name. With a power of attorney, you're giving your agent a blank check over your assets. You must have complete faith in your agent before handing over a signed power of attorney. Your agent is legally required to use the money for you only, not for the agent or the agent's family. Unfortunately, abuses can arise. Thieves prey on the elderly, often approaching with offers of help. What they're really after is a power of attorney over the elderly person's assets, which they then use to drain the person's bank accounts and other assets. Once the money's gone, they move on to the next victim. Also, a child may badger a parent for a power of attorney and then use it improperly.

A huge advantage of a durable financial power of attorney is that you—not a court—get to decide who has power over your money. If something happens to you and you can't speak for yourself, your loved ones won't have to go to court and have you declared incompetent so that they can manage your affairs. A power of attorney preserves your dignity and saves your loved ones the time, expense, and anguish of having to hire medical personnel to declare you incompetent and going to court in a public proceeding. And if family members—say your spouse and your children from a previous marriage—disagree about who should be in charge, things can turn ugly.

Because the agent doesn't have to make a lot of reports to loved ones or a court, it's not always clear how the agent is handling the principal's assets. If someone suspects that the agent is using money for other purposes, it's difficult and costly to prove it. By contrast, a guardian or conservator who is appointed by a court must keep good records and make regular reports to the court. But given the expense and hassle, on balance most people prefer powers of attorney over court proceedings.

Financial powers of attorney terminate at your death. After that, the person named in your will (your executor) or trust (successor trustee) takes over, and your agent has no more power over your assets.

Be sure you make your power of attorney consistent with your overall estate plan. For example, if you have set up your will to ensure that the bulk of your estate passes to your children from a prior marriage, consider carefully whether to give your spouse a power of attorney. If you give your spouse power over your assets, you're setting up a situation that could lead to a different overall result than you intended. You may want to choose a grown child instead.

> EXAMPLE: Sarah and Al are remarried. Each conscientiously keeps assets separate. In her will, Sarah leaves the bulk of her estate to her two children, and names them coexecutors of her estate. If Sarah were to also give Al a power of attorney, then Al would have more control over Sarah's assets during her life than after her

death. He would have a legal responsibility to use her assets only for her benefit, but her children might still not be happy about having him serve as agent. Sarah's plan would be more consistent if she named one or both of her children as her agent. Al would still have control over his separate assets, but not over Sarah's.

Most powers of attorney don't have an expiration date. Still, you'll want to sign a new power of attorney from time to time, at least every three years. Banks and other financial institutions prefer to rely on powers of attorney that have been executed within the past few years. Longer than that, and there's a risk that the bank will not want to honor the power of attorney. They get skittish because they don't want to be held liable for giving money to an unauthorized person even though there may be laws shielding the bank from liability. If a bank initially rejects a power of attorney as stale, it doesn't mean that the power of attorney is legally invalid or that the bank will never accept it. Your agent may be able to give the bank more information and convince it to honor the power of attorney. So, help your agent out and sign new powers of attorney from time to time.

Revocable Living Trusts

For many people, the revocable living trust (RLT) is another way to authorize someone to handle their financial matters if someday they can't. With an RLT, a trustee you've selected can take charge if you become disabled. Your trustee will use the trust funds for things you've specified in the trust document such as health care expenses, your home, and support.

RLTs are designed to last for many years, and banks are accustomed to dealing with them. A bank is more likely to honor a request made by a trustee under a 15-year-old RLT than one by an agent under a 15-year-old power of attorney.

Another advantage of RLTs is that they're designed to last after your death. Unlike a power of attorney, which terminates at death, an RLT continues in effect. With an RLT, you can have a seamless transition from its purpose during your life (providing for you and your needs) to its purpose following your death (providing for your loved ones).

In most cases, you would be the initial trustee of your trust. Your chosen successor would take over only if you became disabled. The successor can be a family member, a professional, a corporate trustee, or a combination. (See Chapter 10 for more on how to pick someone.)

> **EXAMPLE 1:** Regina establishes an revocable living trust and names herself as initial trustee. If she ever becomes incapacitated, the trust provides that Brad, Regina's husband, would become trustee. If he were unable or unwilling to serve, Regina's son John would step in.

> **EXAMPLE 2:** Josh establishes an RLT with himself as initial trustee. The trust provides that if he becomes incapacitated, his son Elliott and Mega Trust Company, N.A., would become cotrustees. If Elliott were unable or unwilling to serve, Mega Trust would serve as sole trustee.

> **EXAMPLE 3:** Juanita establishes an RLT. Years later, she develops Alzheimer's disease and becomes gradually unable to care for herself. When she can no longer manage her own affairs, the successor trustee she named in the trust (her daughter) will have the exclusive right to manage Juanita's trust assets for Juanita's benefit. At Juanita's death, there will be a seamless transition from her lifetime trust to her bequests at death.

Even if you have a living trust, you'll still want a power of attorney so that your agent could transfer to the trustee any assets that aren't in the RLT. For example, you might have checking accounts, real estate, or other property in your name that would need to be transferred to the trust so the trustee could manage it. You can limit your agent's authority to transferring any assets in your name to the trustee at your disability. (For more on RLTs, see Chapter 6.)

Health Care Issues—Who Makes Decisions If You Can't Speak for Yourself?

In addition to the financial concerns posed by disability, you'll want to address the health care issues that could arise if you were ever unable to speak for yourself and needed medical care. With the right documents (discussed below), you can:

- choose, in advance, whom you want making health care decisions for you
- lessen the chance of conflict among your loved ones over who has the right to speak for you, and
- declare your stance regarding end-of-life decisions.

	What is it?	Why have one?
Living will	A document that lets you say what you want to happen if you can't speak for yourself and you're in a coma or have a terminal illness and you're not expected to recover or regain consciousness	You get to state what you want to have happen
Health care power of attorney	A document that lets you appoint someone to make medical decisions on your behalf	You get to choose who speaks for you
Advance directive (also called an advance medical directive or medical directive)	A catchall term that can refer both to living wills and health care powers of attorney	All of the above

Choose Your Representative in Advance

You know your family members—their strengths, their weaknesses, who brings everyone together and who tends to cause conflicts. Knowing this, you may have a preference for someone you want to make health care decisions for you if you can't speak for yourself. You can make your choices known by signing an advance directive. You can choose your spouse, an adult child, or a trusted friend to be your health care representative.

If you don't have an advance directive, you can still get medical treatment if you can't speak for yourself. Before beginning a procedure, medical professionals will want your spouse to consent to your treatment. If your spouse is unavailable, doctors will look to your adult children to consent to your treatment. If no one is available, two or three physicians would have to sign the consent for you. Failing to sign an advance directive can cause delays and confusion when what you really want is people focusing on your care.

> **EXAMPLE:** Lucinda is in a car accident and needs emergency surgery. She is unconscious. Her husband, Wendell, can consent to the surgery on her behalf. If he is not available, one or both of Lucinda's children would be able to authorize the surgery.

An advance directive is a lot like a financial power of attorney, except that you're giving your agent the power over your care as opposed to power over your checkbook.

> **EXAMPLE:** Maria and her husband Charles are both in good health. She signs an advance directive allowing Charles to make medical decisions if she is unable to speak for herself. If Maria suffers a stroke and later breaks her hip in a fall, then Charles will be able to make decisions regarding Maria's treatment if she can't communicate her wishes. If needed, Charles could authorize surgery to repair Maria's hip.

Not only do you want to choose someone for initial medical care, you want someone who can authorize treatment for you down the road if your condition persists and you remain unable to speak for yourself.

An advance directive allows you to specify whom you would want to serve as your guardian in the event you are no longer able to care for yourself.

Without an advance directive, your loved ones may have to go to court to seek a guardian for you. To get a guardian, the court will require that they demonstrate your incapacity through the testimony of witnesses and doctors. This is a time-consuming, public, embarrassing, and costly process that everyone wants to avoid.

> EXAMPLE: Evelyn, who doesn't sign an advance directive, develops Alzheimer's and is no longer able to speak for herself. She needs constant care. Her husband Larry goes to court to be declared Evelyn's guardian to obtain the continuing right to oversee her care. Three months later, after thousands of dollars spent with attorneys and a public hearing featuring testimony of medical professionals and Evelyn's family members as to her incapacity, Larry is appointed guardian.

Avoid Family Fights

By having the power of attorney, you lessen the likelihood of a dispute between your spouse and your children over who is best suited to take care of you. These kinds of disputes can be common in blended families if a stepparent and stepchildren disagree over what's best for the children's parent.

> EXAMPLE 1: Maria does not sign a health care power of attorney. She suffers a stroke and later breaks her hip in a fall. Based on the advice of Maria's doctor, her husband Charles wants to authorize surgery to repair Maria's hip. Her children disagree, saying they "don't want to put mama through any more pain." If Maria had authorized Charles or her children to make the decision, then there's less of a chance that they would end up in a fuss, with the medical staff caught in the middle.

Will My Loved Ones Get the Information They Need?

Another good reason to have a health care power of attorney is to make sure your loved ones have access to information on your medical condition so they can help make the right choices. A federal law called HIPAA requires doctors and hospitals to keep your medical information confidential and provides for fines and other penalties if they don't. Consequently, medical providers can be very stingy when it comes to sharing information—they don't want a HIPAA violation.

As long as you can speak for yourself, you can authorize your medical providers to share information with your spouse, your children, or friends. In your advance directive, you also can authorize your medical provider to share information with your agents.

But if you can't speak for yourself and you haven't signed a health care power of attorney, the medical provider has to decide whether sharing your information would violate HIPAA. As a result, your children might be unable to obtain information regarding your medical care.

> EXAMPLE: Maria does not sign a health care power of attorney. She suffers a stroke, falls and breaks her hip, is unable to speak for herself, and needs constant assistance. Her husband Charles wants to authorize surgery to repair Maria's hip. Her children fly in from out of state wanting more information, but Charles objects. The doctor, citing HIPAA concerns, agrees to share information only with Charles. Because the doctor has never seen Maria's children before and doesn't know what Maria's wishes are, he's not willing to risk a HIPAA violation by sharing information with the children.

EXAMPLE 2: Steve, who has not signed an advance directive, develops dementia and needs constant care, which his second wife Emily provides. Emily and Steven's children don't get along. One day, Emily is served with court papers filed by Steven's son seeking to be appointed his guardian. In response, Emily files her own papers and contests the son's petition. If Steven had authorized Emily to make his health care decisions, then there's less of a chance that Emily and Steven's son would be embroiled in a dispute over who should be Steven's guardian.

Declare Your Stance on End-of-Life Decisions

Have you ever seen a friend or a loved one spend their final days or weeks in a hospital, hooked to a respirator, and thought that person would have never wanted that?

An advance directive gives you the chance to make your most personal choices known regarding your final treatment. With an advance directive, you can spare your spouse and children the agony and disagreement over what your wishes are in the event you cannot speak for yourself.

The laws of each state vary as to when and how advance directives apply in end-of-life decisions. Generally, it's going to require a determination by your primary physician and a second physician that your condition meets the standard set by your state (terminal condition, unconsciousness, or coma), that you are unresponsive, and that your condition is unlikely to improve with treatment.

In an advance directive, you can specify what treatment you wish, if any, if that unfortunate situation should occur to you. For example, you can specify whether you wish:

- to extend your life as long as possible using whatever measures are necessary, regardless of cost
- to allow your natural death to occur—alleviate pain, but don't give you food and water, don't put you on a ventilator, don't administer CPR if you go into heart failure, or

- to specify a middle ground—don't use heroic measures to save your life, but continue to give you certain treatment. With this approach, you likely will be able to choose whether or not you want:
  - to have food and water provided to you by a tube if you can't eat or drink
  - to be put on a ventilator if you can't breathe by yourself, and
  - CPR to be used if you have heart failure.

The laws of your state will likely dictate the form of the advance directive and your treatment options. By doing some online research (check out the resources below) or asking a local hospital, you should be able to see the form used in your state and start thinking about the decisions that are available to you.

It's painful to think of these things happening to you. But by acting while you're healthy, you can make sure your wishes are known and spare your loved ones the agony of wondering what you would have wanted.

RESOURCE

More on advance directives.

- www.caringinfo.org has a wealth of brochures on advance directives and end-of-life decisions. This website also offers free downloads of advance directive forms for each state
- www.mayoclinic.com offers resources on advance directives, including health care powers of attorney and living wills
- www.webmd.com also has a section on advance directives, and
- www.nolo.com also offer free articles on these issues and products that let you create advance directives and powers of attorney tailored to each state.

Working With Lawyers

How to Find the Right Lawyer for You 244

    Where to Look 245

    How to Make Sure the Attorney Is Knowledgeable 246

    The First Meeting 247

You Are the Client 248

How Lawyers Advise Couples 249

How Lawyers Bill 251

    Flat Fee 251

    By the Hour 252

    The Hybrid Approach 253

How Much Should It Cost? 253

The Estate Planning Process 253

    The Engagement Letter 254

    Getting Started 254

Pulling Together the Information You Need 255

    Documents 258

    More Meetings 259

    Signing the Documents 260

How to Help Your Lawyer (and Lower Your Bill) 260

Other Members of the Team: Accountants and Financial Advisers 262

Your estate planning journey
Begins and ends with an attorney
Whose expertise and learning
Will give shape to all your yearning.

Unless you're a professional athlete prone to hanging out in nightclubs or a troubled pop star fending off the paparazzi, you probably don't have a covey of lawyers on staff. Most people don't deal with lawyers very much.

If you aren't sure how to go about finding the right lawyer, or how or how much a lawyer charges for estate planning, you might be a little apprehensive about going to a lawyer and getting the help you need.

Especially if your last experience with a lawyer was during a contentious divorce, you may feel less than eager to seek out another lawyer. But estate planning is different—it's collaborative and cooperative, not adversarial. It's all about making sure that what you want to have happen happens.

Look forward to working with your lawyer in your estate planning. Your planning will flourish when you find a qualified lawyer who is interested in you and your family and with whom you're open to discussing your cares and concerns. There's a bunch of lawyers who qualify out there; you just have to find one.

This chapter will help you find a good lawyer, know what to expect, and learn how you can help the whole process along.

How to Find the Right Lawyer for You

As a member of a blended family, you might have a number of loved ones with competing goals vying for your resources at your death. It's critical that you get your planning right to avoid family disputes. That's why I recommend you not try to do this on your own. You want advice from someone who is well-versed in estate planning for people in your situation. It doesn't mean you have to get the Rockefellers' family lawyer, but it probably does rule out your Uncle Larry's cousin's nephew who produces one will a year.

Where to Look

If you or your business has a current lawyer, ask the lawyer for a recommendation. Or if friends or colleagues have recently completed their estate plans, ask them. Finding someone who is trusted by others you know may point you in the right direction.

If those don't produce a good candidate, you'll have to do a little detective work. You want to make sure you get a lawyer who is licensed to practice in your state. If you've moved from a common law state to a community property state (more on that in Chapter 13), or vice versa, you want a lawyer who knows something about the other state's laws. Some resources are listed below.

RESOURCE
Where to find lawyers.
www.martindale.com. For decades, Martindale-Hubbell directories have been a standard reference that businesses and lawyers have used to find qualified lawyers. Now searchable online, Martindale allows you to find lawyers in your city who have identified trusts and estates as a practice area. Martindale also has a rating system for its lawyers. The ratings are based on other lawyers' assessments. Although lawyers pay to advertise in the Martindale listings, they can't buy a favorable rating—that has to come from their peers.

www.actec.org. Members of the American College of Trust and Estate Counsel (called Fellows) have a minimum of ten years of concentration in estate planning. Many have served in leadership positions in bar groups, and published and taught in the area of trusts and estates. Membership is by nomination only—a lawyer cannot apply for membership. To find members in your state, go to www.actec.org and click "Find an ACTEC Fellow."

www.nolo.com. The publisher of this book, Nolo, offers an attorney directory. Primarily suited for residents of larger, metropolitan areas, Nolo's website helps you find attorneys who identify themselves as trust and estate specialists. You'll find information not only on qualifications and experience, but also on how listed attorneys approach the practice of law.

State and local bar associations. You can search online to find your state or local bar association, which is a group of lawyers. Within a bar association, there are often committees or sections dedicated to specific practice areas like trusts and estates (sometimes called fiduciary law). Any of these may show lawyers in your area with trust and estate law listed as an area of interest. In states that offer attorney certification, you may be able to find a lawyer certified in trust and estate law.

Try to get two to three names, and call your first choice to set up a meeting.

How to Make Sure the Attorney Is Knowledgeable

Any licensed attorney in your state can claim to be able to write a will for you. There is no requirement, for example, that someone who mentions a proficiency in estate planning has actually done a certain amount of estate planning work or had special training.

How can you do your homework on your attorney? Use the resources mentioned above and the attorney's own website to check out the following:

- length of practice
- membership in professional associations (is the attorney a member of the attorney's state or local bar associations for estate planning, or any other associations dedicated to estate planning?)
- certification by the state in trusts and estates. Some states do certify lawyers as specialists in trusts and estates. Generally, certification requires passing an exam administered by the state.
- areas of concentration. Are trusts and estates featured on the attorney's website? Where is estate planning on the list? How many other areas are listed?
- writing or speaking on estate planning. Does the attorney lead workshops for attorneys or consumers in this area?

The First Meeting

One meeting will probably give you a good idea of whether or not this is someone you want to trust with important family matters. You're not just looking for qualifications; you're looking for personality as well. You want someone with whom you feel comfortable sharing some of your most personal information. You want someone you can feel open and honest with, because that's when you'll get the most out of your planning.

At the initial meeting, you'll discuss your goals and concerns and look at whether there seems to be a good fit for moving forward. The lawyer may ask you to bring certain documents (deeds or other records) with you; others use the initial meeting simply as a getting-to-know-one-another session, and assign homework to be completed before the next meeting.

You should also discuss fees and billing at the first meeting—so if the lawyer doesn't mention fees, ask. You need to know what you're getting into. (Billing is discussed in detail below.)

Should You Have to Pay for the Initial Meeting?

Some lawyers charge for the initial meeting, some don't. It may depend on custom in your area or just on the lawyer's philosophy. I don't charge for the first meeting if the client decides, for whatever reason, not to move forward. I think it's better for both of us to know that there are no strings attached to the first meeting—if it works for both of us, that's great. If not, all we've lost is our time. Find out your lawyer's practice in advance so you'll know what to anticipate. The lawyer also should let you know whether the lawyer intends to do all of the substantive work, or whether you can expect to see time spent by a more junior lawyer, paralegal, or staff member on your bill.

If you don't like the lawyer or feel the fit is wrong, now's the time to speak up before either of you spends any more time on this matter. As a lawyer, I recognize that different clients have different goals and like different things, so my feelings are not hurt if a potential client senses the client will be better served elsewhere.

Be polite but clear in letting the lawyer know if you're not interested in moving forward. You don't want the lawyer going off and doing a bunch of work—for which you get hit with a bill—when you weren't really interested and hadn't thought you'd hired the lawyer. Keep working down your list until you find one who's right for you.

You Are the Client

Your lawyer represents you in your estate planning. If your spouse agrees, your lawyer will represent both of you. However, unless your lawyer specifically consents in writing, your lawyer won't represent anyone else in this matter, including any of your children, grand-children, or other beneficiaries. Because of confidentiality rules, your lawyer can't share details with your children about your estate plan unless you consent ahead of time.

A lawyer's job is to work with the client to draw up the documents needed in the client's planning and to help make sure the client's wishes are respected. The lawyer is looking out for the client and the client's wishes, no one else. The lawyer wants to make sure each client is able to have an open and honest discussion about goals. That's why lawyers get uneasy when clients want to bring a child with them to listen in on the meeting. They don't want the client influenced by one child into doing something the client doesn't want to do, or something the other children are going to object to down the road. Lawyers look critically at a child who insists on participating, particularly if the child is slated to receive a larger share of the estate than his brothers and sisters. Lawyers don't want to get caught in the middle between siblings.

You should feel free to discuss your plans with your children and get their input between meetings with your lawyer. You don't really want to take them with you to the meetings. Your lawyer shouldn't be asked to give your children legal advice—they should get their own lawyer if necessary.

To make it absolutely clear who the client is, most lawyers send you an "engagement letter" when you make the hiring official. The letter also sets out other terms of your attorney-client relationship. (See "The Engagement Letter," below.)

How Lawyers Advise Couples

Commonly, married couples hire just one attorney to advise them on estate planning, and share information freely. But especially in second marriages, some couples decide that the process will be more fair—to the whole blended family—if the lawyer gives each spouse individual guidance and advice. And some couples go even further and hire separate lawyers—though this is unusual unless large amounts of assets are involved.

If your representation is joint, the lawyer will explain that there are no secrets between you and your spouse. In other words, although what you share with your lawyer for the purpose of seeking legal advice will be privileged as to the rest of the world (that is, the lawyer can't be compelled to divulge it), you can't share something with your lawyer and ask your lawyer not to share it with your spouse.

> **EXAMPLE:** Paula and Simon engage Coolidge as their lawyer and agree that he represents them jointly. Anything Paula or Simon shares with Coolidge as part of seeking legal advice is privileged and won't be shared with third parties. One day, Paula calls Coolidge and asks him to make a change to her draft will and keep it a secret from Simon. Coolidge cannot comply with Paula's request and may have to resign from further representation if Paula refuses to let him share the information with Simon.

Separate representation, which is much less common, means that your lawyer agrees to treat the information your spouse and you give the lawyer as confidential from each other. It's like you've each gone to a separate lawyer, only the separate lawyer is the same person (confusing, I know). If you give the lawyer confidential information, the lawyer won't share it with your spouse. You might want separate representation if there's some information you and your spouse have agreed not share with one another, like the size of a trust that a family member set up for one of you. Before agreeing to represent you separately, the lawyer will want to make sure that your interests don't conflict to such an extent that the lawyer can't represent both of you and still be fair to each.

> **EXAMPLE:** Patty and Ben engage Coolidge as their lawyer. They agree that he represents them separately. Anything Patty or Ben shares with Coolidge as part of seeking legal advice is privileged and won't be shared with the other spouse or third parties. Patty and Ben want the separate representation because Patty is the beneficiary of a large trust her grandfather set up. Her family has a history of being very reserved when it comes to financial matters, which Ben respects. Ben doesn't expect anything out of the trust. As long as Patty's and Ben's interests are not in conflict, the lawyer may agree to the separate representation.

If your and your spouse's interests are so divergent that the lawyer cannot represent both of you, the lawyer may recommend that each of you get your own lawyer.

> **EXAMPLE:** Phyllis and Herman, new in their second marriage, go to see an estate planning lawyer, Ron. They are looking at whether to amend the existing prenuptial agreement they negotiated heavily before they married. They have firm but friendly disagreements over what each should receive at death or divorce and how to divide the new house they're building. Phyllis wants to split everything equally; Herman wants each to keep separate accounts. Ron recommends they seek separate counsel so that each will have an advocate as they revisit their prenuptial agreement.

How Lawyers Bill

Abraham Lincoln's remark still holds true 150 years later: "A lawyer's time and advice is his stock and trade."

Lawyers don't sell a tangible product. Although you may have a pile of papers at the end, what the lawyer really provides is time, advice, and expertise. The value in what you're getting may not always be readily apparent to you. It's not like taking your car to the mechanic because it's making a funny noise and then getting it back running quietly. If the lawyer does his or her job right, you may never know, but your family will surely appreciate it.

You should expect to receive a letter or an agreement to sign that tells you what the lawyer is going to do, how the lawyer will bill you, and when you'll need to pay. No matter how your lawyer bills, you should request an estimate up front as to a likely range of fees so there won't be any surprises. Some states require a written fee agreement that specifies the charges you'll be expected to pay.

Most estate planning lawyers bill one of two ways: by quoting a flat fee or by the hour.

Flat Fee

A flat fee means the lawyer quotes you a fixed amount up front for what the work will cost. The quoted fee isn't absolute. If you change from the plan that you've initially set, the lawyer may charge you more. Some lawyers prefer to bill this way because it eliminates the "meter is running" anxiety clients often feel when working with a lawyer. And lawyers who have a lot of experience can usually gauge what's fair based on the time they'll most likely spend on a new client's estate plan.

Estate planning clients generally prefer flat fees—understandably, they want to know how much this is going to cost in advance. But a flat fee means the lawyer "loses" if the matter takes more time than anticipated. Many lawyers don't like to take that risk.

By the Hour

Billing by the hour means that the lawyer adds up all of the time spent on your matter and multiplies it by the lawyer's hourly rate. Hourly rates vary wildly across the country, from $150 per hour at the very low end in smaller communities to $400+ in major metropolitan areas. Billing by the hour is the most common form of billing. Most lawyers prefer it because no two estate plans are ever identical.

In hourly billing, the lawyer charges for all the time spent working on your file: writing letters, doing research, meeting with you, talking with you on the phone, talking with your advisers, talking about your file with the lawyer's colleagues and staff (some of whom may also bill you), drafting documents, and meeting with you to sign your documents. Everything is written down, and everything is billed. (Some lawyers even bill for the time they spend billing.)

Lawyers use timekeeping systems that capture the time spent. Depending on the system or the lawyer's policy, the smallest increment the lawyer may charge may be a tenth of an hour (six minutes) or as much as a quarter of an hour (15 minutes). If the lawyer spends ten minutes in a 15-minute system, it's rounded up to 15 minutes.

My firm's system collects time in six-minute increments, which is a tenth of an hour. If I'm billing by the hour, I usually charge a minimum of 12 minutes (two-tenths) for any telephone call, because by the time I've dropped what I was working on, take the call, make notes and give my assistant any instructions on what needs to happen based on the call, and then go back to the matter I was working on, it takes at least that long. If I don't write those calls down and charge for them, I end up with a full day spent working at the office and a lot of holes in my day that I don't get paid for. So if your lawyer bills by the hour, don't be surprised if every phone call you make shows up on the bill and lasts a bit longer than you thought it did. It may be the same for meetings, because the lawyer will take time to prepare before the meeting and then draw up an action plan afterward.

The Hybrid Approach

Some lawyers attempt to balance a client's wish for certainty with their own need to protect against being upside-down on a fixed-fee matter that takes longer than expected. They have adopted a hybrid approach. The lawyer quotes a flat fee for the part of the process that's easy to predict and control: preparing routine documents. But the lawyer charges an hourly rate for meetings, phone calls, and revising documents, the part of the process the lawyer can't control.

How Much Should It Cost?

Under any billing system, simple wills that don't contain any trusts or tax planning may cost less than $1,000 each for a husband and a wife. Complex wills and revocable trusts easily can run into the thousands of dollars, from $2,000–$4,000 per person and up. What you can expect to pay varies greatly from area to area, your particular needs, and the practitioner you choose.

When do you have to pay? Some lawyers want to get all of their money up front. Others ask for a retainer, which can be equal to the fee for all or a portion of the time they expect to spend. You may receive a monthly bill or just a final bill when you sign all of your documents.

The lawyer will send you a bill with a description of the work performed, the time spent, and the total amount due. You may get a lot of detail or the short phrase "For Services Rendered" and an amount. If you have any questions about a bill, don't be shy about asking. Your lawyer wants you to be satisfied with your experience so you'll refer friends and colleagues to your lawyer. Talking about it before you become emotional can often clear up any misunderstanding.

The Estate Planning Process

Each lawyer follows his or her own process, which the lawyer will discuss with you in advance. Generally, the process consists of:

- signing an engagement letter or fee agreement
- providing substantive information
- having follow-up meetings to answer questions and provide additional information
- getting and reviewing drafts of your documents
- finalizing your documents, and
- meeting to sign your documents.

The Engagement Letter

After the initial meeting, when you've decided to move ahead with your estate planning, your lawyer will likely send you a formal letter called an engagement letter or a fee contract. The engagement letter will set out what you're hiring the lawyer to do and how you will pay for it. It should state the lawyer's hourly rate or flat fee, tell you how often you'll receive bills, and explain how the retainer will be used, if that's part of the arrangement.

The letter will probably also mention who will be working on your estate planning: the lawyer you met with, any other lawyers at the firm, and any paralegals or legal assistants.

If your lawyer has agreed to represent both you and your spouse, there also will likely be language in there as to whether the lawyer represents you jointly or separately. You (and your spouse if the lawyer is representing both) will be asked to sign and return the letter, along with a retainer fee if the lawyer requests one.

Getting Started

After your initial consultation, you will likely have a few meetings with your lawyer to discuss ways to proceed, go over draft documents, or talk about issues that have come up. In your meetings, you should feel free to ask your lawyer any question you have about your proposed plan.

Pulling Together the Information You Need

To work with a lawyer in building a tailored estate plan, you need to gather a lot of financial and other information. Many lawyers use an estate planning questionnaire like the one in this book so that they'll have the information at hand to best advise clients. If you have this completed questionnaire in hand, you can get it to your lawyer in advance of your meeting, or use it as a resource to complete your lawyer's form.

The questionnaire will ask for basic information about you and your family, your assets and property, insurance and retirement benefits, and what your wishes are. Answering the questions completely and accurately gives your lawyer a good start for crafting a plan that is in your best interests. Your lawyer will use the information for insight about your goals and to recommend techniques that will work for you and your property.

> **EXAMPLE:** Judy and Bill hire Roscoe to be their lawyer. Roscoe asks for copies of their brokerage account statements. Bill is uncomfortable sharing this information and doesn't understand why Roscoe wants it. Roscoe explains that reviewing the state-ments will help him understand whether changes are needed in how the accounts are set up in order for the amounts in the accounts to pass how Judy and Bill wish. Roscoe assures Bill that the information in the statements will be kept in the highest confidence.

If you haven't yet, take a look at the questionnaire (in Appendix A) to see the type of information you'll be expected to have. Many lawyers will send you a list of what you need to bring to your initial meeting; by assembling it now, you'll be ahead of the game. It may take a little time to get it together. So start now and avoid getting slowed down later by a scavenger hunt for a piece of paper.

What to Take to Your First Meeting With a Lawyer

- Advance medical directives/living wills
- State or federal estate tax returns (IRS Form 706) filed on behalf of a deceased spouse or parent
- State or federal gift tax returns (IRS Form 709) you may have filed
- Bank account statements, including any POD ("payable on death") forms
- Brokerage statements for the most recent month and year-end statements from the last two years
- Community property agreements
- Deeds to your house and any other real estate you own
- Deferred compensation agreements
- Disability insurance policies
- Divorce/settlement agreements and decrees
- Life insurance policies (including beneficiary designations—usually part of application)
- Long-term care insurance policies
- Names and addresses for you, your children, stepchildren, parents, and siblings
- Powers of attorney (health care and financial)
- Prenuptial and postnuptial agreements
- Recommendations or plans from other estate planning attorneys
- Retirement plan statements
- Shareholders/operating/buy-sell/partnership agreements for any business in which you own an interest
- Trust account statements
- Trust agreements in which you or anyone in your family is a beneficiary or serves as trustee
- Wills.

> **TIP**
> **Getting organized early will save you money.** The more information you can gather and the sooner you do it, the less you'll spend on legal fees. Having information at hand means you'll be better able to respond in meetings with your lawyer and move things forward.

It may be hard to understand why the lawyer asks for some of this stuff. Don't worry, your lawyer is not trying to pry or judge you. The lawyer needs this information to advise you best and tailor your estate plan to your desires. To illustrate, when I'm reviewing a questionnaire and discussing it with a client, I'm looking for the following:

- Whether the estate is large enough so that federal or state estate tax may eventually be owed.
- Information about the blended family—how long the couple has been married, the children, and the age difference between spouses. This helps me begin to assess what techniques may be best for the couple to accomplish their desires.
- Whether the couple has ever lived in a community property state, which can affect their estate planning no matter where they live now.
- Clues to any special needs that require attention. Caught in the challenges of their particular situation, most people don't realize that substance abuse issues, children born outside marriage, or a child or a spouse who lacks expertise in financial affairs are extremely common.
- The couple's probate and nonprobate assets. As I've discussed, wills and trusts generally govern only the disposition of tangible, probate assets (houses, cars, and so on), not policies or accounts with beneficiary designations, such as life insurance policies or retirement accounts. I want people to realize early on that their beneficiary designations are an important part of their estate plan.
- What resources are available upon disability or death—and whether either spouse has disability or life insurance. For younger couples, an early disability can be devastating and is much more

258 ESTATE PLANNING FOR BLENDED FAMILIES

likely than a premature death. If I see an older couple worried about nursing home and assisted living costs, I talk to them about long-term care insurance.

- How assets are titled—whether most property is held separately or jointly, whether assets are held with right of survivorship (meaning the survivor inherits automatically), and whether there's a disparity in wealth between one spouse and the other.
- The circle of family and friends, where they live and their ages, to see who are the best candidates to serve as executors or trustees. Estates and trusts can't do their job without people (personal representatives, trustees) to carry out your wishes.

Documents

Based on your information and meetings, the lawyer will prepare draft documents and send them to you to review. Your lawyer may include a short letter explaining the documents. You'll want to read everything in advance of your next meeting with your lawyer. (No need to pay the lawyer for time you spend sitting in his or her office reading.)

When reviewing your documents, you should focus on the information that's specific to your goals and concerns, which you'll probably find in the front half to two-thirds of the document. First, look to make sure: your estate passes the way you intend. That means making sure that:

- your decisions regarding what your spouse and children receive are in there, as well as any bequests to charity or other loved ones
- your special mementos are included if you aren't using a separate list for them, and
- you've named the right people as executor of your estate and as trustee of any trusts and have appointed successors if any of these people cannot or choose not to serve.

You also need to understand what happens if:

- you die first
- your spouse dies first

- you and your spouse die simultaneously or within 90 days of each other, or
- a child or grandchild dies before you do.

For blended families, it can be especially important to take a look at a couple of issues to make sure they are covered in a way that suits your family situation. Standard, "boilerplate" clauses might not have the results you would want. So take a look at:

- **Payment of estate tax.** If you expect your estate will owe estate tax, how will taxes be paid and from which assets? In blended families, there's always the chance that a set of beneficiaries from one spouse gets their full inheritance, while the other set is left paying the taxes.
- **What happens in a catastrophe.** If everyone (you, spouse, children) died—highly unlikely, but maybe something you want to plan for—you want to make sure that your assets would be divided appropriately among the surviving family members, so that it's not one-side-takes-all.

And don't forget to do plain old proofreading, to make sure your beneficiaries' names are spelled correctly and that names are up-to-date based on marriage or divorce.

In any estate planning document, there's also going to be a lot of language that is not specific to your family's situation but is included because of state and federal law, and local practice. This is the boilerplate. Boilerplate is important—often, a lawyer will add new provisions in a form to avoid an undesirable result that happened to someone else the lawyer has read or heard about. Boilerplate may help qualify your trusts for tax-favored treatment. Boilerplate is difficult to read and understand. You can really put in a lot of effort and not get a lot of benefit if you spend most of your time trying to read the boilerplate rather than the stuff that's particular to you.

More Meetings

You might have one or more meetings to review the draft documents. Again, feel free to ask questions and make changes. You have a right to understand what you'll be signing. In my experience, the people who get the best results are the ones who spend the most time reviewing the documents, asking questions, and running various "what if" scenarios.

Signing the Documents

The big day arrives.

Each lawyer works from a different script. Normally, you'll be in a conference room with your lawyer and several witnesses. (I keep threatening to use the haunting organ music from *Phantom of the Opera* to set the mood, but so far I have yet to do so.) Your lawyer may ask you some questions to establish your mental capacity in front of the witnesses. You'll verify that these are your final documents and confirm that any changes made since the last draft are in there. And then, you'll sign. Some lawyers will ask you to sign every page of an important document; others have you initial the pages.

After you sign your primary document, one or more of the witnesses may leave, and you will finish up by signing any financial powers of attorney, health care advance directives, living wills, or health care powers of attorney.

And that's it. You and your lawyer will discuss how many copies you want—typically, your lawyer will keep one, you'll have the originals plus at least one copy, more if you wish to share with family members or a proposed trustee.

How to Help Your Lawyer (and Lower Your Bill)

If your lawyer bills by the hour, you can help reduce the cost of your planning, plus get a better result in a shorter period of time, by doing the following.

Be organized. Rather than handing your lawyer a shoebox of names, insurance policies, and deeds, have everything listed out neatly.

Be prepared. Read this book. Know up front what your intentions are about:

- how you want to divide your estate
- whether you wish to be buried or cremated, and
- end-of-life decisions.

Keep it moving. Agree on a schedule with your lawyer as to when you'd like to have your planning completed and stick with it. I meet with a lot of people every month. It's hard to keep up with everyone. It's much harder when I meet with someone, then don't hear from them for a couple of months, then we meet again, then it's another couple of months. When there's a lot of stopping and starting, there's a lot of file review to get back up to speed on things, which the client will have to pay for if the lawyer is billing by the hour.

Be open to your lawyer's recommendations. Based on this book, you may have an idea of what you would like to do and the tools you would like to us. (And if you do, you'll be way ahead of 90% of all clients.) Still, based on your situation or the laws of your state, your lawyer may have other ideas. Keep an open mind when talking with your lawyer, who will be able to help you better if you are willing to discuss alternatives to address your goals.

Share your personal information. Even if it's painful, you need to let your lawyer know about children out of wedlock, children with addiction issues, and other family matters that can have a big impact on your estate planning issues. Your lawyer needs to know these things to give your estate plan the greatest chance for success. Many people who come to see me have something painful they'd rather not share. What they don't realize is that a lot of people have these issues. So, if there's something that makes your stomach flop at having to share, don't despair. Your lawyer is not going to judge you. Your lawyer is not going to tell anybody. Your lawyer will use the information solely to help with your planning.

Establish rapport with the lawyer's assistants. If your lawyer is hard to get in touch with or your documents are a little late in getting to you, assistants in the law firm office can be your best advocates. No one has ever seen their matter neglected by being too nice to the staff.

Deal with staff when possible. Most lawyers bill out time for paralegals at a rate that is one-third to one-half that of the lawyer's. (A paralegal or legal assistant is a nonlawyer who has had specific legal training.) Some also bill for administrative or secretarial assistance, at rates even less than a paralegal's. But many lawyers don't bill for administrative or secretarial time—it's included in their overhead, so their time is free to you. To save money, your goal is to get to the person who charges you the least but can help you. Many times this is the secretary or paralegal, so try them first. They can always put you in touch with the lawyer if necessary.

Other Members of the Team: Accountants and Financial Advisers

Lawyers work best when they're united with the rest of your financial team. If you have an accountant or a financial adviser, you'll get a better result if you'll let them all speak to one another. Normally, this happens after your first or second meeting with the lawyer. Describing your proposed plan with others who know your finances helps give your lawyer a complete picture. It also helps your other advisers know what you're planning.

Encourage your lawyer to ask your accountant to review your proposed plan. Your accountant may know something about your particular situation that you didn't know or remember to share with your lawyer.

> **EXAMPLE:** Bennie and Amanda are talking about selling a piece of rental property and putting the proceeds in an irrevocable trust. Joanna, their new lawyer advises them generally about capital gains tax that might be imposed on the sale. Joanna checks with the accountant to confirm the advice she's given and finds that Bennie and Amanda are subject to the alternative minimum tax, which would mean more tax would be due if they sold the rental property. The accountant's knowledge of Bennie's and Amanda's tax situation improves the advice Joanna is able to give them.

Similarly, your financial adviser can assist your lawyer by providing up-to-date information on your financial assets, making sure your accounts are titled appropriately, and confirming that any beneficiary designations you've made (for example, naming someone to inherit a retirement plan account or life insurance proceeds) are consistent with your plan. Your financial adviser will be able to help you change beneficiary designations to fit with your lawyer's recommendations.

Financial advisers can also run projections based on the assets they're managing for you. This can help your lawyer advise you regarding how much will be left to spread among your loved ones at your death, and let you know if estate tax (federal or state) might be a concern.

You may have to consent in writing before these advisers will share information with your lawyer. Check with them to make sure that you've authorized them to get your lawyer what your lawyer needs.

Keeping Your Plan Current

Where to Keep Your Important Documents..266

When to Update Your Plan 268

You Have a Child...268

Your Marital Status Changes..269

Tax Laws Change...269

Your Financial Condition Changes 270

Your Job or Nonprobate Assets Change..271

You Move to Another State...273

An Executor, Trustee, or Guardian Is No Longer the Best Choice.................275

You Change Your Mind..276

t's not enough for your estate plan to work on the day you sign all of the documents. You want it to work as of the date of your death. Hopefully, there will be many years for you to enjoy before your documents are ever needed. During that time, you may have life changes that affect your estate planning. Trusts you set up to protect your children while they were minors may no longer be needed. Your financial or marital status may change. You may move to a new state. You may just change your mind about what is best for your spouse or your children.

Think of your estate plan as a jar of pickled peaches in the pantry. It may last a long time before going bad, but it won't last forever. You want to take it out and look at it every once in a while to make sure that it's still good.

Where to Keep Your Important Documents

You won't be able to review your estate planning documents if you can't find them. You have a couple of choices where you can keep your estate planning documents once they're signed.

The safest place is a bank safe deposit box. But the critical part of using a safe deposit box is making sure your loved ones can get access to it soon after your death. This requires that (a) they're on the permitted access list at your bank and (b) they can find the key. If they're not on the list, but they have the key, in some states the bank may be able to open the box for the spouse or child solely for the purpose of looking for the original will. In other states, getting into the box to find the will requires going to court and getting an order. This is costly and may be time-consuming. You don't want to rely on that, so make sure the right people are on the list and that they know where the key is.

Another good option is keeping the documents at your home, ideally in a fireproof safe. This eliminates the need for a trip to the bank to open a safe deposit box. If you use a safe, make sure that your loved ones will be able to open it after your death.

Let two people know where your original documents are kept. Your lawyer also will keep a copy.

In this age of digital documents and scanning, don't decide to "go paperless" by scanning your estate planning documents into your computer and destroying the original signed will or trust. It's fine to keep a scanned copy on your computer, but it's no substitute for the signed original. Your loved ones are going to need to file your original will with the court. Filing a photocopy may require additional court filings, may increase the possibility of a challenge by disgruntled heirs, and adds unnecessary cost—all things you're trying to avoid by doing your planning in the first place.

> EXAMPLE: Betty's original will is lost. Her husband, Ray, submits a photocopy of the will to the probate court. Betty's daughter, Veronica, objects and claims that Betty revoked the will by destroying the original. Veronica argues the court should instead accept an earlier will of Betty's that was more generous to Veronica.

Some other tips: Keep stapled pages together, and don't write on your documents. Your goal should be doing nothing that will later give someone an opportunity to challenge your planning.

While you're at it, make sure you gather all of your important papers together to make the job easier for your executor. If you do a lot of stuff online, you'll want to write down your passwords and put them in a safe place.

RESOURCE

More advice on getting organized. If you're interested in additional information on how you can make life easier for yourself and your executor, Nolo publishes a couple of books you may want to check out:

- *The Executor's Guide: Settling a Loved One's Estate or Trust,* by Mary Randolph
- *Get It Together: Organize Your Records So Your Family Won't Have To,* by Melanie Cullen and Shae Irving.

When to Update Your Plan

You'll want to take a fresh look at your plan from time to time to make sure that it still reflects your wishes. Aim to do it every three to five years, more frequently if one of the following should happen:

- you have another child or a child predeceases you
- your marital status changes
- a significant tax law change affects you
- your financial condition changes dramatically (for better or worse)
- you change jobs, insurance policies, or benefits and you receive new policies or benefits for which you have to make beneficiary elections
- you move to a different state
- someone you named as executor, trustee, or guardian is no longer the best choice to serve, or
- you change your mind about what's best for your spouse or your children.

Now let's take a look at these big changes and what they might mean for your estate planning.

You Have a Child

The birth or adoption of a child can undo your will, although most modern wills and trusts avoid this result with language providing that the will survives. Still, your will or revocable living trust (RLT) may not reflect your current wishes or be the best vehicle under your new circumstances. At the very least, you'll want your will to name a guardian for the child and make some financial provisions.

Should you lose a child, then you'll want to look at your plan to make sure that the inheritance your child would have received passes to your other children, the child's spouse, or to your grandchildren of that child, based on your wishes. If you decide that the property should pass to the grandchildren, then you may need to revise your will or RLT to include a trust for the grandchildren to make sure the inheritance passes at the correct ages.

Your Marital Status Changes

If you become divorced or widowed, then you'll want to take a fresh, close look at your plan. Divorce may partially or completely revoke your will so your ex-spouse won't inherit under it. But in many states, divorce won't keep your ex-spouse from inheriting from you if you don't update your living trust or beneficiary designations (for life insurance policies or retirement plan funds, for example) you've signed. Should your spouse predecease you, you'll want to check your existing will or living trust and make appropriate revisions consistent with your wishes.

Tax Laws Change

In 2009, you can pass $3.5 million tax free of federal estate tax to anyone other than your spouse or a charity. In 2010, the annual exclusion amount is unlimited. In 2011, it reverts to $1 million. If Congress doesn't act before 2011, a lot of people who currently aren't subject to estate tax may find themselves with an estate tax problem. In other words, unless Congress acts, if you die in 2011 or after, your estate may owe a lot of tax that it wouldn't have if you had died in 2009 or 2010.

But the federal estate tax laws are likely to change in 2009, probably to set the exclusion amount at around the 2009 level, at least for a while. But no one knows with certainty what will happen. If your net worth is at or above about $1 million, keep an eye on federal and state estate taxes to see if changes affect you.

RESOURCE

Estate tax updates. To keep up with Congress, search "federal estate tax" at any of these websites:

- www.nolo.com
- The Wall Street Journal (http://online.wsj.com/public/us)
- www.kiplinger.com
- www.smartmoney.com.

Your Financial Condition Changes

As we're all somewhat painfully aware, economic conditions can change rapidly and unpredictably. Many couples have seen their finances swing drastically in the last year or so. Ordinarily, your estate plan should have enough flexibility to ride out the peaks and troughs of a financial cycle, and won't need to be revised. Should there be a lasting, systemic change to your finances after you adopt your plan, you'll want to look at whether your plan still works as you would wish.

Things to look out for include specific gifts of money that may no longer be appropriate given the size of your estate.

> EXAMPLE: Susannah's will leaves large cash gifts to her children from her first marriage, and everything else to her second husband, Michael. When she signed the will, she expected that Michael would inherit the bulk of her property. But now her assets are worth far less, and the cash gifts would leave him very little.

If your estate plan includes trusts, especially ones aimed at reducing estate tax, definitely take a look if your finances change. You might need to make adjustments to ensure that there will be enough money to establish some or all of them at your death as you originally wished.

> EXAMPLE: Micah's plan includes a credit shelter trust and a QTIP trust (discussed in Chapter 6). At the time Micah sets up his plan, his net worth is $6 million. If the applicable exclusion amount is $3.5 million at Micah's death, then $3.5 million would go into the credit shelter trust and $2.5 million into the QTIP trust.
>
> If Micah's net worth declines to $2 million, then the credit shelter trust will get the full $2 million, and the QTIP trust won't be used. Although credit shelter trusts and QTIP trusts both provide for surviving spouses, there are important differences. A QTIP trust must distribute income at least every year to the surviving spouse and can be used only for the surviving spouse during the surviving spouse's lifetime. A credit shelter trust doesn't have

to distribute income to the surviving spouse—all distributions are discretionary. Children also can request distributions from the trustee, which may reduce what's available for the surviving spouse. If Micah is relying on the QTIP trust to provide for his spouse, then he will want to revisit his plan.

Also, if you divided up your assets specifically in your will or RLT to leave different assets to different beneficiaries, you may want to revisit your plan from time to time to make sure that the division is still fair.

EXAMPLE: At the time he signed his will, Bernard divided his estate equally among his wife and two children. Bernard left his daughter a beach house, his son some rental property, and his wife his retirement account, all of which were worth about the same amount. Since then, the retirement account has increased in value, the beach house has gone down significantly, and the rental property has remained about the same. Bernard decides to redo his plan to fix the imbalance caused by the changes in market value.

Of course, your net worth could increase substantially because of business success, job promotions, or inheritances from your relatives. If that happens, then new planning opportunities may be right for you. Taxes that weren't a concern may now be an issue.

Your Job or Nonprobate Assets Change

As I've discussed throughout this book, your will or revocable living trust can do only so much. You must also title your nonprobate assets appropriately, and name beneficiaries for these assets, to ensure your plan remains coordinated.

Nonprobate assets (discussed in Chapter 6) consist of:

- property that you and another own where the title says the survivor takes all at the first person's death (joint tenancy with right of survivorship, tenancy by the entirety, or community property with right of survivorship)

- 401(k) and similar retirement plans
- Keogh and other retirement plans
- Individual Retirement Accounts
- life insurance policies
- annuities, and
- payable-on-death or transfer-on-death accounts.

It's your responsibility to make sure your beneficiary designations remain consistent with your estate plan and to change beneficiary designations where appropriate. Keep these beneficiary designations in mind as you make new investments, buy insurance, change jobs, or otherwise acquire additional nonprobate assets or retire old ones.

> **EXAMPLE:** Corey has a term life insurance policy with a death benefit of $1 million and other assets of $1 million. He wants to split his estate 50/50 between his children and his second wife, so he makes his children beneficiaries of the life insurance and leaves his wife everything else. Later, he buys a new $2 million life insurance policy to replace the existing one. Corey needs to make sure his new policy has the right beneficiary designations. He'll also want to take into account the additional $1 million benefit. If he leaves all of the life insurance to his children, they'll be getting twice as much as his wife, which may not be his intent.

To name or change beneficiaries, you'll need to comply with the requirements of the insurer or benefit provider. If you're designating someone other than your spouse to receive certain kinds of benefits, you'll need to get your spouse's consent to keep your spouse from being able to claim an interest in the proceeds after your death.

> **EXAMPLE:** Lacy's estate plan provides that at her death, her interest in her house will pass to her husband, and her retirement benefits will go to her children. Lacy gets a new job with new benefits. She needs to coordinate her beneficiary designations for the new retirement benefits—401(k) plan, employer-sponsored life insurance—with her estate plan. Lacy will need to get her

husband's consent if she wants to leave the 410(k) plan (and possibly the life insurance) to her children, rather than to him.

You Move to Another State

If you move from one state to another, have a lawyer licensed in your new state take a look at your plan. In blended families, state law is very important to your overall plan. The laws of the new state may grant your spouse rights to your home or an additional share of your estate regardless of what your documents say or what you intended.

Moving to or From a Community Property State

As discussed in Chapter 3, estate planning can be very different in community property and common-law property states. If you move from one kind of state to the other, you'll probably need to revise your estate plan.

Community Property States

The states listed below are community property states. All others are common law states.

Alaska*	Louisiana	Texas
Arizona	Nevada	Washington
California	New Mexico	Wisconsin
Idaho		

* In Alaska, couples can elect to treat their property as community property.

Moving from a community property state. If you move from a community property state, your new lawyer will need to know that property you acquired previously may be owned jointly by you and your spouse, even if it's only in one spouse's name. There may be tax advantages to keeping property together even though under the rules of your new state, additions to the property could now be separate.

Once community property, always community property, unless you and your spouse change it with a valid signed agreement. If you acquired community property while living in one state, that property stays community property even if you move to a non-community-property state. You look at the state of your residence when you acquired the property to determine its character.

> EXAMPLE: Neferti and Raj move from California (community property state) to Oklahoma (common law state). While in California, Neferti and Raj saved $200,000 from their jobs. Under California law, it's community property. It stays community property in Oklahoma, so it's still owned equally, even if $199,999 came from Neferti's salary and only $1 from Raj's. However, if Neferti and Raj continue to save (and don't mix their new savings or combine them with the old community property savings), the new savings will not be community property.

Moving to a community property state. If you move to a community property state during your marriage, you might find that your spouse is now a part owner of your salary, bonuses, or other property that previously was yours alone. This can restrict your ability to leave property to your children if you and your spouse don't enter into an agreement to keep the property separate.

Your tax adviser may also wish to elect to have some of your previously separate property treated as community property because of the favorable tax treatment of community property at death. (See Chapter 3.) If so, your attorney can prepare an agreement giving the property the treatment you wish.

Property you acquired when residing in a non-community-property state may take on some aspects of community property if you die a resident of a community property state. In that instance, your surviving spouse may be considered to have an ownership interest in half of that property as if you had acquired it while a resident of the community property state. (This is called quasi-community property.) Again, check with your legal adviser so your estate plan won't be only quasi-correct.

TIP

Keeping things separate takes work. If you want to keep each spouse's property separate in a community property state, you'll need to keep good records and be careful never to mix (commingle) assets. See Chapter 3.

Other State Law Differences

Your new state's law might differ substantially from the old one's. For example, the new state might give a surviving spouse very different rights, which could complicate matters in a blended family.

> EXAMPLE: Jimmy and Heather move from New York to Florida. As part of their estate plan, they have each decided to leave everything to their children from previous marriages, rather than to one another. They've said in their wills that their spouse should not receive anything at their death, and they've both signed documents waiving their right to claim any of the other's estate under New York law. Jimmy and Heather need to have their wills reviewed under Florida law to make sure that at the first spouse's death, the survivor can't get the house or make a claim against the other spouse's estate based on Florida law. Unlike New York, Florida law gives a surviving spouse rights to the family home in some circumstances no matter what the will says. So Florida law might override the plain language in their wills. A Florida attorney may recommend a postnuptial agreement, special trust, or other agreement to avoid an unintended result.

An Executor, Trustee, or Guardian Is No Longer the Best Choice

Many people name parents or other trusted relatives to serve as executors, trustees, or guardians. And that may work well for a time, while everyone is still relatively young and up to the task. But as these relatives age, they may be less able to take on the demands of the job you've given them in your will or trust. If you have named a parent as trustee, and you note that your parent's capacity for the job appears to be diminishing, you need to revise your documents to appoint a suitable successor. The same holds true if someone dies, or a bank or financial institution you've named goes out of business.

Friends or relatives you named as guardians for your children may no longer be the best choice after a few years have passed. People move, relationships change. Your children may become close to an aunt or uncle they didn't know well before, for example. Keep an eye on the individuals and companies you've named to make sure they're still the best candidates for the job.

You Change Your Mind

Sometimes, there isn't a dramatic change in your fortunes, the tax laws, or other external circumstances. You just change your mind.

Your children may become more responsible than you once thought. (Or less.) Or you saw something happen to a friend's family that you'd rather not repeat. Or you signed your will back when you and your spouse were newlyweds, and now you're happy old married people. Or you've just got a few more years under your belt.

Estate plans can contemplate a lot of things, but changing your mind is not one of them. Change your mind and you'll need to change your plan. It probably won't mean repeating the whole process to set up your plan, but a tinker here and there to get it right. If you don't sign a new will or trust or change an existing one, your change of mind won't be given effect.

• • • • • • • • •

I hope you've enjoyed your journey through this book. I've certainly enjoyed sharing it with you. I wish you the very best in your planning and your life.

Selected Glossary

For definitions of many more legal terms, see www.nolo.com or *Nolo's Plain-English Law Dictionary*.

Advance directive. A generic term to describe an individual's expression of wishes and treatment for medical care, including a designation of a representative to act on behalf of that person should the person be unable to speak for himself or herself. Advance directives may include a durable power of attorney for health care, a living will, or a document that combines both.

Annual exclusion gift. A gift that can be made without the donor incurring a federal gift tax. These gifts are called annual exclusion gifts, because there is a maximum amount (in 2009, $13,000 per year, or $26,000 for couples electing to split gifts) that may be given to any one person in a single year. Generally, these gifts may be made for any purpose to any person (in other words, the recipient can be anyone—he or she doesn't have to be a child or relative of the giver). Certain payments for tuition or training made to an educational organization or to any medical care provider aren't subject to the gift tax and don't count against the annual exclusion gift amount, but they must be made to a provider, rather than the individual who benefits from them.

Applicable exclusion amount. Generally, the amount remaining in an estate after payment of debts and expenses that may be transferred free of federal estate tax to someone other than one's spouse or a qualifying charity. You look at the applicable exclusion amount for the year of death to determine how large (or small) the amount is. For 2009, the applicable exclusion amount is $3.5 million. Unless the federal estate tax laws are changed, in 2010 the estate tax will be repealed, and there will be an unlimited applicable exclusion amount; in 2011 the tax will return with an applicable exclusion amount of $1 million.

Credit shelter trust. A trust created most typically for the primary benefit of a deceased person's children. However, credit shelter trust property may be used for the benefit of the surviving spouse. The primary purpose of a credit shelter trust is to use fully the decedent's applicable exclusion amount and so reduce overall estate tax. Credit shelter trusts are most commonly included as part of a will, rather than as a separate trust funded during the lifetime of the donor.

Durable power of attorney for health care. A document that authorizes another to make decisions regarding medical care if the person signing the power of attorney isn't capable of speaking for himself or herself.

Durable power of attorney for property management (durable financial power of attorney). A document that authorizes another to conduct financial transactions on behalf of the person signing the power of attorney. This may take effect immediately, or be structured to take effect only upon disability.

Estate equalization. The process of using lifetime transfers between spouses so that each spouse's estate contains a roughly equal amount of liquid and other assets. This process may include retitling real estate, securities accounts, or other deposit accounts in one spouse's name. This process is important if the couple is concerned about federal estate tax, because it lets the applicable exclusion amount of each spouse be used, regardless of which spouse passes first. From time to time, there have been discussions about making the applicable exclusion amount portable, which would allow the second-to-die spouse to use any unused applicable exclusion amount from the first-to-die spouse. If portability were made part of the estate tax code, then estate equalization would not be needed.

Estate tax. The federal tax that may be payable upon an individual's death for amounts left in excess of the applicable exclusion amount to someone other than a surviving spouse or a qualifying charity. If applicable, federal estate tax can be severe; the 2009 federal estate tax rate is 45%. Some states also impose estate tax, at a much lower rate.

Gift tax. A federal tax that may apply when someone makes a gift in excess of the annual exclusion gift amount. However, gift taxes generally do not apply when making a gift to a spouse or a qualifying charity. The giver, not the recipient, is primarily responsible for the payment of gift tax.

Irrevocable life insurance trust (ILIT). A trust established to hold one or more life insurance policies. If the trust is properly structured and maintained, life insurance benefits paid at death to the ILIT are not included in the deceased person's gross estate for federal estate tax purposes. Without an ILIT, policy proceeds payable to a deceased person's estate or to heirs are generally included in the deceased person's taxable estate. ILITs are usually created as stand-alone trusts during life, not as part of a will.

Last will and testament. A document that provides for the distribution of assets upon death, and names executors, guardians, and (in some cases) trustees. It also may contain one or more trusts (such as a credit shelter trust or QTIP trust) to provide for the surviving spouse and/or children.

Living will. A document that authorizes another to make certain end-of-life decisions regarding whether to continue life support, nutrition, and hydration if the person who signed the living will isn't capable of speaking for himself or herself.

Marital deduction. The unlimited deduction from the calculation of a taxable estate for amounts left to the surviving spouse. Certain requirements must be met: the spouse must receive a "qualifying interest" and must be a citizen of the United States. A qualifying interest is property transferred outright or placed in a trust that meets the technical requirements of IRC § 2523(e) or (f), such as a QTIP trust.

QTIP (Qualified Terminable Interest Property) trust. A trust for the primary benefit of the surviving spouse. Properly structured, the QTIP trust qualifies for the unlimited marital deduction so that, regardless of how much is placed in the trust, there would be no estate tax payable on that amount upon the death of the first spouse. QTIP trusts are commonly included as part of a will or created as a separate trust funded during the lifetime of the donor.

Revocable living trust (RLT). A stand-alone trust that provides for the distribution of assets upon death, and names guardians and trustees. It also may contain one or more trusts (such as a credit shelter trust or QTIP trust) to provide for the surviving spouse and/or children, and may provide for management of trust assets if the person setting up the trust becomes incapacitated.

Sample Estate Planning Questionnaire

Part 1. You and Your Family 282

    Prior Marriages 283

    Children 284

    Your Parents 288

    Brothers and Sisters 289

    Prior Service/Experience as Fiduciary or With Process 289

Part 2. Your, Yes, YOUR Goals 290

    Goals 290

    Concerns 291

    Failure of Beneficiaries 292

    Final Arrangements 292

Part 3. Financial Information 293

    Retirement Plans 294

    Life Insurance 294

    Real Estate 295

    Financial Summary 297

    For Business Owners 299

Part 4. Whom You Want to Put in Charge 300

Part 5. Information to Bring With You 302

Part 1. You and Your Family

Husband's name _____

Wife's name _____

Home address

_____

_____

_____

Business address

Husband	Wife
_____	_____
_____	_____
_____	_____
_____	_____

Preference for receiving correspondence

☐ at home   ☐ at husband's business   ☐ at wife's business

☐ other _____

_____

_____

Telephone numbers (check the number you prefer to be reached at)

	Husband	Wife
Work	☐ _____	☐ _____
Home	☐ _____	☐ _____
Mobile	☐ _____	☐ _____

email address (☐ check here if you do not wish to be contacted by email)

Husband	Wife
_____ @ _____	_____ @ _____

Date of current marriage _____

	Husband	Wife
U.S. citizen?	☐ yes ☐ no	☐ yes ☐ no
Number of years you've lived in this state	_____	_____
Other states you have lived in, including dates	_____	_____
	_____	_____
	_____	_____

Prior Marriages

	Husband	Wife
Previous spouse's name	_____	_____
Dates of marriage	_____	_____
Marriage ended in	☐ divorce ☐ death	☐ divorce ☐ death
Previous spouse's name	_____	_____
Dates of marriage	_____	_____
Marriage ended in	☐ divorce ☐ death	☐ divorce ☐ death
Previous spouse's name	_____	_____
Dates of marriage	_____	_____
Marriage ended in	☐ divorce ☐ death	☐ divorce ☐ death

Obligations (alimony, life insurance) to or from former spouse

	Husband	Wife
Child support payments	_____	_____
Child support received	_____	_____
Separate maintenance payments	_____	_____
Separate maintenance received	_____	_____
Life insurance	_____	_____
Other	_____	_____

Children

Children from previous relationships

[If either of you has more than two children, copy and add sheets as necessary]

	Husband	Wife
Name of child	_____	_____
Birthday	_____	_____
Occupation	_____	_____
Marital status	_____	_____
Spouse's name	_____	_____
Spouse's occupation	_____	_____
Address	_____	_____
	_____	_____
	_____	_____
Parents	_____	_____
	_____	_____
Is this child financially independent?	☐ yes ☐ no	☐ yes ☐ no
Is this child likely to develop a significant net worth apart from his inheritance?	☐ yes ☐ no	☐ yes ☐ no
Does this child have any special needs?	☐ yes ☐ no	☐ yes ☐ no
Rank child's emotional maturity by circling	1 2 3 4 5 low high	1 2 3 4 5 low high
Rank child's financial abilities by circling	1 2 3 4 5 low high	1 2 3 4 5 low high
Any other comments about this child	_____	_____
	_____	_____
	_____	_____

Children from previous relationships, cont'd.

	Husband	Wife
Name of child	_____	_____
Birthday	_____	_____
Occupation	_____	_____
Marital status	_____	_____
Spouse's name	_____	_____
Spouse's occupation	_____	_____
Address	_____	_____
	_____	_____
	_____	_____
Parents	_____	_____
	_____	_____

	Husband	Wife
Is this child financially independent?	☐ yes ☐ no	☐ yes ☐ no
Is this child likely to develop a significant net worth apart from his inheritance?	☐ yes ☐ no	☐ yes ☐ no
Does this child have any special needs?	☐ yes ☐ no	☐ yes ☐ no
Rank child's emotional maturity by circling	1 2 3 4 5 low high	1 2 3 4 5 low high
Rank child's financial abilities by circling	1 2 3 4 5 low high	1 2 3 4 5 low high
Any other comments about this child	_____	_____
	_____	_____
	_____	_____
	_____	_____

Children from current relationship
[If you have more than two children, copy and add sheets as necessary]

	Child	Child
Name of child	_____	_____
Birthday	_____	_____
Occupation	_____	_____
Marital status	_____	_____
Spouse's name	_____	_____
Spouse's occupation	_____	_____
Address	_____	_____
	_____	_____
	_____	_____
Parents	_____	_____
	_____	_____

Is this child financially independent?	☐ yes ☐ no	☐ yes ☐ no
Is this child likely to develop a significant net worth apart from his inheritance?	☐ yes ☐ no	☐ yes ☐ no
Does this child have any special needs?	☐ yes ☐ no	☐ yes ☐ no
Rank child's emotional maturity by circling	1　2　3　4　5 low　　　　high	1　2　3　4　5 low　　　　high
Rank child's financial abilities by circling	1　2　3　4　5 low　　　　high	1　2　3　4　5 low　　　　high
Any other comments about this child	_____	_____
	_____	_____
	_____	_____

Are additional children likely from your current marriage? ☐ yes ☐ no

Grandchildren

[If you have more than three grandchildren, copy and add sheets as necessary]

	Husband	Wife
Name of child	_____	_____
Age	_____	_____
Names of parents	_____	_____
	_____	_____
Address	_____	_____
	_____	_____
	_____	_____
Name of child	_____	_____
Age	_____	_____
Names of parents	_____	_____
	_____	_____
Address	_____	_____
	_____	_____
	_____	_____
Name of child	_____	_____
Age	_____	_____
Names of parents	_____	_____
	_____	_____
Address	_____	_____
	_____	_____
	_____	_____

Do you have any deceased children with surviving children? ☐ yes ☐ no   ☐ yes ☐ no

If yes:

Date of death _____ _____

Does the child have living grandchildren? ☐ yes ☐ no   ☐ yes ☐ no

Your Parents

Husband

	Father	Mother
Name		
Birthday		
Occupation		
Living or deceased	☐ living ☐ deceased	☐ living ☐ deceased
If deceased,		
Date of death		
Cause of death		
Spouse's name		
Address		

Do you expect to receive a significant inheritance from this parent? ☐ yes ☐ no   ☐ yes ☐ no

Wife

	Father	Mother
Name		
Birthday		
Occupation		
Living or deceased	☐ living ☐ deceased	☐ yes ☐ no
If deceased,		
Date of death		
Cause of death		
Spouse's name		
Address		

Do you expect to receive a significant inheritance from this parent? ☐ yes ☐ no   ☐ yes ☐ no

Brothers and Sisters

Husband

	Sibling No. 1	Sibling No. 2
Name		
Occupation		
Marital status		
Spouse's name		
Spouse's occupation		
Address		

Wife

	Sibling No. 1	Sibling No. 2
Name		
Occupation		
Marital status		
Spouse's name		
Spouse's occupation		
Address		

Prior Service/Experience as Fiduciary or With Process

Have you ever served as an executor or trustee?   ☐ yes ☐ no

If you have had a close member of your family die, is there something from your experience with the last illness that you'd like to address in your planning (as in a living will or advance directive)? _____

_____

_____

What was your experience either serving as the executor or trustee or dealing with the executor or trustee?   ☐ positive ☐ negative ☐ neutral

If there were problems in that experience you would like to avoid, please explain.

_____

Part 2. Your, Yes, YOUR Goals

Goals

Check the five goals that resonate most with you as what you'd like to accomplish with your estate planning.

Husband	Wife	
☐	☐	Providing for your spouse at your death
☐	☐	Providing for your spouse if you become disabled
☐	☐	Providing for children from your current relationship
☐	☐	Providing for children from a previous relationship
☐	☐	Providing for stepchildren
☐	☐	Providing for grandchildren
☐	☐	Protecting children from losing their inheritance if the surviving spouse remarries
☐	☐	Ensuring a child won't lose their inheritance in divorce
☐	☐	Providing a college education for your children
☐	☐	Being fair to your spouse, children, and stepchildren in the division of your estate
☐	☐	Keeping property, art, jewelry, or mementos you've inherited in the family
☐	☐	Keeping a business in the family
☐	☐	Minimizing estate tax
☐	☐	Providing for a child with special needs
☐	☐	Providing for children in a manner that avoids "too much/too soon" and gives each child the incentive to get an education and establish a career
☐	☐	Providing for charity
☐	☐	Avoiding probate
☐	☐	Other: _____
☐	☐	Other: _____
☐	☐	Other: _____

Now, rank the ones you've checked, listing from most important to you to least important (try to avoid ties, but in case you truly can't prefer one to another, it's okay to put them on the same line).

	Husband	Wife
1.	_____	_____
2.	_____	_____
3.	_____	_____
4.	_____	_____
5.	_____	_____

Concerns

Check the five things that you are most trying to AVOID or that you are most concerned about with your estate planning.

Husband	Wife	
☐	☐	Your assets going to someone other than your children
☐	☐	Assets coming under the control of an ex-spouse
☐	☐	Assets coming under the control of a stepchild instead of your children
☐	☐	Assets winding up in the hands of a new spouse should your spouse survive you and remarry
☐	☐	Not having enough money to meet everyone's needs
☐	☐	Estate taxes
☐	☐	Putting assets in the hands of someone who lacks the financial expertise or maturity to handle them properly
☐	☐	Losing control of your assets during your life
☐	☐	Children losing their inheritance through their own divorce or to creditors
☐	☐	Disputes among your loved ones
☐	☐	Depletion of your estate because of nursing home costs
☐	☐	Other: _____
☐	☐	Other: _____
☐	☐	Other: _____

Now, rank the ones you've checked, listing from most important to least important (again, try to avoid ties, but if you truly can't prefer one to another, it's okay to put them on the same line).

	Husband	Wife
1.	_____	_____
2.	_____	_____
3.	_____	_____
4.	_____	_____
5.	_____	_____

Failure of Beneficiaries

If you, your spouse, and your children were all to perish, whom would you like to receive your assets?

_____

Final Arrangements

	Husband	Wife
How would you like your assets divided upon the death of the second spouse?	☐ Divide among my children/my spouse's children ☐ All of my assets to my children ☐ _____	☐ Divide among my children/my spouse's children ☐ All of my assets to my children ☐ _____
Do you wish to be buried or cremated?	☐ Buried ☐ Cremated	☐ Buried ☐ Cremated
Have you made funeral, burial, or other arrangements?	☐ yes ☐ no	☐ yes ☐ no
If yes, Name of company	_____	_____
Location (city, state)	_____	_____

Part 3. Financial Information

Husband's checking accounts

Name(s) on account _____

Location of account _____

_____ Balance _____

Name(s) on account _____

Location of account _____

_____ Balance _____

Husband's saving accounts

Name(s) on account _____

Location of account _____

_____ Balance _____

Name(s) on account _____

Location of account _____

_____ Balance _____

Wife's checking accounts

Name(s) on account _____

Location of account _____

_____ Balance _____

Name(s) on account _____

Location of account _____

_____ Balance _____

Wife's saving accounts

Name(s) on account _____

Location of account _____

_____ Balance _____

Name(s) on account _____

Location/type of account _____

_____ Balance _____

	Husband	Wife
Do you have a safe deposit box?	☐ yes ☐ no	☐ yes ☐ no
If so,	_____	_____
Who is on the access list?	_____	_____
Where is the key?	_____	_____

Retirement Plans (current balances)

	Husband	Wife
Name of employer	_____	_____
Employer-provided retirement plans		
Profit sharing	_____	_____
401(k)	_____	_____
Other	_____	_____
IRA	_____	_____
Other	_____	_____

Life Insurance

	Husband	Wife
Amount	_____	_____
Insured	_____	_____
Owner of policy	_____	_____
Primary beneficiary	_____	_____
Contingent beneficiary	_____	_____
Date purchased	_____	_____
Type of policy	☐ term ☐ universal ☐ whole life ☐ _____	☐ term ☐ universal ☐ whole life ☐ _____
If this is a term policy, how many more years are left on it?	_____	_____
Is this an employer-sponsored insurance plan?	☐ yes ☐ no	☐ yes ☐ no
Other Insurance (amount)	_____	_____

Disability or long-term care insurance policy (nursing home assistance policy)

Policy number _____ _____

Carrier _____ _____

Expected benefits _____ _____

Premiums _____ _____

Real Estate

Real Estate held as husband's separate property

Location _____

Title held as _____

Purchase price _____ Market value _____

Debt on property _____ Equity (value less debt) _____

Location _____

Title held as _____

Purchase price _____ Market value _____

Debt on property _____ Equity (value less debt) _____

Location _____

Title held as _____

Purchase price _____ Market value _____

Debt on property _____ Equity (value less debt) _____

Real Estate held as wife's separate property

Location _____

Title held as _____

Purchase price _____ Market value _____

Debt on property _____ Equity (value less debt) _____

Location _____

Title held as _____

Purchase price _____ Market value _____

Debt on property _____ Equity (value less debt) _____

Location _____

Title held as _____

Purchase price _____ Market value _____

Debt on property _____ Equity (value less debt) _____

Real Estate held as joint separate property

Location _____

Title held as _____

Purchase price _____ Market value _____

Debt on property _____ Equity (value less debt) _____

Location _____

Title held as _____

Purchase price _____ Market value _____

Debt on property _____ Equity (value less debt) _____

Location _____

Title held as _____

Purchase price _____ Market value _____

Debt on property _____ Equity (value less debt) _____

Financial Summary

	Husband	Wife	Joint Property
House	$_____	$_____	$_____
Vacation house	_____	_____	_____
Other real property	_____	_____	_____
Marketable securities [1]	_____	_____	_____
Business ownership	_____	_____	_____
Interests	_____	_____	_____
Checking accounts	_____	_____	_____
Savings accounts	_____	_____	_____
CDs	_____	_____	_____
Car 1	_____	_____	_____
Car 2	_____	_____	_____
Boats	_____	_____	_____
Other toys	_____	_____	_____
Jewelry [2]	_____	_____	_____
Collections	_____	_____	_____
Other property	_____	_____	_____
Retirement plans	_____	_____	_____
Other	_____	_____	_____
_____	_____	_____	_____
Total Gross Estate	_____	_____	_____
Liabilities	_____	_____	_____
Mortgages	_____	_____	_____
Other debts	_____	_____	_____
Net estate	$_____	$_____	$_____

[1] Marketable securities are stocks and bonds.

[2] How much insurance do you have on your jewelry? _____

Members of husband's estate planning team

Lawyer _____

Accountant _____

Financial adviser _____

Broker (if different from adviser) _____

Insurance advisor/agent _____

Other _____

Members of wife's estate planning team

Lawyer _____

Accountant _____

Financial adviser _____

Broker (if different from adviser) _____

Insurance advisor/agent _____

Other _____

List any assets and beneficiaries of specific gifts you wish to make to individuals:

_____

_____

_____

_____

List assets and beneficiaries of any specific charitable gifts you wish to make:

_____

_____

_____

_____

Describe any significant health problems you or any of your children have:

_____

_____

_____

	Husband	Wife
Are you currently the beneficiary of any trust or estate?	☐ yes ☐ no	☐ yes ☐ no
How much, if any, do you anticipate inheriting in the near future?	_____	_____
Have you ever created a trust, except as part of a will?	☐ yes ☐ no	☐ yes ☐ no
Have you previously signed a living will?*	☐ yes ☐ no	☐ yes ☐ no
Have you previously signed a health care power of attorney?	☐ yes ☐ no	☐ yes ☐ no
Have you previously signed a financial power of attorney?	☐ yes ☐ no	☐ yes ☐ no
Have you ever filed a state or federal gift tax return?	☐ yes ☐ no	☐ yes ☐ no
Do you have a prenuptial or postnuptial agreement?	☐ yes ☐ no	☐ yes ☐ no
Have you ever executed a community property agreement?	☐ yes ☐ no	☐ yes ☐ no

* A living will is an advance directive in which you state what you would like to have happen upon a terminal disease or coma.

For Business Owners

	Husband	Wife
Business name	_____	_____
Address	_____	_____
	_____	_____
Type	☐ corporation ☐ LLC ☐ limited partnership ☐ general partnership ☐ sole proprietorship	☐ corporation ☐ LLC ☐ limited partnership ☐ general partnership ☐ sole proprietorship
Approximate value of business	_____	_____
Percentage ownership	_____	_____
Percentage ownership by immediate family members	_____	_____

Part 4. Whom You Want to Put in Charge

Personal Representative/Executor (manages the probate of your will, the division of your estate, and the settlement of your estate)

	Husband	Wife
1st Choice	_____	_____
Name	_____	_____
Address	_____	_____
	_____	_____
1st Alternate	_____	_____
Name	_____	_____
Address	_____	_____
	_____	_____
2nd Alternate	_____	_____
Name	_____	_____
Address	_____	_____
	_____	_____

Trustee (manages assets for the benefit of your loved ones)

	Husband	Wife
1st Choice	_____	_____
Name	_____	_____
Address	_____	_____
	_____	_____
1st Alternate	_____	_____
Name	_____	_____
Address	_____	_____
	_____	_____
2nd Alternate	_____	_____
Name	_____	_____
Address	_____	_____
	_____	_____

Guardians for your minor children (responsible for your minor children if something happens to both of that child's parents)

	Husband	Wife
1st Choice	_____	_____
Name	_____	_____
Address	_____	_____
	_____	_____
	_____	_____
Relationship	_____	_____
2nd Choice	_____	_____
Name	_____	_____
Address	_____	_____
	_____	_____
	_____	_____
Relationship	_____	_____
3rd Choice	_____	_____
Name	_____	_____
Address	_____	_____
	_____	_____
	_____	_____
Relationship	_____	_____

Part 5. Information to Bring With You

Please bring copies of the following:

- Advance directives/living wills
- Any estate tax returns (IRS Form 706) filed on behalf of a deceased spouse or parent
- Any gift tax returns (IRS Form 709) you have filed
- Community property agreements
- Current wills
- Deeds to your house and any other real estate you own
- Deferred compensation agreements
- Divorce/settlement agreements and decrees
- Disability insurance policies
- Health care or financial powers of attorney
- Life insurance policies (including beneficiary designations—usually part of application)
- Long-term care insurance policies
- Prenuptial or postnuptial agreements
- Previous recommendations from other estate planning attorneys
- Recent brokerage statements
- Shareholders/operating/buy-sell/partnership agreements for any business in which you own an interest
- Summary statements from each retirement plan
- Trust agreements in which you or your family has an interest or serves as trustee.

Sample Estate Plans

Pete and Cynthia: Young Couple of Modest Means 304

    Goals and Concerns..304

    The Plan 305

    Plan Highlights 307

Randy and Andrea: Grandparents Whose House

    Is Their Primary Asset 308

    Goals and Concerns..308

    The Plan 309

    Plan Highlights 313

Tom and Callie: Young Couple With Wealth 314

    Goals and Concerns... 315

    The Options... 315

    The Plan 316

    Plan Highlights 319

Jack and Lynn: Successful Couple With Age and Wealth Differences.......... 319

    Goals and Concerns... 319

    Factors to Consider.. 321

    Jack's Plan 322

    Lynn's Plan 326

    Coordinating the Plans Through a Community Property Agreement 326

    Plan Highlights 327

Pete and Cynthia: Young Couple of Modest Means

Pete and Cynthia are recently married. Pete, 33, has a nine-year-old son from a previous marriage and shares custody of him with his former wife. Cynthia, 26, has no children. Both have jobs with good benefits: Pete teaches at a local middle school, and Cynthia is an assistant principal in an elementary school. Neither has net worth over $100,000.

Their principal assets are:

- their home and its contents, valued at $150,000 in the current market, approximately equal to their outstanding mortgage and home equity loan (leaving them net equity of $0)
- $20,000 in retirement assets ($10,000 each), and
- about $3,000 in checking and savings accounts.

Other than the mortgage and credit card debt of approximately $7,000, neither has any significant liabilities. They don't expect their combined net worth to ever exceed $1 million.

Goals and Concerns

Pete and Cynthia have similar goals: provide for one another and any children they may have together. Pete also wishes to provide for his son from his previous marriage.

Pete is concerned about paying for his son's education if Pete were to die prematurely. Pete understands that his ex-wife would be his son's guardian, but doesn't want to leave her a large sum of money to care for their son. Pete also wants to help Cynthia stay in their home, realizing that it would be difficult for her to pay the mortgage and keep up the house without his income.

For similar reasons, Cynthia would like to make it possible for Pete to stay in the house should she predecease him.

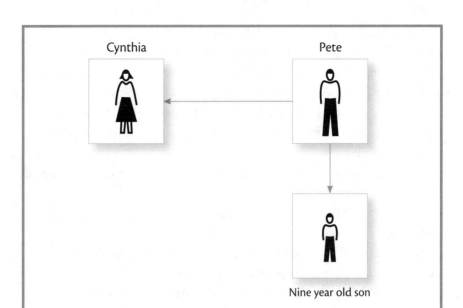

The Plan

Because of their age and incomes, a premature death or disability of either Cynthia or Pete could significantly strain the other spouse's resources. Both Pete and Cynthia need to look at ways to compensate for a loss in income.

Life and disability insurance. Pete and Cynthia meet with an insurance agent to discuss life and disability insurance options. The agent points out that the cheapest life insurance available is through their employers; however, the amount offered would only provide temporary assistance to the surviving spouse, and wouldn't allow the surviving spouse to stay in the house or pay for a child's education. The agent recommends that they buy more life insurance to supplement the employer-provided insurance. The agent shows them term and whole life insurance options (discussed in Chapter 6). They elect to go with term life insurance, which is the cheapest.

Pete buys $250,000 in life insurance coverage, naming Cynthia as beneficiary. This would provide enough funds to pay off the mortgage and still leave some money for Cynthia. To provide for his son's education and support should something happen to Pete, Pete buys an additional $100,000 term policy and names his brother as trustee to hold the benefit for Pete's son and spend them on Pete's son's education and support.

Cynthia chooses to purchase $250,000 in term life insurance only, naming Pete as beneficiary to enable him to pay off the house and have additional funds.

Cynthia and Pete agree to revisit their life insurance and plan should they have a child together.

To protect against a loss of income from disability, Pete and Cynthia obtain quotes from their insurance agent for a long-term disability policy. Because of the cost of individual coverage, Pete and Cynthia decide to participate in the group coverage offered by their employers. Again, should they have children together, they agree to revisit.

Retirement accounts. Because neither spouse has significant assets in a retirement account, each spouse agrees to name the other as beneficiary and to revisit this decision should they have children together.

The house. Each spouse decides to leave his or her interest to the other spouse at death. The surviving spouse can use the life insurance proceeds to pay off the mortgage or invest them carefully to provide funds to keep paying the mortgage over time.

Health Care Issues

Pete and Cynthia are probably too young to consider long-term care insurance. They both have health insurance through their employers. Pete and Cynthia decide to name one another as their primary health care representatives, and authorize the other to act on their behalf in case they're ever unable to speak for themselves. If the spouse is unable or unwilling to act, their advance directives name trusted family members as alternates.

Financial Issues

Pete and Cynthia sign powers of attorney giving the other the right to act on their behalf in the event of disability or incapacity.

At Pete's death (should he die first), the plan looks like this:

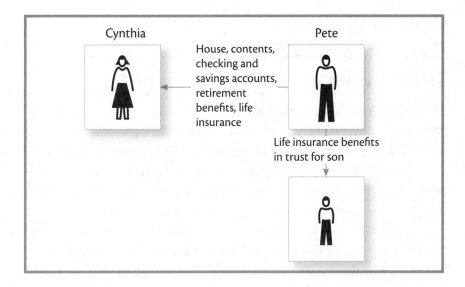

At Cynthia's death, the remainder of their estates would be distributed as she wishes.

Plan Highlights

- Each spouse signs a simple will leaving everything to the other spouse.
- The spouses purchase life insurance for one another to assist the surviving spouse in paying off debts and providing a small cushion.
- Pete purchases additional life insurance, which he leaves to a trust for his son.
- Each spouse names the other as executor under the will.
- Each spouse names the other spouse as primary beneficiary for retirement accounts.
- The spouses set up joint checking and saving accounts as joint accounts, so that the survivor will automatically own all the funds in the accounts when the first spouse dies.
- Each spouse signs an advance directive indicating his or her wishes regarding health care and end-of-life decisions.
- Each spouse signs a durable financial power of attorney granting the other spouse power over the couple's assets in the event of disability.
- Each spouse agrees to revisit the plan and the amount of insurance that will be needed in the event they have a child together.

Randy and Andrea: Grandparents Whose House Is Their Primary Asset

Randy and Andrea are in their mid-60s and live in a cozy, fully restored 1930s arts and crafts bungalow in the Grant Park neighborhood of Atlanta. Randy has three grown sons from a previous marriage; Andrea has a daughter who lives in South Carolina. The children are largely self-sufficient and get along well with their parents and stepparents. Neither Randy nor Andrea has support obligations to a previous spouse.

Randy worked as a graphic designer for a number of years before joining the full-time faculty of the Art Institute of Atlanta. Andrea is the office manager for a small veterinary practice. Before their marriage, they jointly bought and renovated their home, paying cash and exhausting most of their savings in the process.

Their principal assets are:
* their home and its contents, which together have a current value of approximately $500,000
* $200,000 in retirement assets ($100,000 each), and
* about $50,000 in various checking and savings accounts.

Neither has any significant liabilities. They don't expect their combined net worth to ever exceed $1 million.

Goals and Concerns

Randy's and Andrea's goals and concerns are very similar. Both wish the surviving spouse to enjoy living in their home as long as they wish, and to have their interests in the house pass to their children after the surviving spouse dies. They have some personal items (Randy's vintage motorcycle and collection of leather chaps; Andrea's jewelry and scrapbooking equipment) they would like to leave to their children. They want their children to receive what remains of their retirement plan assets following their death. Because the retirement plan assets are going to the children, Randy and Andrea would like the surviving spouse to receive the amounts in the checking and savings accounts.

Andrea wishes to keep the house for the time being if something happens to Randy; however, she sees the possibility of moving closer to her daughter and grandchildren if Randy were to pass before her.

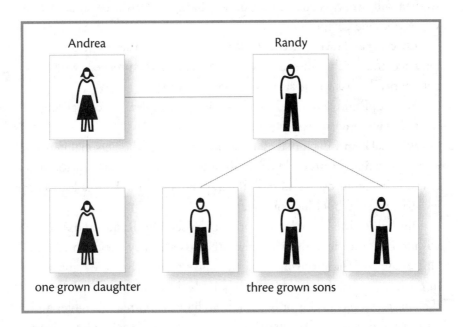

The Plan

To make sure their assets are distributed how they wish regardless of which spouse passes first, Randy and Andrea need to address both their probate and nonprobate assets. A will governs only the disposition of probate assets; nonprobate assets pass according to the beneficiary or survivor designation. (See Chapter 6.)

First, Randy and Andrea will want to ensure that the disposition of their nonprobate assets is consistent with the estate plan. This means they'll need to check the beneficiary designations on their life insurance policies, retirement plan assets, and any other nonprobate assets they may have, as well as check the way in which their checking and savings accounts are set up.

Retirement accounts. Because each spouse wants any remaining assets in these accounts passing to his or her children at death, the retirement accounts need to be set up with the children as the primary beneficiaries. For example, Randy will name his sons as primary beneficiaries of his account; Andrea will name her daughter as primary beneficiary of hers. Andrea will need to consent to Randy's change of 401(k) beneficiary and vice versa. (See Chapter 6.)

Checking and savings accounts. Randy and Andrea set these up as joint accounts with rights of survivorship, so that the proceeds will automatically pass to the surviving spouse at death.

Second, Randy and Andrea will each sign simple wills containing the following provisions:

Personal items. Each makes a specific bequest of the personal items each would like for his child or children to have at his death. In Randy's case it is his motorcycle and related paraphernalia, and Andrea leaves her jewelry and scrapbooking equipment.

The house. The home is their principal asset, and Randy and Andrea wish to treat it differently than their other assets. They decide to create a "life estate" for the survivor—that is, to give the survivor the right to live in the house until death. After both have died, each spouse's interest in the house will pass to his or her children: half to Andrea's daughter and half to Randy's sons. (Because Randy has three sons, each will receive a one-sixth interest in the home ($\frac{1}{2}$ x $\frac{1}{3}$ = $\frac{1}{6}$).)

To do this, the title to the house will need to be examined carefully to ensure that they own it as "tenants in common" and not in a way that ownership would automatically pass to the survivor (for example, as joint tenants with right of survivorship, tenancy by the entirety, or community property with right of survivorship). If the house is currently set up to pass by survivorship, Randy and Andrea will have to sign a new deed terminating the survivorship feature. This should be fairly simple.

Because Andrea might wish to move closer to her daughter and grandchildren, the life estate should authorize the surviving spouse to sell the home as long as the proceeds are invested in a new home or other property, in which case the surviving spouse's life estate would carry over to the new property. For example, let's say Andrea does sell the house and reinvests the proceeds in a new home outside Charleston so she can be closer to her daughter and grandchildren. At Andrea's death, Randy's children would receive an interest in the Charleston home comparable to the one they would have received in the Atlanta home had Andrea not sold it.

A life estate can cause tension between the person occupying it and the children waiting to inherit it, but Randy and Andrea know that their children get along well with their stepparent and aren't worried about conflict. They decide to let the survivor use the funds from the checking and savings accounts for insurance, property taxes, maintenance, and upkeep.

A life estate doesn't work in all situations, but it may be the best alternative for Randy and Andrea because:

- all the stepchildren get along well with their stepparents
- there's no mortgage on the house
- the surviving spouse will need the house
- the house is the primary asset in the estate
- the spouses are already in their 60s, so probably the life estate, once it's created, will not last for too many years.

Life estates are discussed in Chapter 6.

Health Care Issues

Because they're in their mid-60s, Randy and Andrea are probably past the age at which long-term care insurance is affordable (see Chapter 6). They do have health insurance. Randy and Andrea decide to name one another as their primary health care representatives, and authorize the other to act on their behalf in case of they're unable to speak for themselves If the spouse is unable or unwilling to act, their advance directives name their children as alternates.

Financial Issues

Randy and Andrea sign powers of attorney giving the other the right to act on their behalf in the event of disability or incapacity.

At Randy's death (should he die first), the plan looks like this:

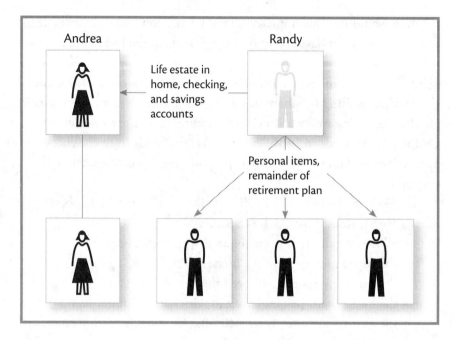

Then, at Andrea's death, the remainder of their estates would be distributed:

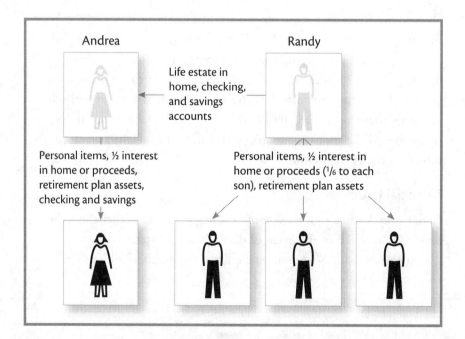

To minimize conflict at the second spouse's death and avoid shared ownership of the house among the children, the wills could authorize the executor to sell the home at the second spouse's death so that the proceeds would be divided equally between the two sets of children.

Plan Highlights

- Each spouse signs a simple will leaving personal items to his or her children.
- Each leaves a life estate in their house to the surviving spouse. At the second spouse's death, the children will receive equal shares of their parent's interest in the house or an equivalent cash payment once the house is sold.
- Each spouse names the other as executor under the will. As alternates, each spouse names an adult child.
- Each spouse names his child or children as primary beneficiary on their retirement accounts.
- The spouses set up joint checking and saving accounts as joint accounts, so that the survivor will automatically own all the funds in the accounts when the first spouse dies.
- Each spouse signs an advance directive indicating his or her wishes regarding health care and end-of-life decisions.
- Each spouse signs a durable financial power of attorney granting the other spouse power over the couple's assets in the event of disability.

Tom and Callie:
Young Couple With Wealth

Tom (44) and Callie (42) were in their late 30s when they began dating. Tom, a prominent real-estate developer, was previously married and has two sons, aged nine and seven. Callie, a successful account executive for a commercial builder, has a daughter, Amber (age five), from a previous marriage.

Tom's net worth is approximately $4 million; Callie's is approximately $1 million. Both anticipate that their incomes and net worth will continue to increase over the next five years.

Although Tom and Callie have no plans to have more children, they've talked about it and have decided to "let whatever happens, happen."

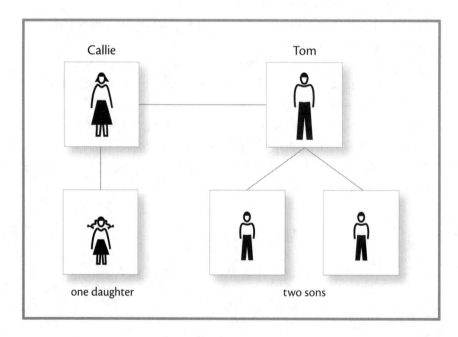

Goals and Concerns

Tom's goals are to provide for Callie and his two sons should something happen to him. Because of his wish to provide for his boys, Tom doesn't want to leave his entire estate outright to Callie. Although he is close to his stepdaughter, he feels that Callie and her ex-husband will adequately provide for his stepdaughter and does not wish to make separate provision for her. Should Tom and Callie have children, he wants to benefit their children. Tom would like to save on federal and state estate tax.

Callie's primary goal is to benefit Amber. Callie feels that Tom has more than enough to meet his needs if she were to pass away.

The Options

In meeting with his and Callie's attorney, Tom emphasizes his desire to benefit Callie and his sons. The attorney recommends that Tom put a portion of his estate into a credit shelter trust that could provide for Callie, Tom's sons, and any children Tom and Callie have together. A credit shelter trust can shield up to $3.5 million from federal estate tax, plus provide for a surviving spouse and children. So Tom could put up to $3.5 million of his $4 million estate into the trust.

From Callie's standpoint, the drawbacks to a credit shelter trust are that she would have to go to a trustee for funds and would have to vie, along with the other trust beneficiaries, for distributions. If Tom were to put the full $3.5 million in the trust, she would have $500,000 left that is dedicated to her and her needs.

The attorney gives Tom a couple of decisions to make:
- how much to put in the credit shelter trust, and
- whether to leave the balance of his estate outright or in a separate trust for Callie. Tom could use a marital trust, commonly known as a QTIP trust. (Credit shelter and QTIP trusts are discussed in Chapter 6.)

Using both trusts would give Tom the most control over his estate—at Callie's death, anything that remained in the trusts would go only to Tom's descendants, his sons and any children he has with Callie. If Tom leaves a portion of his estate outright to Callie, then she could decide out of that portion what to leave and to whom.

The Plan

After meeting with their attorney and discussing things further, Tom and Callie decide that they both want the surviving spouse, whoever it is, to inherit the house outright. Also, because Tom appreciates Callie's wish to not have all of Tom's assets left to her in trust, Tom decides to leave Callie an outright bequest of a substantial portion of his estate. Tom wants to make sure Callie receives at least $2 million outright at his death.

Tom provides in his will that the outright amount going to Callie will be $2 million, and that his credit shelter trust will be funded with whatever remains.

Because Tom does not need anything from Callie's estate should she predecease him, she concentrates her planning on her daughter. She decides to set up a trust for Amber in which all of her assets (except her interest in the family house, which would pass outright to Tom) would be held for Amber's benefit until she reaches age 25. At that time the trustee (Callie's sister) would begin to distribute trust assets to Amber in thirds, with the final distribution at age 35.

The house. Each spouse decides to leave his or her interest to the other spouse at death.

Retirement accounts. Because each spouse wants any remaining assets in these accounts passing to his or her children at death, the retirement accounts need to be set up with the children as the primary beneficiaries. For example, Tom will name his sons as primary beneficiaries of his account; Callie will name her daughter as primary beneficiary of hers. Callie will need to consent to Tom's change of 401(k) beneficiary and vice versa. (See Chapter 6.)

Checking and savings accounts. Tom and Callie set these up as joint accounts with rights of survivorship, so that the proceeds will automatically pass to the surviving spouse at death.

Health Care Issues

Because they're in their early 40s, Tom and Callie are a bit young to consider long-term care insurance. Both have health insurance through their employers. Tom and Callie decide to name one another as their primary health care representatives, and authorize the other to act on their behalf in case they're unable to speak for themselves. If the spouse is unable or unwilling to act, their advance directives name trusted family members as alternates.

Financial Issues

Tom and Callie sign powers of attorney giving the other the right to act on their behalf in the event of disability or incapacity.

At Tom's death (should he die first), the plan looks like this:

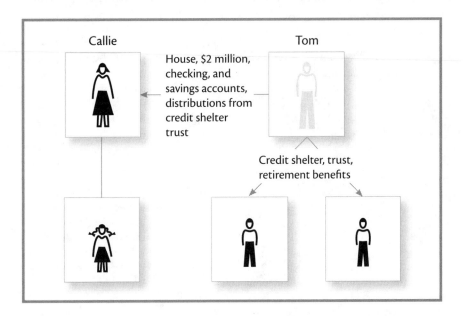

Ultimately, they sign their wills and leave the attorney's office, holding hands and making plans for a celebratory dinner.

Plan Highlights

- Tom signs a will leaving the house and $2 million outright to Callie, and the rest in a credit shelter trust for the benefit of Callie and his sons.
- Each spouse names the other as executor under the will.
- Each spouse names his or her children as primary beneficiary for retirement accounts and gets the other spouse's consent.
- The spouses set up joint checking and saving accounts as joint accounts, so that the survivor will automatically own all the funds in the accounts when the first spouse dies.
- Each spouse signs an advance directive indicating his or her wishes regarding health care and end-of-life decisions.
- Each spouse signs a durable financial power of attorney granting the other spouse power over the couple's assets in the event of disability.
- Each spouse agrees to revisit the plan in the event they have a child together.

Jack and Lynn: Successful Couple With Age and Wealth Differences

Jack, 46, is a successful cardiac surgeon in Santa Fe, New Mexico. He married his previous wife, Carol, during his fellowship at the University of Texas. Jack and Carol's divorce was bitter, and Jack still bristles when thinking of how much Carol received in the divorce settlement. Jack and Carol have two children, Jack, Jr. and Matthew, who are 11 and 13. Jack shares custody with Carol. He has ongoing support obligations to his children, but not to Carol, who directs an art gallery in Albuquerque.

Lynn, 28, is a registered nurse at a regional medical center. She has sole custody of her one child, Carter, age four, from a previous relationship. Lynn and Carter have had virtually no contact with the father since she started seeing Jack a couple of years ago. Lynn went to court and filed a petition for abandonment against Carter's father, which resulted in the termination of his parental rights.

Jack and Lynn have been married for eight months and are thinking about having children together. Jack would like Lynn to give up her job at the hospital and work at his office, at least until she has a baby.

Jack has a net worth of a little over $7 million, some of which is based on his earnings and investments before his marriage to Lynn, and some of which he inherited from his wealthy grandmother. Jack also has a $1 million life insurance policy for the benefit of his sons. Lynn has less than $100,000. They expect their joint net worth to increase based on the success of Jack's practice and the recovery in property values in the Santa Fe area.

Goals and Concerns

Jack's goals are to provide for Jack, Jr. and Matthew, as well as any children he may have with Lynn. His concerns include losing control of his assets should he and Lynn get divorced. Jack also doesn't want to pay his ex-wife, Carol, any more than he is required to under the divorce and wants to make sure anything he leaves his two sons does not come under her control.

Jack is concerned about leaving Lynn a large sum of money outright because he doesn't really trust her skills in handling money. (As a wedding gift, he paid off some credit card debt she owed.) He'd like for her to live comfortably, but wants his two boys to receive the bulk of his assets. Jack also is concerned about how his money will be managed if he should become disabled.

Lynn's goals are to provide for Carter and make sure he receives a college education. Lynn was the first of her family to go to college. (Carter's father attended one year of junior college on a basketball scholarship before dropping out.) She also wants to make sure that should something happen to Jack, she and Carter would have a place to live. Lynn feels that Jack doesn't trust her enough with money—she is proud of how she was able to support Carter and herself without a lot of assistance.

Lynn is excited about the opportunity to work more closely with her husband at his office, but is concerned about losing her autonomy and identity, not to mention the generous benefits offered by the hospital. Jack has assured Lynn she has nothing to worry about, and says he can't wait for the day she's at the office keeping an eye on things.

Neither Jack nor Lynn has any expectation of a significant inheritance from either family.

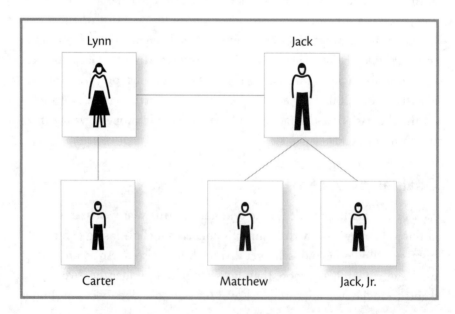

Factors to Consider

At first glance, Jack and Lynn would appear to be well-served by his leaving assets in standard credit shelter and QTIP trusts. As discussed in Chapter 6, that way, he can provide for Lynn during her life, while ensuring that his assets ultimately end up in the hands of his sons. However, some factors might make that plan less than optimal.

Jack's child support obligations. Jack has ongoing obligations to his two sons from his divorce. He needs a plan that incorporates those obligations while honoring to the extent possible his desire to avoid giving his ex-wife access to his sons' inheritances.

The age difference. Jack is 18 years older than Lynn. Lynn has a statistical life expectancy of 49 more years. If Jack's sons don't get the bulk of their inheritance until her death 49 years from now, Jack, Jr. would be 62, and Matthew would be 60. Both of them would have already bought homes, raised their families, paid for educations, and tried to maintain a standard of living comparable to their parents—without the benefit of a substantial part of their inheritance.

In a standard will or RLT incorporating credit shelter and QTIP trusts, the boys could receive some distributions of income and some need-based distributions of principal from the QTIP trust, but wouldn't receive most of their inheritance until Lynn's death. That would unnecessarily delay the sons' inheritance. Jack needs a strategy that gets money to his sons earlier, but out of the hands of Jack's ex-wife.

The wealth disparity. Jack and Lynn are fiscal unequals, which typically raises both emotional and financial issues. Already you can see some tension brewing: Jack is mildly critical of Lynn's money managing abilities; Lynn is somewhat defensive. This tension might increase if Lynn were to work full-time for Jack. (Chapter 7 discusses planning in this situation.)

Jack's estate would (under current tax law) be subject to federal estate tax; Lynn's would not. If Lynn dies first and has less than $100,000 in her name, most of her applicable exclusion amount of $3.5 million would go unused. On the other hand, if Jack could use Lynn's applicable exclusion amount, he'd be able to pay less tax and thus pass more down to his sons than he could without it.

Lynn's goal of college for her son. A standard plan for Jack wouldn't protect Carter and ensure his access to a college education, which is very important to Lynn.

New Mexico is a community property state. Before implementing any plan, the couple needs to review carefully with their attorney what is community and what is separate property. Each spouse will likely be deemed a co-owner of assets or income acquired or earned during the marriage. Jack's income before the marriage and his inheritance from his grandmother shouldn't be considered community property as long as he's careful to keep these funds separate during his marriage, but he doesn't want to take any chances. Jack fears his sons won't receive the inheritance he wishes if Lynn makes a successful claim against assets titled in Jack's name at his death. (Chapter 3 discusses community property issues.)

Jack's Plan

Here are the main features of the plan Jack decides on.

Irrevocable Life Insurance Trust

In his divorce settlement agreement, Jack agreed to maintain a $1 million life insurance policy he currently has for the benefit of his sons. If Jack simply names his two sons as beneficiaries of the policy, then after his death, each will get his portion of the proceeds outright as soon as he becomes an adult. Until then, the proceeds would be under Carol's control, which is not what Jack wants.

A better option would be to put the life insurance into an irrevocable life insurance trust (ILIT). That way, if something should happen to Jack, the proceeds from the policy won't automatically pass to his children or be under his ex-wife's control. The proceeds would be payable to the life insurance trust, which could hold the assets until the boys were of the proper age to receive them. Jack will want to check with his attorney, because he may need to get the divorce settlement agreement amended to provide for holding the life insurance in a trust.

There are also potential estate tax benefits. If Jack lives for at least three years after putting the insurance policy into the trust, his taxable estate won't be considered to include the life insurance proceeds, provided the ILIT is appropriately maintained. The ILIT allows those proceeds to escape estate tax at Jack's death.

If Jack is in good health and is insurable, he may wish to have the trustee buy additional life insurance in the name of the trust, to provide more cash to his sons at his death. This would be another way of making assets available to the sons sooner than if they had to wait for Lynn's death to receive the bulk of their inheritance. (See Chapter 6 for more about life insurance trusts.)

Lifetime QTIP Trust

How can the plan honor what appear to be competing objectives: give Lynn access to funds during her lifetime and fully use her applicable exclusion amount, to reduce overall estate tax?

A good option here is a lifetime QTIP trust. (These trusts are discussed in Chapter 6.) QTIP trusts can take effect at death (testamentary) or during life (lifetime). Either way, the assets qualify for the unlimited marital deduction, so no federal tax (gift or estate) need be paid when the trust is set up. There are a few wrinkles. A lifetime QTIP trust is normally irrevocable, so once Jack sets it up and signs over the assets into the trust, there's no turning back. Lynn will be entitled to income off of those assets for the rest of her life, even if she and Jack get divorced. (From time to time, Congress has discussed making the applicable exclusion amount portable, which would allow the second-to-die spouse to use any unused applicable exclusion amount from the first spouse's death. If portability is adopted, then Jack wouldn't need a lifetime QTIP to use Lynn's applicable exclusion amount. If he still wanted to use a QTIP trust, he could set it up in his will or RLT to take effect at his death—allowing him to change it if he and Lynn divorce.)

Assets in the QTIP will be deemed to be part of her estate, not Jack's, for estate tax purposes. The income to Lynn is a tradeoff for the ultimate benefit Jack's sons receive in not having the amount placed in the QTIP be reduced by a 45% federal estate tax. If Jack can take $3.5 million out of his estate that would have been taxed and put it into Lynn's estate, then he may be able to leave his sons up to an additional $1,575,000 (45% of $3.5 million) that otherwise would be going to the government.

A lifetime QTIP works as follows: Jack transfers assets to a trustee, who holds and invests those assets. During Lynn's lifetime, she receives income from the assets (and can request distributions of principal as needed) at least annually. At Lynn's death, her applicable exclusion amount (up to $3.5 million) would be used by the assets in the trust and any assets in her name. The assets in the trust can be held for Jack's benefit following Lynn's death, or can be held for the benefit of Jack's sons and any child he might have with Lynn.

At Jack's death, the trust assets would be held for the benefit of his children, with distribution at specified ages or earlier if needed. (If Jack had died before Lynn, then the same thing would have happened at Lynn's death.) Regardless of which spouse dies first, Lynn's applicable exclusion amount is fully used, and Jack's sons ultimately end up with the benefit of the assets undiminished by an estate tax at Jack's or Lynn's death.

So although Jack has lost some control over the assets going into the QTIP, his sons are getting a great benefit (more dollars free of estate tax). Lynn is happy and knows she will have income for the rest of her life regardless of what happens to Jack. Lynn also will get to enjoy the income stream from the assets and can request distributions of principal as needed even if she's not working outside of the home. The assets will be under professional management, so Jack won't have to worry about entrusting Lynn with a larger sum than he feels comfortable with.

Jack's Revocable Living Trust

Jack will need a will or revocable living trust (RLT) to address his remaining assets—the ones not transferred to the lifetime QTIP or the life insurance transferred to the ILIT. Jack is concerned about making sure his finances are managed appropriately should he suffer a disability, so Jack decides to use a revocable living trust (RLT) as his primary estate planning device. Should Jack become disabled, his RLT would name a professional trustee to manage his assets and make distributions for his and his family's benefit for the remainder of his life. Jack also will sign a simple pour-over will that transfers to the RLT at his death any probate assets that he hasn't previously transferred.

To keep his sons from inheriting too late in life, particularly because Lynn is otherwise well-provided for, a modified credit shelter trust in Jack's RLT could be used to avoid estate tax and to provide for principal distributions to his children at specified ages, regardless of whether Lynn is then living.

Probate and Nonprobate Assets

Jack needs to coordinate his probate and nonprobate assets. As to his nonprobate assets (chiefly, the retirement plan accounts) he'll want to think whether to designate Lynn as primary beneficiary and the children as contingent beneficiaries, or to name the children as primary beneficiaries. He'll also need to look at getting Lynn's consent to his naming his sons, which is required for some retirement plans and also because New Mexico may treat all or a portion of the retirement plans as community property.

Section 529 College Saving Plan for Carter

Carter, Lynn's son from a previous marriage, will continue to be Lynn's primary beneficiary. But to ensure his education is paid for, Jack could establish a Section 529 plan for Carter (he could even front-load it with $65,000 today without owing federal gift tax) and continue to fund the plan for Carter until there's enough for college. This would go a long way toward relieving Lynn's fears about what might happen to Carter should she or Jack be out of the picture. (Section 529 plans are discussed in Chapter 6.)

If Lynn has reservations about leaving her job at the hospital (or the workforce should she and Jack have children), Jack's agreement to help fund Carter's education will remove a big worry from her mind. Plus, this will be a nice legacy for Jack to give Carter, who will be raised in Jack's and Lynn's home.

In addition, once Jack implements the lifetime QTIP, Lynn will receive income from it for her lifetime, regardless of whether she works outside the home. These income distributions will be hers to do with as she pleases. She can spend them, or she can put a portion in savings for Carter to inherit eventually.

Lynn's Plan

Lynn needs to do some planning as well. First, she needs a will. In it, she'll name Carter as her primary beneficiary. Until Carter is of age, she can name Jack or another family member as the trustee of any assets left to Carter. Because Carter's biological father's rights have been terminated, Lynn will need to designate a guardian for Carter should something happen to her. That could be Jack, a family member, or someone else.

She'll also want to designate Carter as primary beneficiary of her big nonprobate asset, her retirement plan (she may wish to do this through a trust or the guardian she chooses for Carter while he's a minor). Lynn will want to get Jack's consent when she makes the change so that Jack won't have a claim against a portion of her retirement plan.

To leave more for Carter, Lynn could buy more life insurance for his benefit. Ideally, she would hold this insurance in the name of an irrevocable life insurance trust to keep it out of her taxable estate. Otherwise, there could be an estate tax payable at her death, particularly if the assets in the lifetime QTIP appreciate.

Coordinating the Plans Through a Community Property Agreement

Jack and Lynn don't want to have any misunderstandings about what is Jack's property, what is Lynn's, and what is the couple's joint property. To avoid potential disagreements, Jack and Lynn enter into a community property agreement prepared by their lawyer to specify what property is and will remain separate and what property is joint. Before Jack attempts to convey any joint property to one of his sons, he'll get Lynn's consent to the transfer. Similarly, if Lynn wishes to make a gift to Carter from the couple's joint assets, she'll get Jack's consent. All other property will be treated as the spouses have agreed in the community property agreement.

Health Care Issues

Because of his age and occupation, Jack may wish to look at long-term care insurance; Lynn is too young. Jack and Lynn decide to name one another as their primary health care representatives, and authorize the other to act on their behalf in case they're unable to speak for themselves. If the spouse is unable or unwilling to act, their advance directives name trusted family members as alternates.

Financial Issues

Jack and Lynn sign powers of attorney giving the other the right to act on their behalf in the event of disability or incapacity. Because Jack has an RLT that will take effect upon his disability, his power of attorney only allows his agent to transfer his assets into the RLT so his trustee can manage the assets for his benefit.

Plan Highlights

Jack:
- RLT with credit shelter trust to provide for his sons at specified ages
- simple will with pour-over provisions to transfer to RLT any probate assets in Jack's name at his death
- lifetime QTIP to provide for Lynn and partially fund her applicable exclusion amount
- irrevocable life insurance trust to provide for his sons
- section 529 Plan for Lynn's son, Carter, and
- long-term care insurance.

Lynn:
- will with trust for Lynn's son, Carter, and naming a guardian for Carter
- additional life insurance, ideally in an irrevocable life insurance trust for Carter, and
- retirement benefits to Carter (or to his guardian or a trust established for his benefit).

Both:
- Jack and Lynn sign a community property agreement designating which assets are joint and which are separate.
- The spouses set up joint checking and saving accounts as joint accounts, so that the survivor will automatically own all the funds in the accounts when the first spouse dies.
- Each spouse signs an advance directive indicating his or her wishes regarding health care and end-of-life decisions.
- Each spouse signs a durable financial power of attorney granting the other spouse power over the couple's assets in the event of disability.

Index

A

Accountant
  executor working with, 200, 205, 216
  including in estate planning team, 10, 262, 263
  keeping list of questions for, 12
  for tax advice, 71, 200, 201
  trustee working with, 201, 213, 216
Accounting firm, as executor or trustee, 203, 210
Addiction. *See* Substance abuse problems
Adoption of a child, 268
Advance directive, 221, 236–241, 260
Age difference. *See* May-December relationships
Agent, under durable power of attorney, 231
Age-related disability, 220–221
  advance directive for, 221, 236–241, 260
  financial power of attorney for, 105, 221, 231–234, 235, 260
  long-term care insurance for, 39, 227–230, 258, 327
  revocable living trust for, 234–235, 324–325, 327
Alzheimer's disease. *See* Dementia
Annual exclusion gifts, 88–90, 139, 140. *See also* Split gifts
Annuities, 99, 136, 272
Antiques, 217

Applicable exclusion amount, 74–75
  credit shelter trust and, 128, 132, 133
  in estate tax calculation, 82, 83, 84
  joint revocable trust and, 143, 161
  lifetime credit on taxable gifts and, 89–90
  lifetime QTIP trust and, 144–145, 323
  portable, 77, 323
  QTIP trust and, 128, 132, 133
  scheduled changes in, 74–75, 269
  with unequally wealthy spouses, 143, 158–161
Appraisal, of collectibles and memorabilia, 217
Appraisers, executor's work with, 200
Appreciation of assets, removing from estate
  with gifts, 90–91, 94
  with qualified personal residence trust, 148, 149
Art objects, 217
Ascertainable standard, for trust distributions, 209
Assets. *See* Property
Assisted living. *See* Long-term care insurance
Attorney. *See* Lawyer
Automobile insurance, of wealthier spouse, 163
Avoiding undesired outcomes. *See* Concerns in estate planning; Mistakes in estate planning

B

Bank
as executor, 211
executor working with, 200
as trustee, 203, 211–214
trustee working with, 201
Bank accounts
deciding on disposition of, 56, 57
executor's role with, 200
joint, with right of survivorship, 310, 328
Basis
carryover, 74, 80–82, 89
cash inheritance and, 82
of community property, 36–37
scheduled changes in law on, 81
stepped-up, 37, 74, 80–82
Beneficiaries
consistent with estate plan, 257, 263
of credit shelter trust, 127
deciding on, 37–38
determining portions for, 27, 39–45
executor's duties and, 200, 201
of nonprobate assets, 99–104, 271–273. *See also* Life insurance beneficiaries; Retirement plan beneficiary
of QPRT, 148
of QTIP trust, 127
surprised by estate plan, 24
young, 49–52
Bequests, outright, 109
Bequests in trust, 109
Birth of a child, and updating estate plan, 268
Blended families
defined, 12
estate planning goals common to, 98–99
estate planning mistakes of, 23–24, 72, 98
estate tax mistakes of, 72
tensions in, 26, 166, 203
Boilerplate, 259
Boutique fiduciary, 214
Brokerage accounts
deciding on disposition of, 56
See also Stock
Brokerage companies, trust companies related to, 212
Burial, 56, 110–111, 261, 292
Business. *See* Family business

C

Capital gains tax, 37, 80. *See also* Basis
Carryover basis, 74, 80–82
of gift, 89
Catastrophe scenario, 20, 259, 292
Change in financial condition, 270–271
Changing your estate plan, 266, 268–276
Changing your mind, 276
Charities
as beneficiaries, 45
gift tax and, 88
Children
adoption of, 268
birth of, 268
born outside marriage, 257, 261
communicating plans to, 29, 216
community property and, 32
consenting to parent's medical treatment, 237
death of, 268
in family business, 188–192
lawyer of parent and, 248–249

life insurance owned by, 145, 162
maturity level of, 49–51
from May-December relationship, 173
of older spouse, 166–167, 171–172
relationships with, 52–54, 154, 216
with substance abuse problems, 195, 196, 261
timing of inheritance, 49–51
unprepared to handle money or property, 23, 27
waiting to inherit until death of surviving spouse, 23, 27
See also Grandchildren; Minor children; Providing for children; Stepchildren
Child support agreements, 41, 42
Civil unions, 11. *See also* Same–sex couples
Codicil, 111
Coexecutors, 23, 215
Collectibles, 217
College savings plans, 39
Section 529, 91, 139, 140–141, 325
See also Education of children
Commingling, 36, 275
Common law states, 30–31
Communicating with children
about choice of executor, 216
about your plans, 29
Communicating with spouse
about estate plan, 24
about estate planning issues, 8, 56–65, 154–155
unequal wealth and, 154–155
Community property, 31–37
basic concept of, 31–32
commingled with separate property, 36, 275

defined, 33
difficulty of identifying, 34–35, 36
gifts of, 34
providing for children and, 32
with right of survivorship, 99, 271
tax advantages of, 36–37
Community property agreement, 33, 35, 36, 123, 274
sample estate plan with, 326–327, 328
Community property states, 31–37
couple that has ever lived in, 257
difficulty of classifying property in, 34–35, 36
family business and, 33–35
income on separate assets in, 34, 35–36
irrevocable life insurance trust in, 147
joint revocable trust in, 142
life insurance in, 138–139
list of, 30
moving to or from, 273–275
retirement plans in, 103
same-sex couples in, 33
in sample estate plan, 322, 325, 326–327
Computer passwords, 215, 267
Concerns in estate planning
assessing probabilities of, 20
broad categories of, 19–20
defined, 15
identifying and ranking, 7–8, 22, 291–292
as motivation for finishing, 67, 68
overview of, 14–17
raising with your attorney, 20, 22
reviewing and updating, 8, 23

Conflicts between children and
stepparent, 26, 28, 166–167
Conservation easement, 187
Conservator, 233. *See also* Guardian
Contract to make a will, 123
Control from beyond the grave, 52,
129
Corporate fiduciary, 211–214
Cost of estate planning
vs. cost of not planning, 67
lawyers' fees, 247, 251–253, 254
Cotrustees, 23, 215
Counseling, about unresolved
emotional issues, 66, 67
Creditors
claims against house after QPRT
termination, 149
credit shelter trust and, 133–134
executor's notification of, 200
Credit shelter trust, 117, 119, 121,
127–129, 131–135
change in financial condition and,
270–271
created in revocable living trust,
127, 134
created in will, 127, 135
problem with creditors and,
133–134
sample estate plan with, 325, 327
of wealthier spouse, 162–163
Cremation, 56, 110–111, 261, 292
Custodian, for transfers to minors,
180

D

Death of child, and updating estate
plan, 268
Death of multiple family members,
20, 259, 292

Death of spouse
children inheriting only after, 23,
27
timing relative to your death, 56
updating estate plan after, 269
Debts. *See* Creditors; Liabilities
Decanting statues, 196
Dementia, 220
advance directive and, 240
financial power of attorney and, 232
revocable living trust and, 235
See also Age-related disability
Disability
estate planning lawyer and,
257–258
financial power of attorney and,
221, 231–234, 235, 328
health care directives for, 236–241,
260
planning tools for, 221
premature vs. age-related, 220–221
revocable living trust and, 109, 113,
114, 116, 234–235, 324–325, 327
See also Age-related disability
Disability insurance, 39, 222–227
estate planning lawyer and,
257–258
need for, 222–223
for older persons, 226
paying premiums for, 225–226
in sample estate plan, young couple,
306
shopping for, 223–225
short-term, 224
Distant relative, as beneficiary, 45
Diversification of investments, 202
Divorce
updating estate plan after, 269
See also Ex-spouse

Divorce settlement
  effect on estate planning, 24, 41, 42
  requiring life insurance on
    ex-spouse, 101
  requiring life insurance on self,
    322–323
  unresolved emotions about, 66
Documents, estate planning
  copies for attorney and accountant,
    215
  keeping in safe place, 215, 266–267
Domestic partnerships, 11, 33. *See also*
  Same–sex couples
Donating body to science, 56
Drug abuse. *See* Substance abuse
  problems
Durable financial power of attorney,
  231–234. *See also* Financial power of
  attorney

E

Education of children
  credit shelter trust and, 127, 132,
    133
  direct payments to provider for,
    91–92, 141–142, 157, 158
  helping stepchildren, 156–157
  of May-December relationship, 173
  Section 529 college savings plans,
    91, 139, 140–141, 325
  with unequally wealthy spouses,
    156–157, 158, 325–326
Elderly persons. *See* Age-related
  disability
Elective share statues, 23–24, 31, 40,
  49, 275
Emotional maturity level, of young
  beneficiaries, 49–51

Emotional roadblocks to estate
  planning, 65–67
Emotions about unequal wealth,
  152–153, 154
Encroachments
  on credit shelter trust, 132
  on QTIP trust, 130
End-of-life decisions, 236, 240–241,
  261
Engagement letter, 249, 251, 254
Estate
  change in size of, 270–271
  deciding on division of, 27, 39–45
  enlarging and protecting, 39
  estimating value of, 29, 293–297
  See also Property
Estate plan
  finalizing, 10–11, 259–260
  reviewing periodically, 11, 266,
    268–276
  sample, grandparents with house,
    308–313
  sample, with age and wealth
    differences, 319–328
  sample, young couple of modest
    means, 304–307
  sample, young couple with wealth,
    314–318
  specific assets in, 46–49, 271
Estate planning
  comparing some tools for, 121
  defined, 6
  effective, 7, 260
  estate tax and importance of,
    73–74, 78–79
  failing to complete, 7, 65–68
  finding time for, 67–68
  four steps on path to, 7–11
  length of process, 67

mistakes in blended families,
23–24, 72, 98
motivation for completion of, 21
preparing for, 7–8
process of, 253–260
rewards of, 21
roadblocks in, 65–68
tensions in blended families and,
26, 166, 203
with unequal wealth. *See* Unequally
wealthy spouses
Estate planning lawyer. *See* Lawyer
Estate planning questionnaire. *See*
Questionnaire, estate planning
Estate tax, federal, 73–86
basic features of, 70–71
calculating, 82–84
community property and, 37
concerns about, 22
conservation easement and, 187
credit shelter trust and, 127, 128,
131, 162–163, 325
exclusion from. *See* Applicable
exclusion amount
gifts during life and, 67, 90–91,
92–94, 141–142
importance of planning and, 73–74,
78–79
irrevocable life insurance trust and,
146–147, 162, 322–323, 326
joint revocable trust and, 143
key concepts of, 74
lawyer's estate plan and, 259, 263
life insurance and, 172
lifetime credit for gift tax and,
89–90
lifetime QTIP trust and, 144,
323–324

magnitude of, 73
marital deduction, 74, 75–76, 77,
83, 129
mistakes blended families make, 72
with noncitizen spouse, 75
powers of appointment and, 194
QPRT and, 149
QTIP trust and, 127, 128, 129, 131
raising cash for, 136
same-sex couples and, 77
scheduled changes in, 74–75, 269
stepped-up basis vs. carryover basis
and, 37, 74, 80–82
trustee and, 209
with unequally wealthy spouses,
158–161, 162, 163
who pays, 85–86
Estate tax, state, 70, 87
possible changes in, 269
Executor
bank as, 211
as bearer of bad news, 24, 216
changing, 275–276
choice of, 23, 198–199, 203–204,
205–211, 215, 216, 300
collectibles or memorabilia and, 217
credit shelter trust and, 133, 135
discussing expectations with, 216
duties of, 198, 200–201
enriching himself, 67
as fiduciary, 199
financial power of attorney and,
233–234
heirlooms and, 205
helping, 215–216
lawyer as, 203, 211
lawyer's help in choosing, 258
leaving notes for, 215
named in will, 110

organizing your papers for, 267

pay for, 198, 215

probate and, 114, 115, 200

QTIP trust and, 130, 135

time span of job, 200, 203

trust company as, 211

Ex-spouse

as beneficiary, failing to remove, 23, 98, 101, 102, 269

concerns about assets being controlled by, 19, 22

mistakes giving control to, 23

termination of rights under will or trust, 101–102

unresolved emotions about, 66

See also Child support agreements; Divorce settlement

F

Family business, 188–193

advisers for succession planning, 189, 190

children's role in, 188–192

in community property states, 33–35

concerns about, 20

key employee of, 192–193

keys to planning for, 190

main planning alternatives for, 191–192

selling the business, 192

spouse's role in, 189–190

Farm, 185–188

Federal estate tax. *See* Estate tax, federal

Fiduciary, 199. *See also* Executor; Trustee

Fiduciary boutiques, 214

Financial adviser

executor working with, 200

including in estate planning team, 10, 263

keeping list of questions for, 12

trustee working with, 201

Financial power of attorney, 105, 221, 231–234

revocable living trust and, 235

in sample estate plan, 328

signing of, 260

stale, 234

Fireproof home safe, 215, 266

Flat fee, for legal services, 251, 253, 254

Forced share. *See* Elective share statues

Foreign citizen, as spouse, 75, 92, 140

401(k) plans

as nonprobate assets, 99, 100, 272

spouse's consent to name beneficiary, 30, 272–273

Friend

as beneficiary, 45

as executor or trustee, 203, 205–210

G

Gay couples. *See* Same-sex couples

Generation-skipping transfer tax, 70–71, 95–96

Gifts during life, 51, 67, 90–91, 139–142

annual exclusion gifts, 88–89, 139, 140

carryover basis of, 82

to children of older spouse, 172

of community property, 34

do not become community
  property, 33
estate tax calculation and, 83
of heirlooms, 177–178, 179, 181
to less wealthy spouse, 158,
  160–161
paying education and medical
  expenses, 91–92, 139, 141–142,
  157, 158
Section 529 plans and, 91, 139,
  140–141
Gift tax, federal, 87–92
  annual exclusion gifts, 88–89, 139,
    140
  basic features of, 70–71, 87–88, 92
  charities and, 88
  continuation in 2010, 92
  estate tax and, 90–91, 92–94,
    141–142
  exclusion for paying medical
    expenses, 91–92, 141–142, 158
  exclusion for paying tuition, 91–92,
    141–142, 157, 158
  lifetime credit, 89–90
  noncitizen spouse and, 92, 140
  planning opportunities with, 90–92
  QPRT and, 148
  Section 529 plan and, 91, 141
  split gifts and, 88, 91, 140, 141, 158
  with unequally wealthy spouses,
    158
Goals of estate planning
  common goals in blended families,
    98–99, 117
  control from beyond the grave, 52,
    129
  identifying and ranking, 7–8,
    17–19, 290–291
  as motivation, 21, 67, 68

overview of, 14–17
reviewing and updating, 8, 23
Grandchildren
  generation-skipping transfer tax
    and, 71, 95–96
  providing for, 99
  timing of inheritance, 49–52
Guardian for incapacitated person,
  233, 238, 240
Guardian for minor child, 111, 301
  born after estate plan, 268
  changing designation of, 268,
    275–276
  in sample estate plan, 326, 328

H

Health care directives, 236–241, 260
Health care information, federal law
  on, 239
Health care power of attorney, 221,
  236, 238, 239, 260
Health insurance, for unequally
  wealthy spouses, 161–162
Heirlooms, 176–181
  executor's handling of, 205
  given during life, 177–178, 179, 181
  issues related to, 56
  left to spouse, then children,
    178–179
  letting the recipients choose, 179,
    205
  making intentions known, 180–181
  making sure children get, 120
  tips for, 181
  See also Memorabilia
HIPAA, 239
Hourly billing, for legal services, 252,
  253, 254, 260, 261–262

House
annual upkeep costs of, 185
in division of assets, 41–42, 47, 48, 49
issues related to, 56
life estate for. *See* Life estate
in May-December relationship, 170, 173
QPRT for, 147–149
spouse's statutory right to, 24, 49, 275
in will, 111
See also Real estate; Vacation home
Household items. *See* Personal property
Husband. *See* Spouse

I

ILIT. *See* Irrevocable life insurance trust (ILIT)
Incapacity. *See* Disability
Incentive trusts, 52
Income tax
community property and, 36–37
conservation easement and, 187
on disability benefits, 225–226
state, deduction for 529 plan contributions, 141
See also Capital gains tax
Individual Retirement Accounts (IRAs), 99, 272
Inheritance taxes, state, 87
Insurance
rating organizations for, 225
on real estate inheritance, 185
of wealthier spouse, against third-party claims, 163

See also Disability insurance; Health insurance; Life insurance; Long-term care insurance
In terrorem clause, 112
Inter vivos trust. *See* Revocable living trust (RLT)
Investment adviser. *See* Financial adviser
Investments
diversification of, 202
new, beneficiary designations for, 272
trustee's job in relation to, 201–202, 210, 212, 213, 214
Irrevocable life insurance trust (ILIT), 105, 146–147, 162, 172
in sample estate plan, 322–323, 326, 328
Irrevocable trust
amending with court permission, 196
See also Lifetime QTIP trust

J

Job, change of, beneficiary designations and, 272–273
Joint bank accounts, 310, 328
Joint revocable trust, 108, 142–143, 161
Joint tenancy property, with right of survivorship, 99, 271
Joint will, 123–124

K

Keogh plans, 99, 272

L

Land trust, 187

Law firm, as executor or trustee, 203

Lawsuits over estates
  of children against stepparent, 26, 28
  emotional nature of, 206
  surprises as cause of, 29

Lawyer, 9–10, 243–263
  accountant's communication with, 262, 263
  assistants in office of, 247, 252, 254, 261–262
  billing by, 247, 251–253, 254
  checking qualifications of, 246
  children's input and, 248–249
  client's wishes and, 248–249
  confidentiality and, 248, 249–250, 255, 261
  for couple, 10, 248, 249–250, 254
  documents produced by, 258–260
  engagement letter from, 249, 251, 254
  estate planning process with, 253–260
  as executor or trustee, 203, 211
  executor working with, 200, 205, 216
  facilitating the process with, 260–262
  financial adviser's communication with, 263
  finding, 244–246
  first meeting with, 247–248, 255, 256
  information for, 255–258
  list of questions for, 12
  need for, 10, 244

  raising your concerns with, 20, 22
  recommendations provided by, 10, 68, 261
  resolving differences with help of, 65
  revealing family problems to, 216, 257, 261
  role of, 9–10
  signing documents prepared by, 11, 260
  trustee working with, 201, 216

Lesbian couples. *See* Same-sex couples

Letter to children, to be read after your death, 27

Liabilities, in estimating net worth, 29

Life estate, 117, 119, 124–127, 182–183
  in an heirloom, 179
  in building occupied by business, 190
  comparing features of, 121
  in sample estate plan, 310–311
  for younger spouse, 170

Life insurance, 136–139
  amount of, 138
  to balance farming inheritance, 186–187
  to benefit business owner's child, 192
  to benefit business owner's spouse, 189
  to benefit children of May-December relationship, 173
  to benefit children of older spouse, 172
  buying, 137–138
  in community property states, 138–139

consistency with overall plan,
48–49

divorce settlement requiring, 24,
322–323

estate planning lawyer and, 257

in estimating net worth, 29

executor's role with, 200

issues related to, 56

as nonprobate asset, 99, 100–101,
102, 272

owned by children, 145, 162

in sample estate plan, young couple,
305–306

types of, 137

for unequally wealthy spouses, 162

usefulness of, 39, 136

Life insurance beneficiaries
deciding on, 56
updating the designation of, 23, 98,
101, 102, 104, 269, 272–273
young children as, 100–101

Life insurance trust. *See* Irrevocable
life insurance trust (ILIT)

Lifetime credit on taxable gifts, 89–90

Lifetime giving. *See* Gifts during life

Lifetime QTIP trust, 143–145, 161,
323–324, 326, 327

Limited liability company, to manage
real estate, 184–185

Living trust. *See* Revocable living
trust (RLT)

Living will, 105, 221, 236, 260

Long-term care insurance, 39,
227–230, 258, 327

Long-Term Care Partnership
Program, 229

M

Marital deduction, unlimited, 74,
75–76
estate tax calculation and, 83
QTIP trust and, 129
same-sex couples and, 77

Marital deduction trust. *See* QTIP
trust

Maturity level, of young beneficiaries,
49–51

Maybe-inherit beneficiaries, 38, 48

May-December relationship, 165–174
dos and don'ts for planning in, 174
issues in, 166–167, 174
providing for children from current
relationship, 173
providing for older spouse's
children, 166–167, 171–172
providing for younger spouse,
167–171
sample estate plan, 319–328
younger spouse's estate planning,
167

Medicaid, nursing home care and,
227, 228, 229–230

Medical care
directives for, 236–241, 260
direct payments to provider for,
91–92, 141–142, 158

Mementos. *See* Collectibles;
Heirlooms

Memorabilia, 217

Minor children
claims on estate, 42
custodian for transfers to, 180

as life insurance beneficiaries, 100–101

mistake of leaving property to, 23

See also Children; Guardian for minor child

Mistakes in estate planning, 23–24, 72, 98

Moving to another state, 273–275

Must-inherit beneficiaries, 38, 48

N

Net worth
change in, 270–271
estimating, 29, 293–297

No-contest clause, 112

Nonprobate assets, 99–104
beneficiaries of, 99–104
changing beneficiary designations, 271–273
common examples of, 99, 271–272
consistency with overall plan, 48–49
defined, 99
revocable living trust and, 135
superwill legislation and, 100
See also Life insurance; Retirement plans

Nursing home costs
concerns about, 22
See also Long-term care insurance

O

Older persons. *See* Age-related disability

Older spouse, 166–174

Organ donation, 56

Organizing your estate planning documents, 266–267

Organizing your paperwork, 8, 12, 260

Outright bequests, 109

P

Paralegals, 247, 254, 262

Passwords for computer, 215, 267

Payable-on-death accounts, 23, 99, 272

Permanent life insurance, 137

Personal property
collectibles and memorabilia, 217
issues related to, 56
leaving to children, 41
leaving to friend or relative, 45
life estate for, 124
See also Heirlooms

Poorer spouse. *See* Unequally wealthy spouses

Postnuptial agreement, 31, 122–123

Pot trust, 133

Pour-over will, 113, 134, 325

Power of appointment
for QTIP trust, 130
for trust in your estate, 193–195

Power of attorney
abuse of, 232–233
financial, 105, 221, 231–234, 235, 260, 328
health care, 221, 236, 238, 239, 260

Prenuptial agreement, 120, 122
consistent with estate plan, 24, 158
lawyer for amendment of, 250
on separate and community property, 35

Principal, of durable power of attorney, 231

Private school, direct payments for, 141–142

Probate, 114–115
   concerns about, 20
   examination of will in, 106–107
   executor and, 114, 115, 200
   QTIP and/or credit shelter trust
      and, 135
   See also Will
Probate assets, 109, 110, 111
Promissory note, in planning for
   family business, 189
Property
   dividing up specific assets, 46–49,
      271
   estate planning lawyer and, 257,
      258
   estimating total value of, 29,
      293–297
   executor's handling of, 201
   keeping a list of, 215
   trust assets in your estate, 193–196
   See also Basis; Community
      property; Estate; Family business;
      Family farm; Heirlooms; Personal
      property; Real estate; Separate
      property
Property and casualty insurance, of
   wealthier spouse, 163
Property tax
   conservation easement and, 187
   farming and, 186
   on real estate, 185
Providing for children
   concerns about, 8, 19, 22
   division of estate and, 40–41,
      42–43
   equalizing inheritances, 136
   goals related to, 18, 99
   by less-wealthy spouse, 163–164
   of May-December relationship, 173

of older spouse, 166–167, 171–172,
      174
   with one child inheriting and
      distributing estate, 23
   outright or in trust, 56
   with QTIP or credit shelter trust,
      127–128
   real estate and, 181–185
   with special needs, 43
   techniques for blended families,
      70–71, 117, 127–128
   unequal treatment in, 40–41,
      42–43
   by wealthier spouse, 162–163
   See also Children
Providing for spouse, 39–40
   concerns about, 19
   estate tax and, 74, 75–76, 83, 129
   with gifts, 87, 92, 160–161
   goals about, 18
   leaving assets outright, 117–119,
      120, 121
   mistake of leaving everything to
      spouse, 23
   portion of estate for, 41–42
   so that children ultimately benefit,
      99, 117, 127, 143–144
   statutory share of property, 23–24,
      31, 40, 49, 275
   techniques for blended families,
      70–71, 117, 127–128
   unlimited estate tax deduction, 74,
      75–76, 77, 83, 129
   younger, 166–171, 174
   See also House; Spouse; Unequally
      wealthy spouses

Q

QPRT, 147–149
 reverse, 148
QTIP trust, 117, 119, 121, 127–132, 133, 134–135
 change in financial condition and, 270–271
 created in revocable living trust, 127, 130, 134
 created in will, 127, 130, 135
 lifetime, 143–145, 161, 323–324, 326, 327
 of wealthier spouse, 162–163
Qualified personal residence trust. *See* QPRT
Qualified terminable interest property trust. *See* QTIP trust
Qualifying interest, 75
Quasi-community property, 274
Questionnaire, estate planning, 281–302
 concerns, 291–292
 executor, trustee, and guardians, 300–301
 failure of beneficiaries, 292
 family information, 282–289
 final arrangements, 292
 financial information, 293–299
 goals, 290–291

R

Real estate, 181–185
 life estate for, 124
 spouse's statutory rights in, 31
 See also House; Vacation home
Records
 organizing, 8, 12, 260

 for use of executor and trustee, 215, 267
Remainder beneficiaries of life estate, 125
Remainder of life estate, 117
Retainer, 253, 254
Retirement plan beneficiary
 spouse's consent for, 30, 49, 272–273, 325, 326
 updating designation of, 23, 269, 272–273
Retirement plans
 in community property states, 103, 325, 326
 consistency with overall plan, 48–49
 in estimating net worth, 29
 issues related to, 56
 as nonprobate assets, 99, 272
 spouse's legal right to benefits, 30, 49
 superwill legislation and, 100
 tax-free, 39
Reverse QPRT, 148
Revocable living trust (RLT)
 appropriate situations for, 116
 credit shelter trust created in, 127, 134
 disability and, 109, 113, 114, 116, 234–235, 324–325, 327
 divorce and, 269
 features of, 105–109
 how it works, 113–114
 joint, 108, 142–143, 161
 of less-wealthy spouse, 163
 life estate given in, 124
 probate's disadvantages and, 114, 115–116

promotional pitches for, 116–117
QTIP trust created in, 127, 130, 134
updating, 268, 269, 271
vs. will, 104–109
Richer spouse. *See* Unequally wealthy spouses
Right of survivorship, 99, 258, 271
RLT. *See* Revocable living trust (RLT)

S

Safe combinations, 215
Safe deposit box, 215, 266
Same-sex couples, 11
community property and, 33
federal estate tax and, 77
Second-to-die insurance policy, 137
Section 529 plans, 91, 139, 140–141, 325
Separate property, in community property states
based on written agreement, 33, 35, 36
basic concept of, 31, 32
difficulty of identifying, 34, 36
income on, 34, 35–36
requires work, 275
Settlement agreements
effect on estate planning, 41, 42
See also Divorce settlement
Signing ceremony, 11, 260
Skip persons, 95
Social Security Disability Insurance, 223
Special needs trusts, 43
Split gifts, 88, 91, 140, 141, 158
Spouse
communicating about the issues with, 8, 56–65, 154–155
communicating plans to, 24
consenting to medical treatment of, 237
family business and, 189–190
financial power of attorney given to, 233–234
noncitizen, 75, 92, 140
older, 166–174
resolving differences with, 58, 63–65
as trustee, 206
unprepared to handle money or property, 23, 27
with unresolved emotional issues, 66–67
younger, 166–171, 173, 174
See also Death of spouse; Providing for spouse; Unequally wealthy spouses
Springing power of attorney, 231–232
State estate taxes, 70, 87, 269
State income tax deduction, for 529 plan contributions, 141
State laws
on advance directives, 241
elective share statues, 23–24, 31, 40, 49, 275
moving to new state and, 275
on providing for minor children, 42
on transfers to minor children, 180
trust assets and, 202
See also Community property states
Stepchildren
concerns about assets and, 22
decision whether to help, 156–157
gifts to, during life, 141–142, 158
providing for, 44–45, 99
relationships with, 52–54, 154, 156, 216

timing of inheritance, 49–52

Stepped-up basis, 74, 80–82

with community property, 37

Stock

gifts of, 90–91

See also Brokerage accounts

Substance abuse problems

discussing with lawyer, 257, 261

interfering with estate planning
process, 67

of trust beneficiaries, 195, 196

Succession planning, for family
business, 190, 192

Successor trustee, of revocable living
trust, 113, 114, 134, 235

Superwills, 100

Supplemental Security Income, 223

Surprises, avoiding, 29, 216

Survivorship, right of, 99, 258, 271

T

Tax basis. *See* Basis

Taxes

conservation easement and, 187

corporate trustee and planning for,
213

on real estate, 185

second-to-die insurance policy and,
137

transfer tax overview, 70–72

See also Estate tax, federal; Estate
tax, state; Generation-skipping
transfer tax; Gift tax, federal;
Income tax; Property tax

Tenancy by the entirety, 99, 271

Tenants in common, 310

Term life insurance, 137

Testamentary trusts, 109, 111, 323

Transfer-on-death accounts, 99, 272

Transfer taxes, 70–72

Trust assets in your estate, 193–196

Trust company

as executor, 203, 211

as successor trustee of revocable
living trust, 235

as trustee, 203, 211–214

Trustee

changing, 275–276

choice of, 23, 198–199, 203–204,
205–211, 215, 216, 300

crafting solutions to trust problems,
196

of credit shelter trust, 127, 129,
132–133

discussing expectations with, 216

duties of, 200, 201–202

effective, qualities of, 198, 202

family member paired with
professional, 215

as fiduciary, 199

helping, 215–216

of irrevocable life insurance trust,
146–147

lawyer's help in choosing, 258

long-term role of, 200, 203

pay for, 215

of QTIP trust, 127, 129, 130

real estate managed by, 183

successor trustee of revocable living
trust, 113, 114, 134, 235, 325

See also Trust company

Trusts

amending with court permission,
196

change in financial condition and,
270–271

for children of older spouse,
168–169, 171, 173, 174
contained in will, 109, 201
estate tax and, 75, 76, 79, 85
heirlooms listed in, 180, 181
house contained in, 170, 182
to influence behavior, 52
maturity level of young persons
and, 50–51
powers of appointment and,
193–196
real estate in, 170, 182, 183
special needs, 43
testamentary, 109, 111, 323
for younger spouse, 168–171, 174
for younger spouse and her/his
children, 173
See also Credit shelter trust;
Irrevocable life insurance trust
(ILIT); QPRT; QTIP trust;
Revocable living trust (RLT)
Tuition
direct payments for, 141–142, 157,
158
See also Education of children

U

Unequally wealthy spouses, 151–164
communicating about financial
issues, 154–155
day-to-day finances and, 153–154
different values and, 153, 154–155
emotions about the finances,
152–153, 154
estate planning lawyer and, 258
estate planning tools for, 157–164
estate tax reduction for, 158–161,
162, 163

gender issues and, 155
gifts during life, 158, 160–161
health insurance for, 161–162
helping stepchildren, 156–157, 158
joint revocable trust and, 143, 161
life insurance for, 162
lifetime QTIP trust and, 144, 161,
323–324, 326, 327
prenuptial agreement of, 122, 158
sample estate plan for, 319–328
tools for both spouses, 157–162
tools for less wealthy spouse,
163–164
tools for wealthier spouse, 162–163
Unlimited marital deduction. *See*
Marital deduction, unlimited

V

Vacation home
managed as limited liability
company, 184–185
QPRT for, 147–149

W

Wealth disparity. *See* Unequally
wealthy spouses
Widowhood, and updating estate
plan, 269
Wife. *See* Spouse
Will
challenge to, 107, 112, 114, 115
codicil to, 111
contract to make, 123
cost of, 253
credit shelter trust created in, 127,
135
executor and, 200, 201
features of, 105–109

heirloom gifts mentioned in, 178,
179, 180, 181
how it works, 109–112
joint, 123–124
keeping in safe place, 266–267
language of, 110
of less-wealthy spouse, 163
life estate given in, 124
message to children in, 216
no-contest clause in, 112
parts of, 110–112
pour-over, 113, 134, 325
powers of appointment mentioned
in, 193, 195
public record of, 108, 115

QTIP trust created in, 127, 130,
135
vs. revocable living trust, 104–109
trusts created in, 109, 201
updating, 268–276
See also Probate
Witnesses to signing, 11, 260
Worries. *See* Concerns about estate
planning

Y

Young couples, sample estate plans
modest means, 304–307
wealthy, 314–318
Younger spouse, 166–171, 173, 174

Get the Latest in the Law

Nolo's Legal Updater
We'll send you an email whenever a new edition of your book is published!
Sign up at **www.nolo.com/legalupdater**.

Updates at Nolo.com
Check **www.nolo.com/update** to find recent changes in the law that
affect the current edition of your book.

Nolo Customer Service
To make sure that this edition of the book is the most recent one, call us at
800-728-3555 and ask one of our friendly customer service representatives
(7:00 am to 6:00 pm PST, weekdays only). Or find out at **www.nolo.com**.

Complete the Registration & Comment Card...
...and we'll do the work for you! Just indicate your preferences below:

Registration & Comment Card

NAME _____ DATE _____

ADDRESS _____

CITY _____ STATE _____ ZIP _____

PHONE _____ EMAIL _____

COMMENTS _____

WAS THIS BOOK EASY TO USE?   (VERY EASY)   5   4   3   2   1   (VERY DIFFICULT)

☐ Yes, you can quote me in future Nolo promotional materials. *Please include phone number above.*

☐ Yes, send me **Nolo's Legal Updater** via email when a new edition of this book is available.

Yes, I want to sign up for the following email newsletters:

  ☐ **NoloBriefs** (monthly)
  ☐ **Nolo's Special Offer** (monthly)
  ☐ **Nolo's BizBriefs** (monthly)
  ☐ **Every Landlord's Quarterly** (four times a year)

☐ Yes, you can give my contact info to carefully selected
partners whose products may be of interest to me.

SMAR1

Send to: **Nolo** 950 Parker Street Berkeley, CA 94710-9867, Fax: (800) 645-0895, or include all of
the above information in an email to regcard@nolo.com with the subject line "SMAR1."

NOLO *and* USA TODAY

Cutting-Edge Content, Unparalleled Expertise

The Busy Family's Guide to Money
by Sandra Block, Kathy Chu & John Waggoner • $19.99

The Busy Family's Guide to Money will help you make the most of your income, handle major one-time expenses, figure children into the budget—and much more.

The Work From Home Handbook
Flex Your Time, Improve Your Life
by Diana Fitzpatrick & Stephen Fishman • $19.99

If you're one of those people who need to (or simply want to) work from home, let this book help you come up with a plan that both you and your boss can embrace!

Retire Happy
What You Can Do NOW to Guarantee a Great Retirement
by Richard Stim & Ralph Warner • $19.99

You don't need a million dollars to retire well, but you do need friends, hobbies and an active lifestyle. This book shows how to make retirement the best time of your life.

The Essential Guide for First-Time Homeowners
Maximize Your Investment & Enjoy Your New Home
by Ilona Bray & Alayna Schroeder • $19.99

This reassuring resource is filled with crucial financial advice, real solutions and easy-to-implement ideas that can save you thousands of dollars.

Easy Ways to Lower Your Taxes
Simple Strategies Every Taxpayer Should Know
by Sandra Block & Stephen Fishman • $19.99

Provides useful insights and tactics to help lower your taxes. Learn how to boost tax-free income, get a lower tax rate, defer paying taxes, make the most of deductions—and more!

First-Time Landlord
Your Guide to Renting Out a Single-Family Home
by Attorney Janet Portman, Marcia Stewart & Michael Molinski • $19.99

From choosing tenants to handling repairs to avoiding legal trouble, this book provides the information new landlords need to make a profit and follow the law.

Stopping Identity Theft
10 Easy Steps to Security
by Scott Mitic, CEO, TrustedID, Inc. • $19.99

Don't let an emptied bank account be your first warning sign. This book offers ten strategies to help prevent the theft of personal information.

ORDER ANYTIME AT WWW.NOLO.COM OR CALL 800-728-3555

Prices subject to change.

NOLO *Online Legal Forms*

Nolo offers a large library of legal solutions and forms, created by Nolo's in-house legal staff. These reliable documents can be prepared in minutes.

Online Legal Solutions

- **Incorporation.** Incorporate your business in any state.
- **LLC Formations.** Gain asset protection and pass-through tax status in any state.
- **Wills.** Nolo has helped people make over 2 million wills. Is it time to make or revise yours?
- **Living Trust (avoid probate).** Plan now to save your family the cost, delays, and hassle of probate.
- **Trademark.** Protect the name of your business or product.
- **Provisional Patent.** Preserve your rights under patent law and claim "patent pending" status.

Online Legal Forms

Nolo.com has hundreds of top quality legal forms available for download—bills of sale, promissory notes, nondisclosure agreements, LLC operating agreements, corporate minutes, commercial lease and sublease, motor vehicle bill of sale, consignment agreements and many, many more.

Review Your Documents

Many lawyers in Nolo's consumer-friendly lawyer directory will review Nolo documents for a very reasonable fee. Check their detailed profiles at **lawyers.nolo.com**.

NOLO *Law for All*

Find a Quality Attorney

- *Qualified lawyers*
- *In-depth profiles*
- *Respectful service*

When you want help with estate planning, you don't want just any lawyer—you want an expert in the field, who can provide up-to-the-minute advice to help you protect your loved ones. You need a lawyer who has the experience and knowledge to answer your questions about living trusts, wills, powers of attorney, estate taxes, probate, executors, life insurance and more.

Nolo's Lawyer Directory is unique because it provides an extensive profile of every lawyer. You'll learn about not only each lawyer's education, professional history, legal specialties, credentials and fees, but also about their philosophy of practicing law and how they like to work with clients. It's all crucial information when you're looking for someone to trust with an important personal or business matter.

All lawyers listed in Nolo's directory are in good standing with their state bar association. They all pledge to work diligently and respectfully with clients—communicating regularly, providing a written agreement about how legal matters will be handled, sending clear and detailed bills and more. And many directory lawyers will review Nolo documents, such as a will or living trust, for a fixed fee, to help you get the advice you need.

www.lawyers.nolo.com